School Year Church Year

Customs
and
Decorations
for the
Classroom

Peter Mazar

Art by
Jane Pitz

LITURGY
TRAINING
PUBLICATIONS

SCHOOL YEAR, CHURCH YEAR: CUSTOMS AND DECORATIONS FOR THE CLASSROOM © 2001 Archdiocese of Chicago: Liturgy Training Publications, 3949 South Racine Avenue, Chicago IL 60609; 1-800-933-1800; fax 1-800-933-7094; e-mail orders@ltp.org; Web site: www.LTP.org. All rights reserved.

This book was edited by David Philippart. Marie McLaughlin and Bryan Cones were the production editors. It was designed by Lucy Smith and typeset in Weidemann, Univers and Allure by Kari Nicholls. Printed in the United States of America.

The author and editor offer heartfelt thanks to Vivian Williams, Maureen Como and Jennifer Schmidt Odegard for their review of and suggestions toward improving the manuscript. The author also wishes to thank Virginia Martelle as well as other supporters of LTP for their encouragement that such a book was necessary.

14 13 12 11 10   6 5 4 3 2

Library of Congress Card Number: 00-111595

ISBN 978-1-56854-240-9
SCHYR

Give ear, O my people, to my teaching;

    incline your ears to the words of my mouth.

I will open my mouth in a parable;

    I will utter dark sayings from of old,

things that we have heard and known,

    that our ancestors have told us.

We will not hide them from their children;

    we will tell to the coming generation

*the glorious deeds of the L*ORD*, and his might*

    and the wonders that he has done.

—Psalm 78:1–4

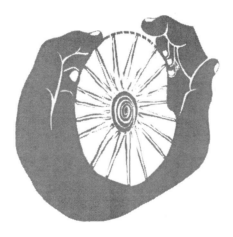

Contents

A Howdy from the Author

*I*n 1995 I wrote a book about decorating the church for the seasons. Its first fan letter was from a teacher or, more specifically, a teacher of teachers, who was recommending the book to parish catechists and school teachers. Amazing, I thought, but teachers deserve their own book.

Writing a book takes months of doing nothing else, plus the consumption (according to my particular way of working) of several hundred thousand chocolate doughnuts. Could my body handle another book?

The catalyst came in the form of a visit to a parochial school early in November. Of course, every room was hung with cardboard Pilgrims, pumpkins, teepees and turkeys—every room, save one, a room that made my heart beat faster and put fresh wind in my sails to complete this project. In this particular classroom a bulletin board was dedicated to photos of the dead—students' deceased relatives, friends and a specially framed photograph of one of the students. Dried, pressed autumn leaves were hung like halos around each photo. A wreath of leaves was placed around the classroom cross.

Instead of a store-bought cardboard cornucopia, in the prayer corner there was a wicker one overflowing with gourds and dried grasses. Nearby was a hamper full of canned goods to be donated to a food pantry. And my favorite, thanks to a biology project in anatomy that was scheduled to coincide with the church's month for remembering the dead, several dozen two-foot-tall paper skeletons, the bones named and labeled, hung from the ceiling and out into the hallway. There was a turkey, too, just one but very large, constructed by students from feathers and oak leaves, which surrounded the classroom clock. Over it was a scroll that said, "Time to give thanks."

What I've gotten together in this book isn't a comprehensive collection of recipes, but a book of tradition, a pep talk about the Catholic way of life. Instead of details about building an Advent wreath (there are other resources that cover the hands-on practicalities), I've used these pages to explore what Advent is. Outfitted with that information, you can decide how best to express the season in your circumstances, with the talents, resources, interests and budget at your fingertips.

I hang wreaths and arrange flowers and change displays in tune with the seasons not because I know the liturgy but because I'm in love with it and am eager to have others fall in love with it, too. That's the goal of my efforts. I'm playing cupid. Tom Ryan, a New Englander, calls this the "orientation of affections."

With gratitude I remember teachers who "oriented my affections." When I was in fourth grade (this is 1961 in New Jersey) I sang in a boys' choir run by Mrs. Coleman. She was gruff and demanding, and was one of those people who knew that most students will try to live up to expectations.

Mrs. Coleman expected us to be at church at ten o'clock on Christmas Eve to rehearse for and then sing at the Midnight Mass. We wore black pants, white starched shirts and red bows—not bow ties, but floppy satin bows that no one knew how to tie. We sang two-part harmony from the Pius X and Saint Gregory hymnals, wonderful songs, including the Huron carol "'Twas in the Moon of Wintertime," the Polish "God Supreme I Know Thee" and the German "O Come, Little Children."

I vividly recollect the decorations in church that year. Indoors, pine garland was hung in great swags throughout the building. The fir trees by the nativity scene were hung strand-by-strand with lead tinsel (which creates a shimmering effect like nothing else). Mass began after a simple ceremony in which the statue of the infant Jesus was placed in the manger, and some good soul had the sense to turn the lights out so the ceremony took place by candlelight. Over the outdoor nativity scene an enormous plaster angel was hung from the steeple, which struck me even as a nine-year-old as a feat of engineering. When we arrived for Mass the outdoor manger was empty; when we left, it was full.

Kids pay attention to such details, don't they?

A year later, in fifth grade, much was different. Someone decided that we were too young to be expected to stay up that late, so no more choirboys at Midnight Mass. No tinsel either, just the trees, and no pine garland. (The interior had been repainted and "the resin might stain the walls.") Lights were on full tilt from start to finish. The statues were all in place when we arrived—even the magi and camels, which in previous years didn't appear until Epiphany.

None of these changes had anything to do with the liturgical reforms going on at the time. Even as a ten-year-old I knew what was afoot in the parish and that it could be described with the words "laziness," "sloppiness" and, worst of all, "convenience."

As an adult, I became determined that hard work (which communicates affection and enthusiasm for our way of life) and a fealty to the fullness of tradition (which shows respect for the ancestors) should mark my own efforts in keeping the year within the parish community. None of this is in any way convenient.

I also saw the need to give credit where it is due: to the fellows who hung the angel from the steeple; to the ushers who got the statues into the outdoor manger at the proper time; to the Altar Rosary Society, who devoted the final nights of Advent to tinseling trees; to Mrs. Coleman, who had the good taste to teach us honest-to-goodness folk carols with melodies that last a lifetime and who went to bat for her choir's presence at Midnight Mass until she was defeated—these folks deserve applause.

Sister Tarcissus, a Sister of Saint Joseph of Peace, my seventh-grade teacher, was a liturgy buff. She taught us the vestment colors. She taught us the vestments. She gave us a tour of the church. We were allowed into the baptistry, in those days a large room off of the vestibule that was hidden behind a marvelous, ornate grate. She pointed out the windows: Jonah and the whale, the crossing of the Red Sea, and the baptism of Jesus in the Jordan. Since I wasn't a server, that was the first time I was allowed beyond the communion rail. She opened a locked box, like another tabernacle, that contained oils, one of which smelled like a Christmas tree. The best was saved for last: We learned that there were bits of *dead bodies* in the altar, stuck in stone.

Sister Tarcissus was also a music buff. She introduced us to Handel's *Messiah* and played its parts in season. She taught us the funeral sequence *Dies irae* and then played the wonderfully creepy version that makes up the final movement of Berlioz's *Symphonie Fantastique.* She taught us the Gelineau settings of the psalms, which gave me a lifelong language: "We will go up with joy to the house of our God"; "My shepherd is the Lord, nothing indeed shall I want"; "Great is God's love, love without end."

In high school, Mrs. Neder opened for us religion beyond the parish. Those were the days folks took the Octave of Christian Unity seriously. We were taught not just who Lutherans, Methodists and Greek Orthodox were but what they sang, saw, heard, touched, smelled and tasted at worship, and even how they danced (or didn't dance) afterward in the parish hall. At times Mrs. Neder's religion class tasted like saffron bread or stollen or baklava. We were taught connections between what happens in church and what happens on the streets and in the workplace. With a Guatemalan family we staged *Las Posadas.* With a Jewish family we ate the Passover seder. From a Muslim family we learned about *hajj,* pilgrimage. For the first time in our lives, Lent included almsgiving, acts of charity.

At the Iowa college I attended in the early 1970s, Mass got goofy. "Reinventing the wheel" would be a good description. I remember sitting down with a group to retool the wording of the eucharistic prayer. That was the first time I gave a thought to this prayer and to its function and structure, and I would liken the experience to taking a car apart and then trying to put it back together. Most times you wreck the car, but it's a way to learn how it works.

The chaplain found out what we were doing, got red in the face and chewed our heads off. Seems it was okay that the "psalm" between the readings was "Bridge over Troubled Waters" and that the priest put on a clown nose during the homily, but adapting the eucharistic prayer? No way!

Enter Sister Mary Rehmann, of the Congregation of the Humility of Mary. Suddenly our energy went into a number of constructive projects as we got reacquainted with tradition. The school's art department was invited to participate in preparing the environment for prayer. We were making beautiful new vessels, vesture, textiles, tapestries—even an Advent wreath as wide as the chapel aisle. Each Sunday an art student prepared an illustration of one of the scripture readings or the psalm. The music department was also able to participate, and where there had only been guitar accompaniments we now had, on occasion, a flute, a cello, or a four-voice schola singing William Schuman or Samuel Barber.

The lesson here, besides the one about giving students some opportunities to disassemble something to see how it works (as long as you don't victimize people with the results), is the great good that is possible when disciplines cooperate.

In the early 1980s I knew Sister Marold Kornovich, OSB, a teacher at the parish school of Saint John the Baptist in Excelsior, Minnesota. I think of Sister Marold as a "parish mystic." That's a term I use for someone formed in liturgy as a way of life, someone who holds in balance the liturgy's spirit and soul, its good order, its "grammar and syntax," its priorities, its vision. I wish every school could have a person like Sister Marold to be a mentor and an inspiration, and that, if the school is so fortunate, the person is nurtured, even pampered. A parish mystic is a precious resource.

One evening at sunset, early in Holy Week, in the middle of the millions of preparations for the Paschal Triduum, Sister Marold and I were crossing the parking lot between school and church. She stopped, looked toward the east and called out, "Look! The paschal moon!" We put aside our other concerns and stood there, watching the full moon as it cleared the horizon. The air was chilly and damp but already smelled of spring. Newly returned robins were singing their hearts out. So, too, were spring peepers, frogs that begin calling for a mate immediately upon emerging from the thawing earth.

Another "liturgical mystic," the Rhode Island artist Adé Bethune, tells about an ancient Christian tomb on which is carved the image of a frog rising from hibernation. Nearby are the Latin words for "in the twinkling of an eye," a reference to Saint Paul's lesson about the transfiguration of the dead on the day of resurrection.

Jewish mystical writers have claimed that each spring God rewrites the book of Genesis. In the parking lot, by the light of the silvery moon, Sister Marold and I watched a chapter rewritten in the sky. Gosh, I needed that moment, and Marold gave it to me. I'm happy to dedicate this book to her.

Editor's Note

Peter Mazar died in 2002, but his insights and wit continue to deepen our appreciation for concrete, poetic ways of expressing the Catholic faith. Thanks be to God for his life and work!

How to Use This Book

Let's begin with a few guidelines for using this book.

First Guideline
**Don't read the rest of this book
until you've digested the introductory sections.**

The "guidelines," "principles" and "nuts and bolts" of these first sections tackle the big picture. True, they aren't as fun as the rest of the book, but they're foundational. Think of it as the extended "Yes, but . . ." to everything that follows.

In other words, let's say you spot something in the Advent section that catches your interest. The introductory material taps you on the shoulder and says, "Yes, but . . . before you do anything for Advent, let's cover some fundamentals: Why do we Catholics have such high regard for visuals? How will the Advent decorations relate to what you do at other seasons? How will the Advent decorations build on the materials used during late autumn and then prepare for the materials used at Christmas and winter?"

Second Guideline
Tradition, no gimmicks!

"Tradition" literally means "hand-me-down." *School Year, Church Year* is a primer in the Catholic approach to the year. At every turn the book will flood you with information on the traditions of the year. Almost all the information in it is a gift from our ancestors in faith, who knew that the church is not a museum even though it's filled with lovely treasures. The church's hand-me-downs are meant to be used, and that often requires painstaking alteration so we aren't handing rags to the next generation.

If something will be done just once and never again, it's probably not worth doing at all. Especially with young children, doing something significant and lovable even once can establish a "tradition." If Saint Nicholas makes an appearance on his feast day this year, expect students to look for his return next year. They have a right to this expectation.

A gimmick wears out quickly. A well-tailored tradition is good for a lifetime. In 1949 Dorothy Coddington wrote these amazing words: "I prefer to cut children's spiritual garments a little large, for them to grow into, as they will in time. And who knows what vivid image or hint of the beauty of God may remain in their mind and memory?"

3 Third Guideline
*D*on't take this book—or yourself—too seriously.

We all work under different circumstances, with different budgets, different attitudes, among many different kinds of people. We are constrained. But we also enjoy unique opportunities. You may be helped or hindered by your administration's policies. The talents of staff and volunteers, along with your own talents, may make something possible that otherwise couldn't happen. And, of course, each year's class brings a different pool of abilities and interests.

This book can't possibly supply the creativity, adaptability, patience, communication skills and compassionate sense of humor required to put the ideas here to proper use. When dealing with visuals—for instance, when a rotting pumpkin tumbles onto the floor in a slimy heap, when a mouse makes a home in your nativity scene, when you discover a hidden Easter egg (and the source of that sulphurous smell) while cleaning the classroom in June—a sense of humor can be your chief asset.

Consider gargoyles. Those are oddball creatures set among the carvings of the saints and angels on the exteriors of medieval churches. What are they doing there, vying for attention with the mysteries of faith? What sort of people thought it was right to pepper their depictions of the citizens of heaven with such comical characters?

Clearly the creators of gargoyles were people of reverence and awe, people of knowledge who had been formed soundly in the language of the church. They also clearly knew how to laugh. And it wasn't just the stone masons who were laughing—it also had to have been the bishops and other administrators and power brokers who shared these attitudes. Their peculiar sense of humor and appreciation for delight must color our work as well, especially when we take ourselves too seriously.

Fourth Guideline
*I*f you do something, do it well.

This book challenges you to do some difficult things, sometimes to buck an established practice in favor of Catholic tradition. In controversial or counter-cultural matters, such as keeping Advent as Advent and not jumping the gun on the Christmas season, halfhearted efforts are likely to cause the same fuss as full-throttle ones, but with less chance of being satisfying and effective over the long haul. You want your efforts to bear fruit, perhaps not this year but certainly in future years.

If you're going to make a ruckus, make it count! It needs to lead somewhere worthwhile. It's better to do nothing if what can be done can't be done well.

Remember, in working with visuals in the classroom you are affecting hearts as well as minds. You are appealing to and challenging the whole person. You want people to react with more than "Oh, that's interesting." The goal is more than getting folks' attention or even imparting information—instead, the goal is "formation." In the use of visuals in the celebration of the seasons, you are forming Christians. You're reorienting spirits. You're shifting affections. You're asking people to fall in love with things. And that doesn't necessarily happen quickly. It can take years.

In making decisions about where to put your priorities, ask yourself: Is it lovable? Is it worth loving? In subsequent years will it return the affection lavished on it? Is it sound and authentic? Genuine Christian tradition has a lofty function: It helps to form us in the image of Christ.

Fifth Guideline
*B*e convinced that visuals are powerful.

Just as "a picture is worth a thousand words," any sort of decoration conveys volumes more than words alone. Like the other arts, visuals have clout. Think for a moment how, say, a jack-o'-lantern affects the senses. There's the pumpkin's lovely cool fatness, which, so it can seem, evokes the entirety of the harvest. In making a jack-o'-lantern there can be that mysterious sense of sacrifice—after the pumpkin is chosen and brought home, a knife is raised over it, the flesh is pierced, and the stringy and aromatic innards are removed.

Were the pumpkin left intact it might last for months, but carving it exposes the flesh to molds that soon destroy it. So in making a jack-o'-lantern you are dedicating that particular pumpkin to a special purpose, and there's no going back! Many of the church's blessings also entail that sense of dedicating a person or an object for the sake of the community.

Used in its new function, the pumpkin takes on symbolic value: Is there any more vivid *memento mori,* "reminder of death" (which is meant to reorient priorities and to challenge us to focus on what matters most in human affairs), than the wizening grin of a rotting, collapsing jack-o'-lantern? There's also the symbolism of the lantern to consider, a light in autumn's deepening darkness that's often set by a doorway so that its golden and grisly face welcomes Halloween pilgrims to the home. Here we see a symbolism found in many of the church's favorite objects—the expression of hospitality. Set by a doorway, a shining jack-o'-lantern can presage the welcome that Christ will offer the living and the dead on that great and awesome day "when all the saints go marchin' in."

In making a jack-o'-lantern you're involved in ritual. Each year calls to mind what has happened before and rehearses the next. Also, you're entering into the mystery of the calendar. After all, the jack-o'-lantern derives much of its meaning from the time of year, when leaves tumble down, birds depart, daylight rapidly dwindles and gardens frost.

Be assured that visuals have transformative energy: Consider all the power within a vegetable, a knife and a burning candle!

A Final Guideline
*T*hink of *School Year, Church Year* as a pep talk
rather than a book of recipes.

The intent of this book is to get blood flowing and spirits up. More important than the practical ideas for the Easter season, for example, is the book's whoop of enthusiasm for the Fifty Days, a rallying cry that those days are worth celebrating and are in fact essential to Catholic identity.

If a few concrete suggestions here appeal to you, put them through the litmus test of your own good judgment, your own particular circumstances and your school's ground rules. Then get cracking!

Twelve Principles

First Principle
Catholicism is a way of life.

Second Principle
Catholics see the world as an icon of God's reign.

Third Principle
The Catholic way of life is sacramental.

Fourth Principle
The Catholic way of life is liturgical.

Fifth Principle
Liturgy is a public, communal action.

Sixth Principle
Liturgy is like a language.

Seventh Principle
This language called "liturgy" has dialects.

Eighth Principle
The language called "liturgy" is a scriptural language.

Ninth Principle
The language called "liturgy" is taught by the Holy Spirit.

Tenth Principle
The liturgical year is the syllabus of the church's "school of formation."

Eleventh Principle
The liturgy calls for the authentic.

Twelfth Principle
Good liturgy evokes wonder, thanks and praise.

School Year, Church Year was written according to a set of principles. If you share them, you're likely to cotton to this book's suggestions. The principles provide a foundation for adapting the book to your needs.

You may be interested in some good reasons why you care so much about how your classroom is set up and decorated. We all have experienced the power of the arts. As Catholic Christians we have a long tradition of bringing the arts into the ways we worship. As members of the church we also have a "theology of the arts." Here we will explore these convictions.

First Principle
Catholicism is a way of life.

Think about what "a way of life" means. It's the homes we make, the songs we sing, the foods we eat, the clothes we wear, the material goods with which we surround ourselves. It's our beliefs as well as our actions based on those beliefs. It's our ceremonies, too, including the ways we welcome a newborn baby, or teach the young, or fall in love, or marry, or work, or grow old, or bury the dead. It's also our calendars, which govern when we do what we do.

In decorating the classroom you're teaching an aspect of a way of life. What goes up, and when, and how it's used—the materials, the calendars and the rituals—these things can support the Catholic way of life or else subordinate it to something else.

Of course, right here we have a problem: Most of us haven't been formed in our religion as a way of life. Instead, we often think of it more as a way of belief, as a doctrinal system for "right thinking," as something that involves mainly the mind instead of the whole body.

The presupposition in *School Year, Church Year* is that religion involves the whole person. When you say "Judaism" or "Hinduism" or "Catholicism," you're talking about music and decorations and cooking and calendars as much as you're talking about beliefs—all these aspects, as much as possible, working in synch, kept authentic, kept in perspective.

Second Principle
Catholics see the world as an icon of God's reign.

The book of Genesis tells us that we were made in the image and likeness of God, and that through our sinfulness the image became clouded. In Greek the word for "image" is *eikon,* icon. The beginning of the letter to the Colossians tells us that the Lord Jesus is God's perfect and unclouded icon: Christ Jesus "is the image of the invisible God, the firstborn of all creation" (1:15). The church is Christ's body, and as the head of the body, Christ brings God's distorted image back to perfection in us.

That's an amazing claim. The poets of the church put it this way: God becomes one with us that we might become one with God. And it's a cosmic event. This transfiguration involves more than just human beings; it touches everything God has made. The letter to the Colossians continues, "Through Christ God was pleased to reconcile to himself all things, whether on earth or in heaven, by making peace through the blood of his cross" (1:20).

Living the Catholic way of life means recognizing the things of the world as icons of God's reign. We have surrounding us mirrors of God's image, windows into heaven. Here is the theological foundation of our use of decorations in the classroom: Even though they may be clouded windows, in some way they can offer a glimpse into eternity.

In the eighth century the Council of Nicaea established a theology of the Christian use of images. Created things are capable of reflecting the light of Christ the way the moon reflects the light of the sun—not perfectly, but with something of the brightness of the source of all light. Sacred artwork "confirms that the incarnation of the word of God was real and not imaginary, and to our benefit as well, for realities that illustrate each other undoubtedly reflect each other's meaning."

Nowadays, the word "icon" is used for two-dimensional religious art, especially the art of the Christian East. According to tradition, before iconographers (literally, "image writers") paint (they would say "write") a new icon, they pray, fast and give an offering to charity. In a sense, when we use decorations in the classroom, we too become iconographers. Our work brings with it a call to holiness.

Like an iconographer, we also might take time before beginning each new effort by pausing for a moment to pray, fast and make an offering of alms to those in need. That's a traditional way to prepare for any endeavor. Each time we begin something new in our work with visuals in the classroom, as part of our fasting and prayer, we can research the allusions to scripture and then consider how these allusions are reflected in our own day. In other words, we humbly open our hearts to wonder. The only fitting approach to our work with visuals is one of humility and awe and thanksgiving.

Saint Augustine is said to have prayed:

O Lord, Savior,
you warn us that much is required when much is given.
We have cast our lot in your goodly heritage.
By means of prayer, fasting and almsgiving,
multiply the fruits of our labors
as we share with others what we so richly enjoy
through Christ our Lord. Amen.

3 Third Principle
The Catholic way of life is sacramental.

The Latin word *sacramentum* once referred to a soldier's oath of allegiance. To us the word "sacrament" means "holy sign." Signs point toward something beyond themselves. A sacrament points toward God's reign. They cheer us by reminding us of our journey's end.

We name seven particular Christian rituals as sacraments. But there is a broader sense of the word "sacrament." Catholics say that, by the power of God's Spirit, the things of this world can be holy signs that lead us into the mystery of God's own life. We say, for instance, that time itself is a sacrament that points toward eternity.

The Catholic way of life is sacramental. It is a way brimming with signs. It is a way of life lived with a particular attitude toward creation.

In the beginning, again and again, God called creation "good." And when creation was complete, God went a step further and pronounced it "very good" (Genesis 1:31). The Catholic genius has been to see in creation signs of the Creator, iconographic signs of the "original goodness."

We recognize as best we can that the things of time become signs of that which is timeless. That's why we often use things in church that fall apart and decay, that slip through our fingers or that waft into the air. Bread and wine, incense and oil, water and wax—we know these especially well and make them emblems of eternity.

The human body, too, is an emblem of eternity. To the church's roster of special signs we never forget to include the least decay-proof material of all, human flesh, which God claimed in Christ to be bound for glory. The sacraments are directed not just toward our souls but also toward our bodies! (Could you have a wedding without a bride and groom?)

Think of these things when choosing a pumpkin, when clipping evergreens, when boiling an egg. Think of these things also when a classroom project crashes down in a tangled heap, when a windstorm wrecks a picnic, when someone forgets the lines during the Epiphany pageant.

As lovely as the word "sign" can be, the Greek word for sacrament is more telling: *mysterion.* That's why you sometimes hear the seven sacraments, especially the eucharist, referred to as "holy mysteries." This word "mystery" nowadays means something unknown, something that needs deciphering. However, in ancient times "mystery" meant a ritual that led the participants into communion with the divine. By means of human actions with certain iconographic objects (objects that are images of the divine), you enter into union with God.

The idea here isn't that you force God's hand to do something for your benefit. After all, a god who is easily manipulated isn't God. Rather, God, in overwhelming graciousness, takes the initiative and welcomes us into the mystery, drawing us into the divine life, embracing us in a love that even death cannot overcome. Entrance into a sacrament, into a *mysterion,* is a gift from God. That's why we say that sacraments impart grace. The lovely word "grace" simply means "gift."

A sacrament is a ritual action. It's more than the objects used in the ritual. It's the interplay of human beings with these objects, these icons that reflect the creator. We have here another of our Catholic inclinations: We are a people who love ritual action. We prefer the active to the passive.

In your work with visuals you too can prefer activity to passivity. Better than setting up a display of beautiful things to look at, you might instead figure out a way to have those things carried in a procession during classroom prayer. Perhaps each morning during prayer, the flowers and candles that beautify the prayer corner can be held by the students. Perhaps during prayer on All Saints Day the gourds and other harvest bounty used as November decorations can be held in the hands of students and then gathered into a handsome basket.

Perhaps the cross or Mary's statue or other year-round art is given a special site on a feast day. Moving the object to the new site, no matter how short the distance, is an occasion for a procession. (Processions are sacramental signs of our journey as a people—our paschal exodus—toward the fullness of God's reign. And, wonderfully, the biggest procession that we're always walking is time itself!)

You can think up ways to "decorate" people and not just things. Students might enjoy wearing special colors or buttons or even costumes in observance of certain days. You can make sure to include traditional gestures and postures and movement in your prayer this year. The sharing of valentines or a birthday treat or even the distribution of a new textbook is a fitting occasion for a prayer of blessing.

You get the idea. Of course, the making of "beautiful things to look at" is part of active ritual, too, and are part of prayer in the classroom.

Fourth Principle
*T*he Catholic way of life is liturgical.

"Liturgy" means "work of the people." In "liturgy" you can see the related words "energy" and "laity" (from the Greek word *laios,* "people"). In the fullest sense of the word, liturgy is everything we do as members of the church. Christian scriptures identify liturgy as the proclamation of the gospel, as thanksgiving to God, and as labor for justice and charity. Service to God is not separated from service to neighbor. (See, for instance, 2 Corinthians 9.) Liturgy is what baptized people do in making their lives—again to quote Saint Paul—a constant prayer.

Specifically, liturgy is the public worship that the church gives to God. In public worship the church sees its fullest, brightest image. In worship the church is most the church, head and members, Christ and us. The Mass is one form of Catholic liturgy and is its crown. Other forms of liturgy are the sacraments, blessings, and Morning and Evening Prayer. And liturgy doesn't always take place in a church building. "Where two or more are gathered" is taken seriously, and so Catholic liturgy happens in funeral homes, around the kitchen table, and in classrooms, too.

Anyone with responsibility for the prayer of others has to be acquainted with all the forms that liturgy can take. Two forms of liturgy that deserve particular attention in Catholic schools are the liturgy of blessings and the liturgy of the hours (Morning, Midday and Evening Prayer). These forms of liturgy are especially suited to Catholic schools or to any group that meets regularly during the week. They're also suited to gatherings of Christians of various denominations. They are forms of prayer in which any Christian can participate.

The liturgy of the hours is the daily liturgy of the church. Somehow, even though Catholics kept the pattern of praying each morning and night, this daily liturgy is lost to most of us. It's being restored, slowly. It's too important to lose. It's too lovely, too.

The pattern of the liturgy of the hours is simple: At morning we may bless ourselves with water in remembrance of baptism. At evening we light a lamp and sing our thanksgiving for the light of Christ. We may also burn incense, the biblical "evening sacrifice" offered to God. Then, morning or evening, we sing a hymn. We also sing the psalms—the heart of our daily prayer. We sing a gospel canticle as well, Zechariah's song each morning, Mary's song each evening and Simeon's song each night. We conclude by pouring out our petitions to God and then joining together in the Lord's Prayer.

Take note that the liturgy of the hours is different from the liturgy of the word, although some people confuse the two. The core of Morning, Midday, Evening and Night Prayer is the singing of the psalms, which becomes the warp and woof of Christian prayer. Without the psalms Christian prayer fails to form "whole cloth."

The liturgy of blessings is essentially twofold: It is "eucharistic" (from a Greek word meaning "to give thanks") in the sense that we give thanks to God who created the thing we're blessing. And it's also "exorcistic" (from a Greek word meaning "to pledge") in the sense that we are setting something aside for a sacred purpose. The church uses the *Book of Blessings* in the liturgy. Every Catholic teacher will want to have a copy of *Catholic Household Blessings and Prayers,* Revised Edition, United States Conference of Catholic Bishops, 2007. The book is full of orders of service and prayer texts that can be adapted for use in the classroom. Another resource prepared just for you is LTP's annual *Blessings and Prayers through the Years* by Elizabeth McMahon Jeep, which contains a number of orders of service for blessing the classroom itself, the classroom cross, the Advent wreath, as well as other seasonal blessings celebrated in the classroom.

 *R*esource Idea

Fifth Principle
*L*iturgy is a public, communal action.

Something astounding we say about liturgy is that, even alone, when we participate in worship we are surrounded by the saints and angels, whose united voice of praise is nothing less than the voice of Christ. Desert-dwelling hermits would paint their huts with images of the saints as a reminder of this truth. If you're baptized, you're in grand company. You're never alone.

Display Idea

That's why Catholics have such affection for statues and other images of the citizens of heaven. They represent the company we keep in prayer. The use of such images is governed by strong and important traditions. It's never right to use these casually or use them only to beautify a room. Ordinarily, statues and religious icons are located in a place of honor and reverence, in a place that can function as a focus for prayer. The images should be cleaned regularly, with flowers and other signs of affection put nearby. It's a great and nearly universal custom to encircle a statue or icon with a wreath of flowers and herbs, or even to clothe and crown the statue in celebration of a feast day.

Take inventory of the school's religious art. Try to ensure that none of it is taken for granted, that all of it is used prayerfully and lovingly.

All are invited! To claim that liturgy is public prayer (and that the "public" aspect of liturgy is without limits of place and time) means that no baptized person may be excluded from participating in it. This principle affects how we should think about decorations. These need to convey a message of invitation and not exclusion. Their purpose always must include a sense of hospitality. They function as invitations when they function well. They enable (and should never hinder) participation and communication.

Here's an example: Let's say you decide to set up an "old rugged cross" for Lent on the parish-school lawn. Think how neighbors will react. Think about the issue of hospitality. Consider the proper reverence due the cross. What are traditions for using the cross outdoors? Consider the "language" that the cross speaks, which in American history has taken a horrible turn and, sad to say, affects the significance of the cross. Consider also what you're ultimately after in decorating for Lent. How can you invite the neighborhood into the celebration of the season in a manner that is traditional, hospitable and reverent?

Here's another example: Look at all the images of Christ or of Mary that are placed throughout the school. Now look at your students, their families and your colleagues. Do all of your images show Jesus and Mary as Europeans, even though your students are also of African and Asian and Hispanic descent? How can visuals help your children to know that all human beings are created in the image and likeness of God?

Public ritual means faith is put on display. Catholic schools are struggling with the issues raised when the student population encompasses people of many different (or no) religious affiliations. There are unwanted effects when non-Catholic students are separated from Catholic students during times of public prayer.

Schools are also struggling with the things that make a school "Catholic." What is Catholic identity? Is it right to compel a person, Catholic or non-Catholic, to participate in liturgy? These are tough issues! One of the reasons that *School Year, Church Year* was written, even as it explores the use of visuals in the classroom, is to open up broad dimensions of the entire Catholic way of life.

This book won't shy away from areas that have been known to separate rather than unite members of a school community. (Celebrating Halloween is an example. Some people today think that it is harmful, but its roots are in Catholic tradition. See pages 126–28.) The book will address the issues and provide you with information you can share—or else send you to some handy sources of information—to help you defuse bombshells even as you deepen communal awareness of the Catholic way of life.

Catholics have a traditional inclination toward inclusiveness, tolerance, hospitality. Despite all the terrible divisions of the church, despite local and even churchwide practices that exclude non-Catholics from Catholic celebrations, and even despite ongoing movements that seek to "purify" the church by throwing almost everyone out of it, in general in our history we haven't been inclined to close doors on people. As Saint Augustine is said to have written, and many people have said ever since, "In essentials, unity, in nonessentials, diversity, in all things, charity."

The word "ecumenical" literally means "concerning one household." The disunity of Christians is essentially a sin against hospitality.

Hospitality is a key Christian virtue. Without it, the church stops being the church. Its importance is expressed in familiar sayings: "A guest in the home is Christ in the home"; "So oft, oft, oft goes Christ in the stranger's guise." The sayings call to mind the hospitality that Sarah and Abraham showed three guests who appeared suddenly one hot summer day. The couple dropped everything and attended to their guests, one of whom was God in human form. The letter to the Hebrews exhorts us: "Do not neglect to show hospitality to strangers, for by doing that some have entertained angels without knowing it" (13:2).

Sixth Principle
*L*iturgy is like a language.

Liturgy, like a language, has a vocabulary, a grammar and syntax, as well as subjects, actions and objects. It's passed down from one generation to another. Each generation has its effect on it but is not free to reinvent it. This generation-to-generation aspect is called "tradition."

This is good news for everyone. It means we don't need to make work when none is needed. We don't need to invent the liturgy; we need to enter into it. We don't exactly *plan* it, either. Instead, we *prepare* it. And part of preparing the liturgy is that we prepare *ourselves* to participate in it.

The comparison with a language is a good one. Like a language, the liturgy must be passed down from one generation to the next fairly intact for it to remain useful. Like a language, each generation adds some words, adjusts the grammar a bit, discovers that certain words have shifted in meaning or, on occasion, may even have reversed meaning completely.

Like a language, liturgy gets full of things that were useful once but that now remain in the background, mostly as curiosities. But on occasion one of these curiosities gets retrieved, dusted off and put to a new purpose to fill a need. Each generation has to retool some of the liturgy, add new "vocabulary," and take care in teaching it to the up-and-coming generations. Some people use the word "tradition" for the oddball stuff that made sense years ago but that nowadays seems quaint and old-fashioned. But that's not what we mean by "tradition," even if some of it falls into this category. Liturgy is a living tradition.

Liturgy, in fact the entire Catholic way of life, like language, involves actions and objects and modifiers and connectives in marvelous interplay. We get ourselves into trouble when we focus too much on the objects and ignore the actions—which would be like trying to speak a language without using the verbs.

The use of visuals within the celebration of the Catholic way of life, like good language, is as complex as poetry. It resists straightforward thinking. If, for instance, you find yourself explaining in so many words what a particular decoration signifies, you're probably on the wrong track. You likely are oversimplifying something that's complex. You likely are stripping the delight from a decoration. An authentic symbol can communicate on its own.

"Explaining" symbols can be an act of irreverence. It may fail to show respect for the richness of a sacred sign, and it can be patronizing and demeaning to the hearers. In the presence of the sacred, sometimes the best response is an awestruck silence.

That's not to say that we don't provide catechesis, although the time for this is separate from the time of celebration. The resources listed beginning on page 293 are a place to start in preparing information to share with students.

Seventh Principle
*T*his language called "liturgy" has dialects.

Just as geography and time create dialects within a language, the liturgical way of life has its variants, too. And it's never tidy. In fact, it's usually downright sloppy. It's important to stay aware of the origins of visual traditions.

A dialect that Roman Catholics "speak" is called the Roman rite. Like dialects of a language, the various rites of the church share important elements, sometimes borrow bits and pieces from one another, and sometimes hybridize. But, in general, because each rite has integrity and a particular genius, borrowing among the church's "dialects" comes with the risk of trivializing them and reducing their intelligibility. If it's done at all, it has to be done carefully.

The use of statuary and other three-dimensional religious imagery is a characteristic of the Roman rite. Another characteristic, some would say, is the straightforwardness of rituals and the simplicity of texts. The liturgical reforms of the past century, eloquently expressed in the *Constitution on the Sacred Liturgy,* called for "noble simplicity" (#34). This reduced repetition and restored some of the simplicity that the church in Rome prized in ancient times.

Regarding decoration and the other arts, the *Constitution* also reminds us that the Roman rite has resisted making any one style its own "but has admitted styles from every period, according to the proper genius and circumstances of peoples." The constitution calls the church the "friend of the fine arts" and says that the "art of our own days, coming from every race and region, shall also be given free scope in the church" (#122, 123).

The church is made up of many cultures, each with a unique expression. Each expression is like a quilt. To stay functioning, there will need to be occasional repairs. Patches of the quilt that wear out need replacement. Borrowed patches need to be sewn into place carefully.

Some traditions represent a way of life no longer lived. We may keep them for nostalgia's sake. Some traditions are kept because of ethnic pride. Instead of being part of the "quilt" of Catholic identity, they instead identify national origin. Instead of being a source of unity, they can become a source of friction.

Sometimes we make tradition a matter of fun and games, and nowadays that's probably the greatest threat to tradition's integrity. This happened to trick-or-treating. In the United States it got pulled away from its mooring as something Catholic people did to begin the celebration of All Saints and became instead a children's activity shorn of religious significance. In seeking to embrace a traditional way of life, our goal is transcendence, not entertainment. We're searching for windows into the mystery.

What are the consequences when the quilt breaks apart into detached patches? Consider what has happened to the observance of special blessings on saints' days. At one time the Catholic year was filled with blessings. It seems that almost everything of the earth, each on a different day in association with the memorials of the saints and other festival days, was lifted up to God in thanksgiving. (For instance, on various days during June a particular parish may have blessed beer, hay, lilies, harvesting equipment, fishing boats, church bells and a merry midsummer bonfire.) In our own day in most parishes in the United States what remains of this cycle of blessings is the blessing of throats on February 3, Saint Blase's Day. We have a single "relic" from a far richer pattern. The full pattern reflected the Catholic sacramental attitude toward life. But what is reflected in observing just one blessing on one day of the year?

Another example of a disjointed tradition is the practice of fasting. The practices have survived mostly in bits and pieces. For centuries both Eastern and Western Christians kept Lent by abstaining from foods made from animals. There were a thousand local variations, but in the main people kept this abstinence. Nowadays we may observe a relic of this tradition not by what we don't eat during Lent but what we do eat before and after the season, perhaps by feasting on doughnuts or pancakes at Mardi Gras, perhaps by feasting on eggs and ham at Easter. Not only has tradition's balance gotten tipped, so have bathroom scales!

Regarding lenten fasting, we're usually left to our own wits to decide what form it will take, if any. Church guidance is mostly missing in this matter; in former times, church regulations governing fasting had been important and exacting, and they derived power not from each individual inventing a personal expression of the tradition but instead from a broad spectrum of the entire community engaging in the tradition. And a key foundation of the sacramental sign of fasting, as we'll explore in the chapter on Lent, derives from its being done by a community, together, for the good of all.

We're living in a time of broken traditions. In our own generation, if we want to live a Catholic way of life, we're often left to pick and choose from among the enormous array of traditional images and folkways. Shall we think of this as an opportunity and not as a problem? Because our parents in faith did not bequeath to us "whole cloth," if we want any "cloth" at all we are compelled to transcend our private, individual and ethnic experiences.

Because we have access to historical and ethnological studies, we're able to open our eyes to the full scope of tradition within the church, to the many forms that life-giving disciplines and customs have taken among the members of the church now and in the past.

We in the United States know all about blending cultures. We revel in it. If the intentions are honest and the efforts sincere, we're able to derive enormous hybrid vigor from the amalgamation of cultures. Think of the ways we keep Christmas, with Mexican poinsettias, New Mexican *farolitos* (luminaries), German stollen, English holly and New England minced pie, as well as the omnipresence of a nineteenth-century Manhattan marketer's version of a Dutch folk character redubbed "Santa Claus."

A number of customs that are kept up to celebrate ethnic identity are in fact nearly worldwide practices that link rather than distinguish different nations. For instance, perhaps you know about the Polish custom of the *oplatek.* An unleavened wafer is broken and shared around the supper table on Christmas Eve. We may know this as a Polish custom, but by other names it's kept by Catholics of several central and eastern European nationalities.

The custom seems to be one of several with a common pedigree. As an "edible prayer" for a year of prosperity and peace, many cultures share a significant food, perhaps a bread, a grain porridge or some other dish prepared from the fruits of the harvest. In Poland the food chosen for this ritual was unleavened bread. Not far away, in Ukraine, where leavened bread is used in the eucharist, a braided and yeast-raised loaf is shared on Christmas Eve. In far-off England, before the Reformation, a porridge called "frumenty" (from the Latin word for "grain") was part of the mystical supper each Christmas Eve. Great minds sometimes really do think alike.

A separate and important issue is the expression of non-Catholic religious traditions in Catholic schools. For instance, perhaps at school you teach about the Jewish festival of Hanukkah, the Hindu festival of Diwali or the Muslim fast of Ramadan. Your desire is to break down walls of ignorance and intolerance, and to bring to the students an appreciation for the marvelous expressions of faith found on this increasingly small planet.

On the one hand, learning bits and pieces from other religious traditions, like learning a few words from another language, or like sampling the cuisine of another culture, can contribute to our respect and even affection for those traditions. On the other hand, we always need to keep in mind that learning a few words isn't the same as learning a language. Eating only the festive and rich foods from many different cuisines results in poor nutrition.

As an example, consider Saint Patrick's Day. In North America the day is an occasion of ethnic pride for Irish Americans. However, in some places the day is also an occasion for anyone of any ethnic descent to "be Irish for a day." There's a certain genius in that approach. By immersing oneself in another culture's music, foods, poetry and folklore, by walking around in someone else's shoes, walls can come down, trust and respect can emerge. An annual one-day immersion accomplishes a beginning to the dialogue between cultures. But it's just a beginning, although a delightful one.

Even as we cautiously and respectfully immerse ourselves in aspects of other religious traditions, we fully immerse ourselves in our own tradition. We may learn "words" from other "languages," but we make sure to learn the "Catholic language" as fully as we can.

Eighth Principle
The language called "liturgy" is a scriptural language.

In *School Year, Church Year* we'll be talking about jack-o'-lanterns, Advent wreaths and Easter eggs. These are Catholic domestic traditions. We'll learn how these things are steeped in the imagery of the liturgy, which is in fact the imagery of the scriptures.

The mothers and fathers of the church, the teachers of the early generations of Christians, had this scriptural language down pat. It was the air they breathed, the breath they exhaled. A number of them lived among peoples of all sorts of religions in the cosmopolitan cities of the nations surrounding the Mediterranean Sea, and so their teaching skills were constantly being tested. Christians had competition! They had to capture an audience's attention. They had to convince people to open their minds to a new way of thinking. Not surprisingly, many of the early church teachers were great speakers, poets, artists and songwriters. They had to be. That's what it often takes to be a great teacher.

If you want to immerse yourself in this language, a language fundamental to Catholic identity, read Ephrem of Syria. Read John of Damascus. Read Ambrose of Milan, Bernard of Clairvaux, Julian of Norwich and Hildegard of Bingen. You'll dive deeply into strange, musical images and homey ones, too, such as roosters welcoming the dawn, schools of newborn fishes reflecting sunlight on their shining bodies, lovers lazily whiling away a summer afternoon—this is how the saints spoke of their church, their faith, their God.

Resource Idea

Their own sources, more than anything, were the scriptural psalms and canticles, and chief among these is the Song of Songs. Jewish and Christian poets alike have called this book the holiest of the Bible, and yet it never mentions God by name! Its utter earthiness seemed the best vehicle, so thought many of the saints, to declare the things of heaven.

If you want to take a bath in the Bible, read the Song of Songs, or, better, make up a melody and sing it! Delight yourself in its language as you keep company with the lovers in their windswept garden, in their bedchamber and in vineyards, among the turtledoves and gazelles, the pomegranate and apple trees, your hands dripping with fragrant nard and embalming myrrh. Here is the language of the church—a language of metaphors.

The word "metaphor" means "carrier." A metaphor is language that carries figurative meaning. Sometimes the word "symbolic" is used to describe metaphorical language. The word "symbol" means "sign," something that points the way to something else. The Greek root of the word "symbol" means "tossing a ball"—in other words, "juggling." That's a great word for what needs to go on in our brains when we make use of visual images. Getting good at appreciating metaphorical language means we need to become skilled at juggling a number of things at once.

Keep this in mind through the year when wondering about the significance of such things as evergreens, valentines, Carnival masks, pretzels, skeletons, May baskets. Like the Song of Songs, they too bear no obvious sign of being about something religious, and yet from generation to generation Christians have used them to express faith and to help it grow strong. They too are part of the metaphorical language of the church.

As a people, we've grown weak in scriptural language, and the weakness makes us grow even weaker. We often fail to hear allusions to the scriptures even when they appear in plain view before us. As one example, how many Catholics know about the scriptural significance of the Christmas tree? And yet most Catholic families decorate a tree for Christmas. A federal judge called a Christmas tree a "secular sign" and saw no conflict with the separation of church and state in the use of a Christmas tree to decorate City Hall. Catholic tradition would beg to differ with the judge. Our tradition attests to the sacredness of the tree of life that we set up among ourselves to celebrate Christ, who in our Christmas festival has called us home to paradise.

Scriptural images are touchstones that all the earth's peoples can claim in common. Yes, biblical images are mostly agrarian and not necessarily close to many North Americans today. Have your students ever gazed at a golden field of ripe wheat rippling in the wind? Have their hands ever been nuzzled by the nose of a newborn lamb? Have they ever experienced the anguish caused by a sudden hailstorm or an untimely frost?

However, the scriptures also make broad use of urban imagery. Heaven itself is described as God's holy city, walled around, with twelve mighty gates. The church has been called a great edifice built of people rather than stones.

We cannot lose this language. Even in our own day it unites poor and rich, the powerless and powerful, those who "give us this day our daily bread" and those who eat the bread. Almost any journey by air lifts us high enough to reduce even large cities to finite dimensions and also sets before us farmers' fields as far as the eye can see. Perhaps that puts agricultural images in perspective. For all the asphalt we have laid down, we remain people of the soil.

One result of learning—or, better, of getting deep into our bones—the scriptural language of liturgy is sheer delight, the delight of a juggler. For instance, it's supposed to tickle us to ponder how the story of the prophet Jonah (whose name in Hebrew means "dove") mirrors the two watery flights of the dove in the story of Noah. (The Bible is filled with such puns.) Then, when reading the Irish legends of Saint Columba (whose name in Latin also means "dove"), the heart should leap up and a smile creep across our faces when we recognize the allusions to Jonah's tale. Each February 10, when we recall once again how Benedict saw a dove winging its way into the sky and then knew his sister Scholastica had completed her journey to God, we should lean back and contentedly say to ourselves, "Of course! That's how God speaks."

Further, an ear tuned to the scriptures will hear in these stories reflections of the Bible's Song of Songs. There the lovers address one another as "my dove." And of course, there's that glorious dove of the Holy Spirit that appeared over Jesus' head at his baptism, when the Father named his Son "my beloved."

Is it clear now? All these stories are really one, long, glorious tale in which all generations link arms and travel together into eternity. When you orchestrate the ornamentation of the classroom at Pentecost with cut-paper doves, if you've become good at juggling metaphors, it will be as if the stories themselves are fluttering overhead among the bright wings.

Ninth Principle
*T*he language called "liturgy" is taught by the Holy Spirit.

In the rites of Christian initiation, the period known as the catechumenate (the time of catechesis) precedes the final period, the time of purification and enlightenment, before baptism. Following initiation comes the period of mystagogy, the "teaching of mystery." The sense here is that those who have received the Holy Spirit at baptism are now able to be guided by the Spirit ever more deeply into the mystery. The Holy Spirit is their teacher.

Of course, the entrance into mystery lasts all life long. The Spirit, like any good teacher, opens eyes to wonder. ("To educate" literally means "to lead into.") The Spirit gives the baptized the necessary gift of insight into the sacramental signs of the church. The Spirit makes those signs effective windows into God's reign and mirrors of the divine life.

You, too, as a Spirit-filled Christian, are called to become a "teacher of mystery." The letter to the Hebrews tells us that God's work must be our own: "For every house is built by someone, but the builder of all things is God" (3:4).

Your work, the work of any baptized person, is the liturgy, "the work of the people," which has been called the church's "school of formation." The liturgical year is the syllabus. The liturgical texts and melodies and rituals offer the lesson plans. Seasonal decorations you use in the classroom, when used according to tradition, are a part of the metaphorical language spoken by the church. They can be sacramental signs, windows into mystery, mirrors of the divine life, made effective by the Spirit.

The word "decoration" is a problem. It usually refers to balloons and streamers and other gaudy materials used to make a party more festive. In *School Year, Church Year* the word is used in its ancient sense, from the Latin root *decus,* which also gives English the words "decent" and "decorous" — "fitting." A real decoration makes a place fit for its purpose. A real decoration makes the classroom a window into mystery.

Decorations are not meant to be pretty distractions, although they work wonders in building spirit and enthusiasm for the season being celebrated. Decorations aren't rose-colored glasses that hide our eyes from reality, although they can make an ugly place more beautiful. Decorations, when used in a traditional manner, under the guidance of the Spirit, are meant to help us see what is most real, most true, most valuable in life. Like all forms of true education, they are meant to offer glimpses into the things that matter most.

Imagine that! And now be convinced: A bowl of gourds in November or a bowl of brightly colored eggs in April is capable of bearing what liturgical writer Robert Hovda called "the weight of mystery"!

Tenth Principle
*T*he liturgical year is the syllabus of the church's "school of formation."

If you're charged with making decisions about the use of visuals in the classroom, about the ways in which you will celebrate the feasts and seasons of the year, you will need to grasp what the year is and what it is not. Let's begin by considering three approaches to the year that have not been helpful and that lead to poor decisions: the year as biography, the year as a series of theological mysteries, the year as a series of themes.

The biographical approach: Somewhere along the line we fell into the mistaken notion that the church's year is a kind of biography of Jesus, that the purpose of the year is to tell about the life of the Lord. But it doesn't work, does it? If it were true, Easter and Pentecost would be celebrated at the end of the year, just before Advent. Before Pentecost the church certainly wouldn't proclaim the Acts of the Apostles, which tells about the events that followed Pentecost. But we do!

If the year were a biography we would hear the gospel story about Jesus' baptism in the Jordan River on the Sunday immediately before we hear about Jesus' forty-day fast in the wilderness, because, according to the gospels, Jesus' fast immediately followed his baptism. But we don't. Each year at the end of the Christmas season we hear about Jesus' baptism. And, several weeks later, at the beginning of Lent we hear about Jesus' fast. On the Sundays in between we hear the early chapters of the gospel that cover events that happened after Jesus came onto the scene following his baptism and 40-day fast.

The year isn't so much about Jesus' earthly biography as it is about the reign of God, which Jesus came to announce. Instead, the church's year continues the proclamation.

The theological approach: Another mistaken and unhelpful notion is that the purpose of the cycle of feasts and seasons is to set before us an ongoing series of theological topics to ponder. For example, according to this approach at Christmas we are supposed to think deeply about the incarnation of the Lord. At Easter we're supposed to explore the mystery of our redemption.

But this cerebral approach doesn't work, either. The Christian theology of the incarnation makes no sense apart from the death, burial and resurrection of the Lord and the sending of the Spirit. Nor can the church speak sensibly about Christmas without making full use of the theology of God's redemption of the cosmos.

The thematic approach: You may have heard people say that "Christmas is the season of light" and that "Easter is the season of life." But this approach doesn't hold up to inspection, either. There's plenty of "life" in Christmas. Why, we even set up the tree of life in our living rooms! There's plenty of "light" in the church's celebration of Lent, the Triduum and Easter. It's not for nothing that the Easter Vigil begins with a bonfire and the lighting of an enormous candle. Even the names "Lent" and "Easter" are based on the imagery of light. "Lent" comes from the same root as the English word "lengthen." "Lent" is an old title for the season when days grow longer. "Easter" is etymologically related to the words "east" and "star" and other words signifying light. Easter is a festival that reaches its mystical fullness at dawn.

If the church year isn't a biography of Jesus and isn't a series of theology lessons or themes, what is it? The poets of the church have described the circle of the year as the wedding band we wear as a sign of our fidelity to Christ. We keep the year faithfully, and it keeps us in faith. The year also has been called King Jesus' crown, a crown given to all who are baptized to be worn as a sign of *noblesse oblige,* the moral responsibilities of the highborn to live compassionately. The brightest jewel in the ring and in the crown is Easter.

Another odd but helpful image of the church's year is of a shop window. Imagine, as the year unfolds, that the mystery of Christ appears before us like a mannequin, clothed in the garments of the seasons. As the year goes by, the garments change but the wearer of the garments stays the same. In April the mystery of Christ comes clothed in cherry blossoms, flooding rivers, green pastures, newborn lambs. In August the mystery is dressed in ripe peaches, sunflowers, enormous thunderclouds, oppressive heat. In November the same mystery comes before us once again, this time enfolded in the imagery of late autumn's mix of nostalgia, contentment and fear as another winter arrives.

The mystery is further clothed by the church in stories, melodies, prayer texts, visuals. In April, for instance, the mystery wears the scriptural stories of Mary Magdalene mistaking the risen Jesus for a gardener, of the disciples meeting the Lord at a lakeside barbecue, of the good shepherd who lays down his life for the sheep. In April evidence of Easter stands in our midst—a babbling font, a volume of flowers, a great candle marked with five grains of incense that represent the wounds of Christ.

We can call this the "iconographic approach" to the year. The course of the year brings before us a series of gradually shifting icons ("images") that open windows into the mystery of Christ, the "paschal mystery." Each "icon" during the year—each season and feast—sets before us not an aspect of Christ or a part of the mystery, but the whole Christ, the fullness of the mystery, seen through the framework of each season's icon, seen clothed in the garments of the year.

The mystery is that of the incarnate Word who died, was buried, is risen in glory, who created us anew as the church in the divine image, whose Body we are, whose Spirit flows through our veins. The paschal mystery isn't celebrated only at Easter. Throughout the year, at every season, we live within this mystery when we offer our prayer to the Father, united by the Spirit in the one body of Christ. In this body, Christ prays to the Father. Our prayer, the voice of the church, is the voice of the Word-made-flesh. This is the Christ who has come and yet for whom we wait. This is the paschal mystery, because Christ, so Saint Paul tells us, is our passover.

If the year is a series of windows, the year's moments of transition, of "passover," seem especially clear as windows into the paschal mystery. Naturally, these moments receive extra attention. These are the times within the season of nature that we have named as the liturgical seasons.

Because we feel that springtime contains such vivid imagery of the mystery of Christ, we pay extra attention to the weeks that surround the vernal equinox, when days grow longer than nights. In fact, we make a point to count the days carefully—first the 40 days we call Lent, then the three we call the Paschal Triduum, then the 50 that at one time were called "the Pentecost," meaning "the fifty days," what we now call the Easter season, the seven weeks between Easter Sunday and the festival of Pentecost.

The numbers 40, 3 and 50 themselves are iconographic, rich in biblical significance. Students and teachers, take note: The custom of counting days (and the traditional devices for keeping count) are an ancient and important part of the time from Ash Wednesday until Pentecost. In the chapters on Lent and Easter we'll talk about the numbers and about customs for counting the days.

We Catholics are a people in love with signs. Once a year, at Easter, it seems that all the signs of the year point in the same direction, straight into the mystery of Christ. In its infancy the church decided that Easter should be the first Sunday after the first full moon after the vernal equinox. At the vernal equinox days grow longer than nights—the first sign of the Easter victory. Since a full moon rises just as the sun sets, when the moon is full there is no moment during the night that it isn't shining in the sky—the second sign.

The third sign, the sign of days of the week, is marvelously complex: We keep the Paschal Triduum from sunset on Holy Thursday until Easter Sunday evening because the span of days corresponds to the biblical sixth, seventh and first days of creation. (Remember, those days begin and end at sundown.) On the sixth day of the week God created human beings. On the seventh day, the Sabbath, God rested. On the first day God created light. Creation began. So, too, in his death on a sixth day the Lord Jesus completed his work. In his burial he rested on the Sabbath day. In his resurrection on the first day he began a new creation.

In observing the Paschal Triduum as the heart of the year, we are celebrating our new creation in Christ. That's why we reserve Easter Eve (the holiest of holy times during the year, the night of the most profound signs) for celebrating the sacraments of initiation—baptism, confirmation and eucharist—which are our entrance into the "passing over" of Christ.

Another turning point in the year is the time before and after the winter solstice. We divide this time in two: Advent and Christmas. The Advent season falls during the darkest days of the year immediately before and during the solstice. The Christmas seasons falls after the solstice, when days ever-so-slowly begin to grow longer, when the year takes its first baby steps toward spring. Here, too, is a time of "passing over," now reflected in the stories of the nativity and baptism of Jesus. We celebrate at this season with lights in darkness, with evergreens and flowers in the dead of winter, with dancing and singing and abundant hospitality as an antidote to our anxieties at this time of year.

Ordinary Time: The summer and autumn days between Pentecost and Advent, and the winter days between the Christmas season and Lent are less structured by the church, but again the paschal mystery gets clothed in the garments of nature's seasons. That readily can be sensed in festival days, for instance, on February 2, Candlemas, or on June 24, the Birth of John the Baptist, or on November 1, All Saints Day. The turning of the year has many such "passovers."

Even in Ordinary Time, the days around solstices and equinoxes get extra attention. September is a rich time of church festivals that fit well into the beginning of the school year. June, too, is packed with special days that kick off the summer. In contrast, the months that follow—October and July—are less rich, as if the church needs a chance to catch its breath after the excitement.

We pay extra attention to daily times of transition. We have special affection for sunrise and sunset, the turning of the day. Noontime and bedtime also seem especially sacred. That's why the liturgical tradition of the church summons us to regard the liturgy of the hours, with its times of prayer each morning, midday, evening and night, as foundational to our lives.

Do you pray at some of these times in the classroom? How do you begin and end the day? How do you mark lunchtime?

We Christians also have great affection for the turning of the week. Sunday, the Lord's Day, is the day of resurrection and the day of the outpouring of the Spirit. Sunday is the first day of creation and the "eighth day" as well, the day that leaps out of time altogether. We believe that when time is done, when our days and weeks and years spiral toward completion, it will be a Lord's Day that ushers in the end of days and the fullness of time. Every Lord's Day is a rehearsal for eternity. Every Lord's Day is a time to "play heaven."

How do you keep Fridays in the classroom? In a sense, Fridays prepare for Sundays. Before we can "play heaven," we try to live as if heaven has broken out on earth. Friday's extra prayer, fasting and acts of practical charity (alms-giving—from the Greek word for "compassion") are the "first course" of the Lord's Day feast.

Somewhere in the classroom, keep a "mite box" (or even a "mite hamper"), **a place to gather donations for charity.** You might use that spot to provide information about the recipients of the gifts. This spot can include students' suggestions for Sunday activities. Also include suggested actions that can help announce God's dominion of justice, that can help reveal heaven's beauty. Tell about forms of recreation that, in the Spirit, re-create the face of the earth.

Our lifetime moments of transition—birth and death, marriage and anniversaries, exams, moving into a new home and changing jobs, beginning and ending the school year, graduation, even such homey activities as buying new shoes or recovering from the flu—these also can be understood as images of the paschal mystery and as especially appropriate times for prayer. How do you celebrate these moments in the classroom?

Say a student is preparing to move to another town and a new school. You might display a photo of the student and her family in the place of prayer. Keep it there after she is gone. Add an intention for her to the intercessions at daily prayer. Perhaps a lovely blank book is set up in the classroom—look for one in a stationery store. Over the course of the month before the student leaves, other students can jot down their recollections, add photos and other mementos, and write their prayer intentions for the student and her family. Then this book of memories is given to the student on her final day. LTP's *Blessings and Prayers through the Year* includes a blessing of a student who leaves during the course of the school year.

If students don't change rooms during the day, the empty desk of someone who's home sick can receive an image, perhaps of the Good Shepherd or of the archangel Raphael. Before tests, one teacher leads the prayer "Come, Holy Spirit, fill the hearts of your faithful . . ." and then lights a red candle that stays burning until the test is done.

Of course, for Catholics, the special observances throughout the year are meant to be more than a way to organize time. They are part of our way of life. They are part of the Christian "school of formation."

This way of life has integrity, an integrity that is compromised when the Catholic year is regarded as "nice but not necessary" and when it is cast aside for the sake of convenience. It deserves pride of place in our lives because when we keep the year, it keeps us. It forms us into who we are. It tells us who we aim to become—as the Holy Spirit transfigures the church into the mystical body of Christ.

It isn't just a season or feast or morning or evening or birthday or first communion day or any other moment of transition that is the icon of the mystery of Christ. It's our living these events within the community of the church. That's the true image. That's what opens a doorway into heaven.

What happens when the liturgical calendar conflicts with other calendars? The church's year is broad and deep enough to accommodate other calendars, up to a point. Much of the academic and civic calendars, for instance, usually dovetails easily into the liturgical one. But sometimes there is serious disharmony. Sometimes it's a matter of too much at once, when observances pile up in one corner of the year, for example. More often there are conflicts in what is being celebrated, as gospel values come into conflict with those of national or commercial interests.

When push comes to shove, in a Catholic school allow the Catholic year to shine most brightly. For instance, in a February that Saint Valentine's Day and the Chinese New Year and Presidents' Day and Mardi Gras vie for attention during the same weeks, let Mardi Gras and the beginning of Lent be given the most attention. Let the other events take a backseat that year.

In any year give the arrival of Lent far more energy than any saint's day or civic holiday. Also, be aware of the natural connections and sympathies among days. For instance, when Easter is early, the Chinese (Lunar) New Year coincides with Mardi Gras. Within two different traditions the occasions are observed as times to hasten the arrival of spring and to cheer the spirit as winter wears on. So is Saint Valentine's Day. Such deeply human and universal impulses are foundational to the Catholic year.

After all, that's just what the word "catholic" means—universal. Our church has a strong tradition of embracing the finest of human cultures and crafting their customs to give witness to the gospel.

In the creed we profess our belief in the church. The church's year is something worth believing in, something worth trusting. It holds within its authentic and living traditions a path toward wholesomeness, toward holiness. With its foundation in a view of the world that is liturgical, scriptural and sacramental, our keeping such a year is meant to make us healthy.

To paraphrase the fourth-century bishop, theologian and mystical writer Saint John Chrysostom, the discipline of the Christian way of life is a medicine. It prepares the spirit for immortality. It fledges our wings for heaven.

Eleventh Principle
The liturgy calls for the authentic.

11 Display Idea

At a birthday party it's likely that you'd only hurt people's feelings by substituting a cardboard picture of a cake for the real thing. Here we have a strong guiding standard in the use of decorations: If you can make use of the real thing, don't use a picture of it. For instance, it's better to use a wicker cornucopia with real fruits and vegetables than to use a picture of one. A real pumpkin always beats cardboard.

If for the sake of classroom safety, perhaps, you aren't permitted to use candles in an Advent wreath, skip the candles entirely. Don't substitute paper candles with paper flames. Use something else. For instance, glass prisms hung from the wreath or over it might effectively and honestly convey the imagery of light as "rainbows" that dart about the room.

True, most real materials are messier and less convenient than artificial ones. Real pumpkins rot. A real birthday cake attracts ants. A beeswax candle, with its distinctive and delicious fragrance, tends to melt more quickly and messily compared to a paraffin one. Real flowers will stink up the water and fall to pieces if left unattended over a warm weekend. Real branches of foliage picked outdoors come along with resident insects and spiders. And yet the spider looping its web on a cluster of Indian corn adds its own window into mystery—and just about demands a compassionate release outdoors when the display is dismantled and the Indian corn is fed to the squirrels.

We Christians love messy things because these mirror a paradox: Our messy, stinky and utterly "inconvenient" flesh is destined by God for glory.

Using real things requires work. You'll need to be vigilant about upkeep. You'll need to be careful about allergic reactions to materials (although artificial materials come with that risk, too). And you may need to skip using certain things in favor of others, but it's worth it. A few real daffodils announce the spring far more loudly than a roomful of polyester flowers.

Two other ways to keep decorations "honest" is to choose handcrafted materials over mass-produced ones, as well as materials that reflect your own climate. To work honestly as Christian images, classroom decorations need to be true to what we observe around us—whether in Vermont, Virginia or the Virgin Islands, whether in rural, suburban or city neighborhoods. An authentic expression of Advent in Florida would not be frosted in fake snow.

Is there an olive tree outside your window? Put it to use in your celebrations. Does an orange tree blossom in your backyard at Christmas? Let its aroma blend with the bayberry candles. Is the winter still very much in evidence throughout Lent? Make your song these words from Psalm 51, "Wash me bright as snow." Learn to recognize an icicle as a sign of the strengthening sun.

 **Activity Idea**

What local events coincide with the liturgical calendar? Perhaps you visit a historical society during November as a way to remember ancestors. Perhaps you make a trip to the planetarium at Epiphany. Perhaps you check out a display of masks at the natural history museum during the days before Lent. Perhaps you visit a farm during the Easter season. Any mementos you bring back to the classroom become signs of the season.

While remaining true to your climate and surroundings, a rural school shouldn't be aloof to the concerns of the city. An urban school shouldn't turn its back on the imagery of the countryside. Classroom decorations and other signs of the season need to strike a balance between what we are and what we aim to be: a community. In his 1998 apostolic letter *Dies Domini,* On Keeping the Lord's Day Holy, Pope John Paul II writes about how the liturgy unifies us:

> *Those who have received the grace of baptism are not saved as individuals alone, but as members of the mystical body, having become part of the People of God . . . . They have become one in Christ (cf. Galatians 3:28) through the gift of the Spirit. This unity becomes visible when Christians gather together: It is then that they come to know vividly and to testify to the world that they are the people redeemed, drawn "from every tribe and language and people and nation" (Revelation 5:9). (#31)*

It's important to keep in mind that the Roman Catholic year is an invention of people in the middle latitudes of the northern hemisphere. In other latitudes on earth, what are the "passovers" during the turning of the year? It's hard to imagine a more dramatic transition than the early summer beginning of the monsoon in India after weeks of oppressive springtime heat, or the coming of the rains in east Africa or in the American southwest, when life erupts out of the suddenly sodden land.

Most liturgical imagery (which is at heart biblical imagery) makes most sense in the lands that surround the Mediterranean Sea. The liturgy puts key Mediterranean agricultural products to important use: grape wine, wheat bread, incense, beeswax (to make candles), flax (to make linen robes), and olive oil. This isn't exactly "Eurocentrism," which gives European images pride of place over those of other cultures. Northern European foodstuffs such as butter, rye and herring are just as overlooked in the imagery of the church as American or African or Asian ones. The predisposition of liturgical language might better be called "scriptural-centrism."

But it's a predisposition and not an absolute. At certain times over the course of history, Christians have adopted non-Mediterranean images. For instance, in Rome, All Saints Day used to be celebrated in springtime. But in the ninth century the church in Rome took a cue from the Celtic calendar's November 1 New Year festival (which was also a harvest-time day to enter into communion with the ancestors) and transferred All Saints Day from springtime to fall. The reason? There was more food available in November than in May to feed festival-goers.

Some traditional Mediterranean images have gotten lost. Losing this language means we have trouble appreciating a number of our ancient poets and mystical writers. For instance, nowadays most Christians don't think about Christmas as the time that rain pours down and almond trees bloom, as happens in the lands around the Mediterranean Sea. But these images were near and dear to the fourth-century Syrian poet Ephrem, who spoke of the newborn Jesus as a rosy almond flower. The annual cycle of the wheat harvest in that region—autumn sowing, winter growth, spring harvest and the summer barrenness of fields—makes little sense to many North Americans, even in some wheat-growing areas. Ephrem also called the newborn Jesus a sprouting wheat seedling. Nor would we think of Holy Cross Day in mid-September as a turning point in the year, when summer's drought breaks, when the rains begin and the land flushes green.

In *School Year, Church Year* we stick closely to seasonal imagery inherited from the Bible, much of which happens to work well in a large portion of North America. But in the use of this book in your classroom, claim your right to use local imagery as emblems of the paschal mystery. South Africans and Australians and Argentineans need to dismiss what's said in this book about November and Advent being a time of deepening darkness. Instead, they can come up with all sorts of marvelous association for their springtime festivals of All Saints and All Souls, and their summer festivals of Christmas and Epiphany.

It's not that we abandon the biblical language. Instead, we read between the lines: During the Easter season, folks in Argentina might focus on the scripture's harvest imagery, which makes little sense in, say, Massachusetts. Californians might dig even more deeply than this book does into Mediterranean imagery, since their climate is similar.

Twelfth Principle
*G*ood liturgy evokes wonder, thanks and praise.

As public action, as communal act, the liturgy exercises the imagination—of the community and of the individual.

Together in class, open your imaginations to the wonders around you. At issue here is this: Our scriptural, sacramental and liturgical way of life requires our ability to see in the world signs that point toward the dominion of God. All of us, by virtue of our baptism, are called in some way to be mystics, conversant in this language of signs.

Of course, this language takes us only so far and then falls apart. Heaven will not be contained. At the very least, this work of ours with materials that are "here today, gone tomorrow" will keep us humble—a word rooted in "humus," the brown, crumbly stuff in soil. "Humus" also gives us "human." After all, we were made from the earth, fashioned from its clay. And we will return to the earth, which will enfold us when we die. Our work will remind us that we are human, and thank God for that! All these "h" words are related to another word—"humor"! Of course!

Decorating the classroom will help lead your students to joy and wonder. While the word "catechist" means "one who teaches by word of mouth" (and the word "catechumen" means "one who learns by hearing"), you know that there is more to learning than simply listening. There is also seeing and smelling and tasting and touching—and doing. And all of this leads to wonder, to awe, to a deep appreciation for "what we have heard, what we have seen with our eyes, what we have looked at and touched with our hands, concerning the word of life" (1 John 1:1).

Yet to evoke wonder, classroom visuals need to be more than just some extra "religious" stuff added to the clutter. They have to be handsome and fun and enjoyable, worthy of being looked at, handled, sniffed again and again. In other words, they have to invite contemplation. This doesn't mean that they have to be expensive or museum-issue. When talking about the quality of objects that go in our churches, the United States bishops said something that applies equally to things we would introduce into classrooms. In their document *Built of Living Stones,* the United States Conference of Catholic Bishops wrote:

> *Quality is perceived only by contemplation, by standing back from things and really trying to see them, trying to let them speak to the beholder. Quality is evident in the honesty and genuineness of the materials that are used, the nobility of the form embodied in them, the love and care that goes into the creation of a work of art, and the personal stamp of the artist whose special gift produces a harmonious whole, a well-crafted work.*

Then the bishops explain why: To be appropriate for liturgy, art must be able "to bear the weight of mystery, awe, reverence, and wonder . . . . Art that is used in worship must therefore evoke wonder at its beauty but lead beyond itself to the invisible God" (#148). Only then does an object evoke wonder, not in the "scratch-your-head-and-ask-what-the-heck-is-that" way, but in a way that moves your students sincerely to exclaim "Cool!" or "Awesome!"—or simply to step back in silence. Such wonder nourishes the basic attitudes of Catholic liturgy: gratitude and praise.

Wonder leads to thanks and praise. For the baptized, learning to live in reverent wonder of God's creation and our salvation is not simply indulging in warm and good feelings. Wonder leads us to be grateful, to say "Thanks!" And gratitude leads us to praise, to lavishly and excessively love the giver of all gifts, to gush and giggle and be glad.

This way of living has strong moral and ethical implications: When wonder moves us to give God thanks and praise for a beautiful bowl of clean water in our prayer corner, we come to realize that we must care for lakes, rivers and streams, and not leave the faucets in the washroom running, and work so that all of earth's people have enough to drink. When wonder inspires in us gratitude that moves us to praise God for frogs and doves and lions and lambs—even cloth ones stuffed with beans!—we come to know that we must care for our pets, respect wild animals and insist on the humane treatment of those we use for our well-being.

Wonder, thanks and praise are a way of life—and so this twelfth principle brings us back around to the first: Catholicism is a way of life. Now, on to the nuts and bolts!

$\mathcal{N}$uts and Bolts

What's It to Be, "Noble Simplicity" or "Festival Excess"?
The Prayer Corner
Tips about Supplies and Storage: Let's Get Practical!
Toward a School Policy on Decorating for the Seasons
Tackling Some Prickly Topics: Decision-Making, Leadership, Coordination
Good Taste: The Prickliest Topic of All

Nuts and Bolts
$\mathcal{W}$hat's It to Be, "Noble Simplicity" or "Festival Excess"?

What's your own practice in the use of visuals? Do you keep things simple, or do you enjoy plenty of color and ornamentation? Are you an immaculate housekeeper, a mess-cat or something in between?

Some classrooms are decorated in a manner that might be called "visual overload." A merry hodgepodge of materials gets stuck on almost every available surface—class art projects, seasonal decorations, posters from the American Dental Association, student papers and overlapping notices. The stuff gets plastered on walls, windows, doorways, bulletin boards, and even hung from light fixtures.

Some teachers, in contrast, take a spartan approach. Everything's plain and focused. Maybe one corner has been dedicated to an upcoming holiday, but even that is kept low-key and dignified. Maybe another corner features (for a few days) student artwork or other projects. Walls, windows and especially light fixtures are never receptacles for decoration.

Most classrooms fall somewhere between these extremes. Generally, the classrooms of younger students tend toward overload and gaudy colors, while older students are given simpler surroundings.

In some high school rooms and most college classrooms, the environment is beyond spartan. There are no visuals at all, and sometimes even no windows! In most of these situations a classroom is used by many teachers, and no one teacher or group of students is responsible for the appearance of a room. In most nonreligious schools it would never be permitted to use decorations as a catechetical tool for forming students in religious traditions. Some educators feel it's best to avoid distracting sounds and sights, but most agree that certain sensory stimulation can be a good thing regardless of the subject being taught.

The rhythm of the church year suggests times for visual simplicity and times for excess. Excess is exceptional, and that makes it more fun, more a signal that something special is happening. The simplicity rests the eye and allows the brain to focus on other matters.

Generally speaking, the church's time of simplicity is Ordinary Time, which lasts fully half the year. (But note that the word "ordinary" in "Ordinary Time" means "counted"—ordinal—not "plain.") The church's times of excess are the seasons of Easter and Christmas. Times of preparation—Lent and Advent—have their own distinctive atmospheres that might be called "visual fasting."

Ordinary Time may be simpler than other times, but it has a shifting texture. Festival days pepper it and color the Catholic keeping of the year. For instance, All Saints Day fits within the Catholic keeping of autumn. Candlemas fits the Catholic keeping of winter. Besides individual days, there are also distinct periods within Ordinary Time, such as Carnival, which precedes Lent, and the month of November, which has its own "flavor" that prepares the heart for the arrival of Advent.

In times of plainness as well as in times of excess, things should be kept orderly, clean and well-tended. Cleanliness includes removing any bits of tape, glue, string or other leftovers when decorations come down. There's never an excuse for dirt, for tackiness or triteness, for neglect, or for a lack of safety. In any case, something left up too long loses impact.

Nuts and Bolts
The Prayer Corner

Most classrooms in Catholic schools have a crucifix and a statue of Mary, and there may be other religious art. What condition are these in? Are their locations appropriate? Are they at least clean?

Repair and refurbishing of art objects are usually tasks for craftspeople. If your religious art can do with repair, do everyone a favor and have it done as soon as possible. Since statuary is easily damaged, you might advertise in the parish bulletin for the help of someone skilled in making repairs. Keep students informed—perhaps the person doing the repairs can show the class how it's done.

Removing a statue and then bringing it back can be an occasion of prayer. One teacher chose the feast of the Nativity of Mary, September 8, to give the statue of Mary to the artist doing the repair. Students surrounded the image with flowers that day and then wrapped it carefully in beautiful padded fabric for its journey to the artist's home. The artist introduced herself to the students, showed them some of her tools and then explained how she intended to make the repairs. The repaired statue was returned just before All Saints Day, and the members of the class had a procession with the statue from the artist's car into the classroom.

Begin by cleaning. Cleaning something can be tricky. Water- or ammonia-based cleaners can dissolve certain surfaces. Oil- or silicone-based cleaners and polishes can discolor quickly or leave a surface streaked. Degreasers can do a great job or else wreck paint and other ornamentation. Test the backside or underside of the object when in doubt. Moving an object for cleaning is risky too. Ask for advice. With the best of intentions, someone diligently scrubbed off a coat of antiquing on a statue that he took for a layer of grime. After this "cleaning" the statue needed major refinishing.

Location, location, location: Perhaps each morning at daily prayer, everyone faces the crucifix, and at times Mary's statue is the focus of prayer. Sacred images need a noble spot. They shouldn't have to compete too much for attention with flags, posters, maps, clocks and bulletin boards. Perhaps a corner of the classroom can be dedicated as a focus for prayer and most of the sacred images can be gathered there.

True, it's probably not your choice where the crucifix is hung, but with some coordination you may be able to make a change for the better. One tradition for the location of the focus of prayer is front-and-center, although that usually means the cross is hung over the blackboard and projection screen. Is that the best spot? Another tradition is to find a place on an eastern wall.

"Orientation," literally, "facing east," is one of the oldest traditions of Christian prayer. It deserves a revival. The custom is similar to the Jewish tradition of facing Jerusalem and the Muslim tradition of facing Mecca in prayer. Christians face east as a sign of confidence in Christ, who, so says our tradition, will appear like the morning sun to raise the dead on Judgment Day.

(This tradition also led to the practice of burying the dead with their feet facing east—so they're ready to leap up and face their Judge!)

Even if the classroom is "disoriented" so that, in facing east, you'd have to face a peculiar direction when you pray, that strangeness will soon become second nature to students and become part of the traditions of their year with you.

Furnishings: Whatever direction you face during prayer, locate the cross there. Mary's shrine can go beneath the cross on a table or a shelf. A really handsome and sturdy shelf beneath the cross would enable you to gather flowers and artifacts there in addition to the statue of Mary. See what works. Surely you can find shelves, a low table, a small cabinet. Perhaps a "shrine cabinet" can be built. You may even come across something like this in your travels.

The primary requirement is that the furnishings are sturdy, able to bear the weight of whatever you will place on them, and located in a spot that is accessible and at the same time free from too much traffic. A secondary requirement is that the furnishings are handsome. Nowadays it's getting easier and easier to locate inexpensive and yet gorgeous hand-carved shelves and small curio cases. You want the furnishings to be something other than the run-of-the-mill classroom furniture. Yes, you can always cover an ugly piece with beautiful fabric, but first choice would be to use something beautiful that doesn't need to be hidden. That's because in certain seasons, such as Lent, it may seem most appropriate to leave the furniture bare.

A useful furnishing is the retablo. Retablos are seen in homes throughout Central America and the North American southwest. This is a shrine that hangs on a wall, basically a box whose horizontal surfaces hold sacred pictures and statues and other objects. It's something like a shadowbox, sometimes with small doors that can be closed to conceal the image at certain seasons, such as Lent.

One teacher created a retablo out of a rectangular basket, which was nailed to the wall. A wooden crate that has been sanded and rubbed with tung oil could also be used as an enclosure for a statue. Of course, thanks to the popularity of southwestern art, it's not difficult to find useful and beautifully crafted retablos made by regional artists.

Almost every culture has its traditions for building domestic shrines. Get to know these traditions. Most would be in scale in the classroom. The Japanese customarily dedicate a built-in cabinet in the home as a shrine. The area around it is kept simple, and in some places the cabinet is opened only during times of prayer and then closed afterward. The "icon shelf" in Russian homes traditionally features a suspended oil lamp in addition to the icons, which, on feast days, are hung with embroidered scarves. Some German homes have "God's little corner," again, a shelf or cabinet that holds the crucifix, statues and the family Bible (with its records and mementos enclosed within it).

The spot you create becomes your "prayer corner." Just as silence is able to focus thoughts, so the visuals used here are meant to direct our attention to communal prayer—"the work of the people" that is the liturgy. The things that go here are materials of special significance: a cross, an image of Mary, a wonderful candle and a bowl of baptismal water, a picture or other icon depicting the feast or season, the Bible and the leader's prayer book, perhaps some carefully chosen flowers and fruits and herbs. Other things that might go here are a book for writing down petitions for prayer and a book with the names or photos or other mementos of the dead. Other books can be open to something that fits the day or season.

Everything that goes here (and that happens here) should be as beautiful as you can make it. As a place of prayer, the materials and gestures should be a bit larger and fuller than is necessary. The songs we sing, the words we speak, the materials we use—all would be deliberate, careful and dignified, but never cold or pompous. Especially in the typical clutter of a classroom, where space is tight, it may be best to err on the side of streamlining and simplicity in this corner of the room.

Details count. Say, on a feast day, you place some fruit near a holy picture. Of course, you don't want fruit juice to mar the beautiful cloth you have beneath the picture. So you use a bit of foil beneath the fruit. Just make sure you can't see the foil. As obvious as this sounds, it's always necessary to step back from the work, take a deep breath, and then spend an extra moment on the details. Take a look at the corner from different angles. And keep a camera handy: Take photos of the prayer corner in different seasons (making sure to include the students), and assemble them in an album.

Invite everyone to be responsible for the upkeep of the prayer corner. Make that spot and the materials there the common property of everyone in the class, a place that everyone has a stake in keeping beautiful. Invite everyone to contribute to the images there, although the use of the contributions will need to be coordinated.

Ingredients for a Prayer Corner

- a cross
- an image of Mary
- a candle
- a bowl of holy water
- the Bible on a book stand
- an alms box
- seasonal items to add and take away

You may decide that an area of your prayer corner is fair game for any and all additions, which can be left a day or a week and then taken home. Set some ground rules first. Have a basket or hamper nearby for offerings to charity. The placement of furnishings should invite interaction. Take into account the height of students and the sightlines.

Try to keep the walls around the prayer corner free from ornamentation. Or at least make sure that nothing nearby is a distraction. In season you can use the free space for appropriate wall art. It can be useful to have nearby a well-anchored hook in the ceiling for hanging (in season) a mobile, the Advent wreath, a hanging lamp or incense burner, or a windsock.

Of course, we can pray anywhere. Every place on earth is holy. Even when King Solomon built God a magnificent temple in Jerusalem, the Holy of Holies in the center of the temple was nothing more than a flimsy tent, as if to say that God cannot be contained. Christian scriptures remind us that God's temple is not made of stone but of people.

In the time of Saint Francis of Assisi, Christians and Muslims were slaughtering one another for possession of the Holy Land. This disgusted Francis— and so, legends say, he began the two customs of the nativity scene and the stations of the cross. Both of these customs are a way of declaring that the "Holy Land" is no farther than one's own hometown. Do you want to make a pilgrimage to Bethlehem? Set up a nativity scene. Do you want to walk the way of the cross through the streets of Jerusalem? Erect the 14 stations and walk them in prayer.

In a sense, the prayer corner is a sign that you regard your classroom as "holy ground," a place to stand, as on Mount Sinai, before the burning bush, a place to hear God's name.

Nuts and Bolts
Tips about Supplies and Storage: Let's Get Practical!

Open your eyes and imagination when gathering materials for the celebration of the seasons. The key to searching for seasonal images is first to learn the language of the seasons. Once you've learned to "speak" this liturgical language, you are prepared to recognize useful materials when you find them.

Begin by taking inventory of what you have. With your eyes fully open and your "liturgical antennae" attuned, you'll be surprised at what you already have that's useful. For instance, a teacher reviewed her collection of beanbag critters. Her grasshopper was perfect to place beside an image of John the Baptist during Advent. The ladybug is an image of Mary. Folklore names the camel, horse and elephant as the creatures who bore the magi. The stork is a traditional emblem of Annunciation Day. The snake, raven, dove, ram, fish and lion are connected with lenten scriptures. The burro is used before Palm Sunday. The lion and the lamb are appropriate at Easter. The frog, an animal that undergoes a metamorphosis and that in spring emerges from hibernation in the earth, is also an Easter image.

The teacher decided these critters were handsome and simple enough to be worthy of the classroom prayer corner. That's a tough decision sometimes. The setting of an object makes all the difference. In traditional Byzantine iconography, things such as animals and plants and other symbols are located in secondary positions, almost tucked into odd corners, half-hidden, as if to say that the symbols are there to surprise you but that they are not essential to the icon's intent. The symbols act as commentary on the primary focus. That same sort of thinking can go into your use of images that grace the prayer corner. It's amazing how much oddball stuff is appropriate when it is positioned correctly and in perspective to the more important elements.

Acquiring materials year-round as you happen to come across them is more efficient than setting out on a particular day to find a certain something. We all know the aggravation of waiting until the last minute to find a particular item. Yes, that means you need to be free to make purchases year round. The ideal here is to be trusted with a credit card or some other method for spur-of-the-moment purchases because you're more likely to pay top dollar if you set out with a shopping list than if you catch-as-catch-can all year through.

When collecting materials, be ready to act at a moment's notice. An August trip to a fabric store might unearth, say, a great batik print of fishes perfect for Lent—and marked down! Suddenly at a sidewalk sale you spy earthenware figurines of doves perfect for the Baptism of the Lord, Candlemas, Saint Scholastica's Day and Pentecost—50 cents each! If you don't nab them you may never see anything like them again. A summer trip to the seashore might include gathering seashells to place around an image of John the Baptist during Advent. A Christmas catalog arrives and in it you see inexpensive teardrop-shape glass ornaments perfect for hanging over the Noah's ark (to represent rain) that you set up in the classroom during Lent.

Some basic supplies you might want to acquire are the things also used by an art teacher: scissors, glue, tape, paints, fabrics, roping, ribbons, papers, foils, sheets of Mylar® film, sequins and other stationery and office supplies. The choices here are bewildering.

With other teachers and the administration (as well as with other groups), coordinate your needs and learn how to work together to create decorations for the school and for your classroom. If there's an interested art teacher at your school, become allies. Another ally is the parish liturgy coordinator and church decorators. There's no substitute for gathering the forces with calendars in hand to focus on upcoming seasons and other events, and to determine how these will be expressed visually. (More about this work of coordination is found beginning on page 52.)

Sometimes when choosing materials we focus too much on one element and ignore others of equal or even greater importance. As an example, let's say it's Lent and you want to use a piece of fabric. Don't just focus on the color when making the choice, but look also at the weave and other elements of the fabric. Certainly a rough-hewn, homespun, woolen blend in earth tones conveys the mood of Lent more strongly than a piece of bright purple polyester. It's not that we want to lose the color purple as an emblem of Lent, but other elements besides color come into play in evoking the season.

Keep an eye out for materials that can be used during several seasons. For example, a sheaf of wheat might be the right ornament in autumn, again at Christmas, again on Holy Thursday, again at Pentecost. (Wheat needs vermin-proof storage.) Rudimentary objects and designs—seashells, boats, fishes, birds, snakes, stars, snowflakes—are useful on a number of occasions. Of course, nonfigural materials are versatile, too, and these should be chosen for beauty of texture and pattern in addition to color. Can you see the "work of human hands" in the objects you use?

Other basic supplies include devices for displaying treasures. You'll want to find handsome picture frames, small easels, matting, book holders, bowls, vases and baskets, as well as some specialty items such as safe and unburnable candle holders, an incense bowl, heatproof trivets, and perhaps sealable containers for ashes, spices and fragrant oil. Small pedestals are expensive but serve as a great way to display something to which you want to draw particular attention.

Be a borrower as long as there's the reasonable expectation that the materials you use won't be damaged or stolen. Be gracious in accepting materials. A good use for almost anything eventually arises. We're responsible to one another to help build up our religious literacy and for opening up our religious imaginations. Decorating the classroom is a joint venture. Students and teachers will want to share the responsibility for the acquisition, upkeep and storage of the materials used to ornament the classroom for the seasons.

If possible, go to a container store and buy clear, waterproof storage boxes, and label them for each season. This is a worthwhile expense. Plastic hampers, plastic milk cartons or collapsible plastic baskets are handy, too. That way you have a proper place to put something no matter when you acquire it, and the end of the season won't see an item "orphaned" and then lost or ruined for lack of a proper receptacle. (Just keep in mind that watertight storage keeps water in, not just out, so if you pack things away on a damp day they're likely to mildew.)

Transparent storage boxes make it easier to spot the treasures within. But it's also handy to have on hand various baskets and other containers made from woven grasses, reeds and wicker. Some of these also can serve to store items when not being used.

Sealable plastic bags are great for storing small items. Collectors of antique Christmas ornaments swear by these for cushioning and protecting even the most fragile pieces. Hardware stores sometimes sell bags much more cheaply than grocery stores. Clean, dry tissue paper (but not facial tissue) is useful in protecting painted materials liable to flake or stick together in storage. Large packs of tissue are sold very cheaply just after Christmas but can be harder to find the rest of the year.

Some materials require special storage techniques. For instance, seasonal window clings (which now seem to be available everywhere for every season) should be stored face-up on their original sheets. Waxed paper can be used to separate the sheets or even used in place of the original backing materials. If you don't go to this trouble, the clings stick together and the designs peel off when you try to separate them.

Eventually insects will make a meal of anything even barely edible. Mice will make nests in unlikely places. Mothballs to the rescue! Even a few do the trick if the storage container is sealed. Mothballs also keep down mildew, as does aerosol disinfectant. You may never have had a problem with mildew or vermin, but eventually they appear when conditions are right, and the results are disastrous. It's wise to take precautions.

A leaking vase or rotting fruit can wreck the material beneath it. Long exposure to sunlight and humidity can discolor or even destroy materials. Most everyone has had the experience of unfolding a cloth to discover that sunlight has faded exposed edges of the folds. When storing cloth, the less folds the better. You might invest in large cardboard rolls to roll cloth instead of folding it.

Container stores, school supply stores and party goods stores are excellent sources for materials. In the past decade or so a few new types of specialty store have opened up that stock materials that are especially useful for teachers and decorators. Container stores are chock-full of surprising and often economical materials—gorgeous papers, cardboards, fabrics, paints, boxes and display cases in an array of simple, pleasing designs.

Party stores also hold surprises. Although much of the material is tacky and "busy," or else covered in commercial emblems, it's possible to find wonderful things—gold cardboard crowns for All Saints Day and Epiphany, a garland of tissue-paper skulls for All Souls Day, a shimmering cardboard dove (in the wedding section) for the Baptism of the Lord, a piñata in the shape of a donkey for Palm Sunday.

Stores for teachers are opening up, too. There are geography stores, science stores, nature stores. A shop sponsored by the local public broadcasting network has a marvelous section devoted to parents and teachers. Again, some of the material is goofy and most all of it is "secular," but these stores can be great sources for simple and basic designs, say, of oak leaves, suns, snowflakes, butterflies. (Of course, you and the students can design these yourselves, although it may be handy to begin with store-bought materials as templates.)

Also available are kits for making your own decorations. For instance, one kit features the right kind of papers in traditional colors for weaving Danish heart-shaped baskets, a delightful Christmas tradition. Another includes patterns for Lithuanian straw ornaments.

The catalogues that arrive by the armful beginning around Labor Day, along with the Internet, can tempt us with an array of beautiful art objects as well as supplies for creating our own handicrafts. Useful material tends to hide among the useless stuff in catalogues. For example, flipping through a recently arrived catalogue reveals a wonderful carved snake from Mexico that would be perfect for Lent. There's a simple lantern made of steel and glass that holds four candles, which would provide a fireproof way to count the weeks of Advent. A verdigris-coated copper grasshopper and bee would be a great decoration to remind us of John the Baptist's diet of locusts and honey. A carved peacock from Guatemala would make a splendid and traditional Easter ornament. A set of small pedestals is a great bargain at $18. A set of three leather and metal filigree boxes (another bargain at $25) would make opulent containers for real grains of myrrh and frankincense, and chocolate coins wrapped in gold foil during the celebration of Epiphany.

The point, of course, is not to go on spending spree and bankrupt yourself. But every so often you may come across something worth acquiring, something that seems to grab hold of and then open up the imagination, something that deserves to be shared in the community of the baptized. It may be practical to keep ownership of certain items and to share these with each successive class in your career as a teacher, although perhaps in some situations these things can be paid for by the school and so become school property.

In any case, for a while at least, for a feast or a season, these treasures are "owned" by the entire class. They become common property.

Learn to be a copycat! Another use for catalogues and Internet stores is to provide pictures of folk crafts that can be copied by student artists. With the picture of the Guatemalan peacock as a guide, students might craft something similar out of strong wire, papier-mâché and tempera paints. Most stores in art museums specialize in books that gather together design patterns—for example, a book of Chinese-style snowflake patterns, a book of Ukrainian egg designs, a book of stylized animal outlines taken from Kenyan pottery. Books of patterns run the gamut from the prehistoric cave paintings of Lascaux to the windows of Frank Lloyd Wright.

Then, of course, there are museum stores and shops that specialize in travel, science or music. You may have access to ethnic shops (these, too, are often attached to museums) or stores that sell handicrafts from around the world. Even department stores have round-the-world sections.

Make an effort to determine if the artisans are being paid fairly for their work. Catholic Relief Services, in partnership with the Church of the Brethren, makes available handicrafts and other products that foster the dignity and self-sufficiency of artists and manufacturers. Call 1-800-685-7572 for a catalog.

Also, get to know local artisans. Make use of their work if possible. Who knows what talents can be unearthed in your own school and parish community? People who make their living as artists deserve to be paid fairly. As accustomed as we are in the church to accepting the work of volunteers and the gifts of the generous, justice demands fair pay for good work. Money may not be available, but keep in mind that something that costs dearly can be valued dearly as well.

Making use of images that are not specifically sacred opens up your "religious imagination." Everything we use as Christians takes on added significance when we begin to "speak the language" of the religious imagination, when ordinary things are understood in the context of biblical metaphor.

The paper oak leaves mentioned earlier would be used in public schools during autumn, of course. In your classroom the foliage takes on added significance when used to ornament the room at that season. It can conjure up, in the imagery of the book of Revelation, the leafy crowns worn by the martyrs. It can call to mind the branches of victory waved to welcome God's Lamb within the new Jerusalem.

It's all in the eye of the beholder.

Nuts and Bolts
*T*oward a School Policy on Decorating for the Seasons

The integrated use of visuals throughout the school complex can be noble, handsome and powerful. In contrast, a haphazard approach is bound to appear sloppy. Sometimes, in order to help students and faculty communicate on the same wavelength about this matter, the school will create a policy for the use of visuals, seasonal and otherwise.

In forming a policy you aim to make clear that your school is a Catholic institution whose mission includes formation in the Catholic way of life. That way of life covers the principles we have been discussing: literacy in scriptural language, a sacramental attitude toward the world, the rights and responsibility of the baptized to "pray constantly" within the lifelong work called "liturgy."

None of this is a drudge. As the traditions of the Catholic year make clear, this is a way of life overbrimming with satisfaction, rapture and passion. Keeping Advent as Advent, keeping all the days of Christmas, keeping Lent

and the Triduum and the Easter season as the church's "holy springtime"—
this is our communal responsibility and our communal delight. Shall we call
keeping the year "the joy of being Catholic"?

**Perhaps this book can spark the formation of and even be a foundation for
a schoolwide policy regarding the use of seasonal visuals.** Perhaps you can
go that extra step and factor visuals into the school budget. In addition to
money for supplies and training, are there funds available for art personnel?

The axing of art and music budgets is one of the scandals in education during the 1980s that was revealed in the 1990s as an enormous mistake. Until
we get wise to this mistake and repair it, we are forming a generation lacking
literacy in the arts and cheating them of their cultural birthright.

A unified approach throughout the building has force. If you've ever had
the opportunity to enjoy the Art Deco architecture of Miami Beach, you know
how powerful it can be when a common approach is taken throughout a neighborhood. Despite the many regulations governing this city, no one would claim
that the result of the restrictions is a squelching of creativity. The same can be
said for a common approach throughout a school in the use of visuals.
Guidelines can foster creativity.

As an added dimension, for Catholics any effort done for the common good
becomes a sacramental sign of the church as a whole, where we're all in it
together, where the one body of Christ is ascending into glory. That's why one
of the loveliest signs of the church is the beehive.

The way something looks has to work together with the way it functions.
For instance, if everyone is going to spend the time of prayer worrying about an
Advent wreath catching fire, the wreath, no matter how pretty it is, is not func-
tioning well as a focus of prayer.

Many school rules about visuals will involve safety concerns, for instance,
rules about the use of fire, a rule against blocking windows and doors or masking alarms and knobs, and rules about the use of foods and other things that
can attract pests or cause allergic reactions. (If common sense were truly common, we wouldn't need such rules.)

For us Catholics, as a sacramental people, candles and water and real plants
and real food are not optional but are indeed necessasry to our communal
prayer and public celebrations. School policy regarding the use of visuals has to
reflect our need for real candles, real water, real flowers and real evergreens in

A Basic Shopping List
• scissors
• glue
• tape
• paints
• fabrics
• roping
• ribbons
• papers
• foils
• sheets of Mylar ® film
• sequins
• picture frames
• small easels
• fishing line
• matting
• book stands
• bowls
• vases
• baskets
• candleholders
• an incense bowl (filled with sand or stones to absorb heat)
• heatproof trivets
• sealable containers for ashes, spices and fragrant oil
• pedestals of various heights

our observance of the calendar. The demands of safety must work together with the need for authentic sacramental signs. This balancing of priorities is hard work that requires wisdom, creativity, patience—as well as communication skills.

A small board of coordinators might be formed to oversee the use of art and decorations in the school. You'll want people versed in art, in matters of scale and appropriateness, in liturgical tradition, and in good order. You'll also want someone able to communicate effectively with the school and parish staff.

One task of a coordinator is the care and storage of materials. Another task is getting materials up and in use when a season arrives, and then down and into storage when the season passes.

In the course of the year, most festivals and seasons arrive as if they were grand surprises, as if they were undeserved gifts, emblematic of God's grace. Especially on the first days of a season or on festival days, it's delightful to enter the school building and see (or even to see from the street) visual expressions of the time at hand. That's why it's important to get things up and to take things down at the right times.

Sit down with a calendar and plot out the times of year that will require extra effort. At a few times of the year you may find it necessary to do things differently than you've done in the past. Perhaps you shouldn't take things down or put them up over a vacation, even though vacations would be a convenient time to do this—which is why these matters require the cooperation of janitorial staff, who use school vacations as times for extra cleaning.

Also be aware that within the church's calendar are certain times of transition that grant us leeway. For instance the days between Ash Wednesday and the First Sunday of Lent traditionally are an "easing into" Lent. This book cues you into those transitional moments and suggests practical times to get your work done in good order.

Nuts and Bolts
*T*ackling Some Prickly Topics:
Decision-Making, Leadership, Coordination

Perhaps you're the one expected to make decisions in the school about the use of visuals and other decorations. If your school has an art department and if your parish has art and environment ministers, certainly you will want to work with these folks. Perhaps you must rely on decisions made by a committee.

Perhaps the principal and pastor establish the ground rules. Perhaps a committee of teachers, students and the pastoral staff form a schoolwide policy on the use of visuals.

Let's take a look at this thing called a committee, in which a group comes to an agreement about what to do. Some committees include only trained individuals, others are made up of a mix of trained and untrained. Some are coordinated by an individual and some are not. Some are made up of members who represent factions (a kind of representational democracy, like a legislature). Some committees make decisions and leave it to others to implement them, and some comprise strictly the hands-on folks who intend to do the work. Some committees are not expected to make decisions. Instead, they work as advisory bodies.

Regardless of the makeup of a committee, it seems unlikely that a group can transcend the collective talents of its members. For instance, if nobody on the committee knows about growing flowers, the group won't be adept at making decisions about planting a schoolyard garden. A functioning committee pools talents, not ignorance.

The "choosing of mediocrity" is a common drawback of group decision-making. Mediocrity seems assured when the opinions of folks with expertise are given the same weight as the opinions of folks who do not have the same amount of knowledge. Also, when responsibility for a decision is diffused throughout a group, where does "the buck stop"?

Sometimes forming a committees seems the "democratic thing to do." However, a decision-making group is less a democracy or even a house of representatives and more a jury, in which individuals are brought together to consider information in order to make a decision or suggest a course of action. Akin to a jury, a fact-finding advisory committee works best when its task is defined, when it's able to gather the right information, and when it includes trained and open-minded individuals.

But the models of leadership we have as members of the church are something other than those found in civic life. One model, reflected in the letter to the Colossians and the letter to the Ephesians (called the "pastoral epistles" because they deal with practical matters of organization and governance), is of the ordered assembly of the baptized whose Spirit-given gifts work together for the common good. That sounds like an excellent model for any parish school.

Within the assembly of believers the Spirit raises up individuals as *episkopoi* (the Greek word for "overseers," in English, "bishops") to ensure that the gifts given to the church build it up as one body. The bishop delegates *presbyteroi* (the Greek word for "elders," in English, "priests"), gifted and knowledgeable people who are commissioned and coordinated by the overseer.

Delegating gifted individuals to coordinate certain tasks seems more effective than forming a "jury" or representational "legislature." The church's model of leadership defines our gifts and talents as Spirit-given and in need of coordination for the sake of the church. This model makes good sense. It works!

If a school committee followed the church's model of leadership, it would best be comprised of talented and trained hands-on workers, each of which has some particular task to fulfill, the work divided according to abilities and interest. The group meets mainly to learn and to *do,* not just to *talk* (although there's plenty of discussion), and focuses on issues or information throughout the year as needed. The coordinator is responsible for dividing the work according to the "big picture," for ensuring that work remains true to established policy, and also for coordinating tasks with other parish and parish-school personnel.

Decision-makers need to take seriously the ritual nature of liturgy. We share the attitude that we aren't so much planning something but instead preparing it, entering into a mystery that is not at our disposal to alter. We do not reinvent the wheel unless, somehow, it breaks. For instance, we keep Lent pretty much the same from year to year. We put the priority where it belongs. For example, we keep the entire season of Lent with more energy and attention than we keep a particular day during Lent. The task would never be to prepare a single event but instead to prepare each season with respect to the flow of the year and to the events being celebrated within that season.

An enormous benefit of coordination is that the entire school community achieves better "ownership" of the language of the seasonal liturgical arts because parts fit into a confluent whole. Each year builds on the previous year and becomes rehearsal for the next.

Earning trust is a key to leadership, whether as a coordinator or as a member of a committee. You earn trust when you know the tradition, when you respect the Catholic calendar and allow it to govern your decisions. You earn trust when you know the liturgical documents, when you know your way around the liturgical books, especially those very important and practical introductions to the books. You earn trust when you struggle with the spirit behind the texts.

You earn trust when you struggle with the elements of craft—with design, with scale, with appropriateness. You earn trust when you respect a key and lovely principal put forward in *Environment and Art in Catholic Worship,* that the materials and ritual actions that make use of these materials must be able to "bear the weight of mystery."

You earn trust when people can count on you, especially at the year's turning points. And this reliability factor, in the workaday world, is a primary reason people are hired and paid to accomplish a task. Also, you earn trust when you bend over backwards to communicate your intentions and to share the reasoning behind a decision. This means assuming (and being commissioned to assume) the role of mystagogue, the "teacher of mystery." You must bring to your work the principles of sound pedagogy.

Part of this "teaching of mystery," and something often lost, is making connections between church, school and home. Much seasonal art nowadays—the Advent wreath and Christmas tree, for instance—has roots in the rituals of domestic prayer. We might wonder what's going on when a traditional focus and tool of domestic prayer, such as an Advent wreath, becomes simply a pretty decoration in the classroom and is not used at daily prayer. We might be especially uncomfortable if we haven't first taught students how to use the Advent wreath as a focus for prayer in the home.

For the most part, you will need to make it clear that your efforts are not self-expressions. Instead, let your work be expressions of this thing called "tradition" and a servant of the liturgical life of the church.

"Tradition" is a word in which we take refuge. It's the foundation of our work with seasonal art. True, it would be less gray, more black-and-white to rely instead on a set of guidelines, on a single document, on laws and principles, or even on this book instead of claiming to stand on "tradition," but the church has no clear-cut guidelines in the use of seasonal art. Yes, the liturgy has its laws and the all-important spirit behind those laws. And on occasion a specific law or guideline touches directly on some aspect of seasonal art. But the specifics are mostly absent.

Take, for instance, the use of the Advent wreath. Aside from what's said in the *Book of Blessings,* the wreath is mentioned nowhere in church documents.

Nowhere do you find the nitty-gritty of what constitutes a fine-looking Advent wreath. And so we rely on "tradition" as our foundation, on bits and pieces of anecdotal information and historical studies regarding the use of the Advent wreath and related customs. We take this information and we balance it alongside the nature of Advent and the practicalities in the classroom. This is an art!

Nuts and Bolts
Good Taste: The Prickliest Topic of All

By decorating a classroom you are forming the affections of the people who share in the use of the room. That's a great responsibility, no question about it. You're under obligation to continue broadening and deepening your knowledge and appreciation of Christian imagery.

In general, the more you know, the better your taste. The more you know, the more options pop into your brain when making decisions. And, most times, the more you know, the better you're able to make good decisions.

However, it's true that the more you know, the more you're likely at first to be confused! The more you know, the more you have to mull over. The more information that goes into a decision, the harder it can be to explain the rationale for the decision. As the biblical prophets demonstrate time and again, confusion is often the first step toward wisdom.

Travel is one of those tried and true ways to "know more," especially the kind of travel that enables you to experience the day-to-day lives of people. (That being said, a little learning really is a dangerous thing. Superficial observations can be deadly.)

There's "armchair travel," too. The Internet makes that easier, but there have always been libraries at our disposal. Just for fun, type the name of a saint into an Internet browser, perhaps your parish patron. You might be in for a delightful surprise unearthing the links. If you're lucky and have the patience and time, you might find beautiful, reproducible images of the saint. You may find some history about the saint, some geography, some folklore, even perhaps some feast-day recipes. (For a few website addresses, see the list beginning on page 294.)

Broadening your knowledge broadens your taste. Add a liberal dose of compassion, good humor and humility when making decisions, and you're on the road to prudence, wisdom and discretion.

August

Entering into the Mystery of August
The 40 Days between August 6 and September 14
Mary's Month—and It's Not May!
Beginning the School Year

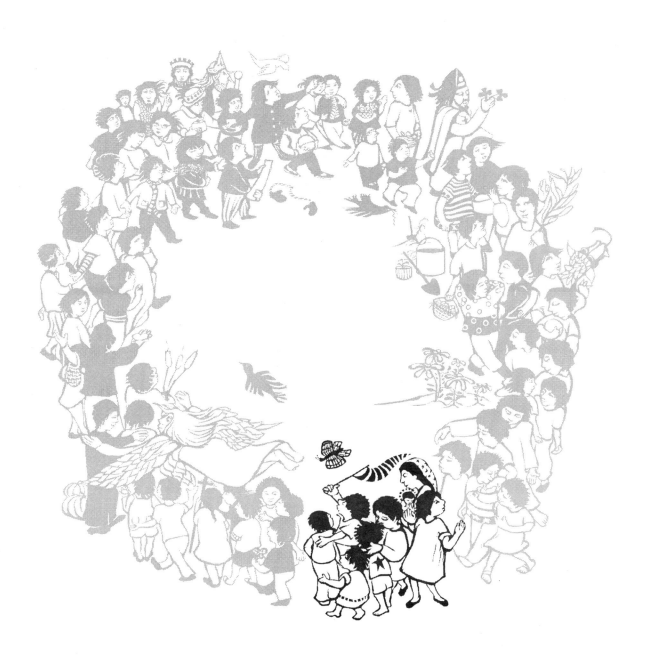

Entering into the Mystery
of August

*T*he Celtic calendar begins the month with **Lammas, the festival of the grain harvest.** We may think of bundles of wheat and rye as an appropriate decoration at Thanksgiving, late in autumn, but the grain harvest is a summer event, and "bringing in the sheaves" is the first step toward gracing the table with "our daily bread."

On the Celtic calendar, Lammas marks the beginning of the darkening quarter of the year, when day lengths decrease dramatically. The quarter is centered on the autumn equinox. November 1 concludes the quarter and is a kind of destination point.

*I*n August enough of summer has passed to turn the world lush. Finally there are garden tomatoes,

eggplants and peaches, although the produce ripens in such overabundance that someone has suggested that August needs a holiday called "Sneak Zucchini onto Your Neighbor's Porch Day."

These are the most fruitful weeks of the year. It's harvest time, and all hands are needed to gather it in. Summer fruits and vegetables don't ripen gracefully. They have to be harvested and preserved at once, otherwise the warm weather makes them ferment rapidly beneath a cloud of flies. Alongside August's fecundity is the smell of death and decay. As if in sympathy, in August the Orthodox and Catholic calendars include the observances of the deaths of Mary and John the Baptist.

The rainless summers in Mediterranean climates guarantee that August is parched and brown. The Jewish calendar observes the ninth day of the month of Av (roughly mid-July to mid-August in most years) as the anniversary of the burning both of Solomon's temple and Herod's temple. That day is the grimmest and most mournful on the calendar.

The old folklore about rain or drought on Saint Swithun's Day, July 15, prognosticating 40 days of rain or drought is not without a meteorological basis. In August most weather systems move slowly. That means that if it's raining it's likely to keep raining, and if it's dry it tends to stay dry. Generally, the weather is near-tropical almost everywhere in North America, as beneficent as it gets—until a hurricane or hailstorm makes the world turn wild.

*N*owadays the droning hum of air-conditioning is August's theme song. Some people spend most of their time indoors as if it were February. But folks over 50 can recall the entire family spending nights on porches or in parks because bedrooms turned into sweatboxes. It was like a neighborhood campout. A power failure can have us doing likewise.

*A*ugust

1 Memorial of Alphonsus Ligouri, bishop, religious founder, doctor of the church

2 Optional memorial of Eusebius of Vercelli, bishop

Optional memorial of Peter Julian Eymard, presbyter, religious founder

4 Memorial of John Mary Vianney, presbyter

5 Optional memorial of the Dedication of the Basilica of Saint Mary in Rome

6 **Feast of the Transfiguration of the Lord**

7 Optional memorial of Sixtus II, pope, and companions, martyrs

Optional memorial of Cajetan, presbyter, religious founder

8 Memorial of Dominic, presbyter, religious founder

10 **Feast of Lawrence, deacon, martyr**

11 Memorial of Clare, religious founder

13 Optional memorial of Pontian, pope, martyr, and Hippolytus, presbyter, martyr

14 Memorial of Maximilian Mary Kolbe, presbyter, religious, martyr

15 **Solemnity of the Assumption of the Virgin Mary into Heaven**

16 Optional memorial of Stephen of Hungary, married man, king

18 Optional memorial of Jane Frances de Chantal, married woman, religious founder

19 Optional memorial of John Eudes, presbyter, religious founder

20 Memorial of Bernard, abbot, doctor of the church

21 Memorial of Pius X, pope

22 Memorial of the Queenship of the Virgin Mary

23 Optional memorial of Rose of Lima, religious

24 **Feast of Bartholomew, apostle**

25 Optional memorial of Louis of France, married man, king

Optional memorial of Joseph Calasanz, presbyter, religious founder

27 Memorial of Monica, married woman

28 Memorial of Augustine, bishop, doctor of the church

29 Memorial of the Martyrdom of John the Baptist

In Short, in August

- Promise to keep the liturgical year as your primary calendar in the classroom, even if this means giving other observances a backseat (or no seat at all).

- Throughout the year make it possible for all the members of the class to share in the work of keeping the place clean and appropriately decorated.

- Begin the year by focusing on some basic visuals—the prayer corner, the classroom cross, the image of the Blessed Mother (more about these in September).

- Find beautiful, noble images of Saint John the Baptist and of your parish and school patronal saints, and keep these in the prayer corner or some other place of honor.

- In all sorts of ways, make use of apples (and other fruit), which have a venerable heritage as symbols of sweet beginnings.

- Schedule and then celebrate the blessing of the classroom in the new school year, and be sure to invite guests to the celebration.

August Ordinary Time
- Seasonal vesture color: *green*
- Some complementary colors: *gold, orange, rose, blue, teal*

Visitors to Europe in August, to their chagrin, discover the tradition of abandoning cities during the month, which can put the kibosh on tourists' plans. It seems that everyone goes "on holiday." Whether or not a person happens to be off from work, everyone's work slows down. It's hard getting things accomplished when so many people are away.

In the United States, in contrast, although some places have kept hold of the practice of beginning the school year after Labor Day, more and more schools are resuming classes in the middle or end of August. And until the first cool breezes of autumn stir the soul, late summer's weather may work against our diving with gusto into the academic year.

But dive we must.

The 40 Days between August 6 and September 14

The year has several 40-day periods. All of them, in some way, are connected to the idea of the renewal of the year. There are 40 days between December 25 and February 2, the 40 days of Lent are familiar to many people, and there are 40 days from Easter Sunday to Ascension Day.

At the end of summer comes another of the year's "quarantines" (meaning "40 days"), between the feasts of the Transfiguration (August 6) and the Holy Cross (September 14). The dating of these two feasts reflects an ancient legend, founded on the biblical imagery of the number 40, that the transfiguration of the Lord took place 40 days before the crucifixion. Summer vacation ends and the school year begins in the context of these 40 days.

Biblically speaking, the number 40 calls to mind the length of a human lifetime. According to the fourteenth chapter of the book of Numbers, when God freed the Hebrew slaves, despite all the many signs and wonders they had witnessed, the people persisted in thinking like slaves. They showed themselves unable to live in freedom. And so God chose to let that generation of former slaves die off in their 40-year wandering in the desert. Their children, a free-born generation, inherited the Promised Land.

That's a difficult tale, painful to read. The great heroes Moses and Miriam were part of the doomed generation, and even their exalted status did not exempt them from the curse. Like us on so many occasions, they looked to their children to inherit a promise they would never see fulfilled.

Of course, another "famous 40" is found in the story of Noah and the flood. Forty days and nights of rain destroyed every creature of the land except the saved remnant aboard the ark. It takes 40 days, in the language of the Bible, to arrive at a new creation.

As if in sympathy with these biblical tales, the holy prophets, Jesus included, underwent 40-day fasts. Moses remained 40 days on Mount Sinai within the cloud of God's presence (Exodus 24:18), and Elijah fasted 40 days on his journey to Mount Horeb (1 Kings 19:8).

*O*bserving a 40-day period marks a transition, a time of intensified introspection, growth, change, renewal. It's no wonder, then, that the 40 days following Christmas or the 40 days of Lent became important to the Catholic calendar. Somehow, the late-summer 40 days got lost, but this too is a time of transition. In fact, for those who must pay heed to the academic year, from mid-August on we're cleaning, unpacking, shopping, mustering our energies, running our feet off and discombobulating our schedules as we get ready for and then settle into a new school year.

Let's take a closer look at the days within this 40-day period. They are the liturgical framework in which the school year begins.

*D*eacon Lawrence: Paradoxically, in the midst of summery fruitfulness, these late summer days bring us in touch with death. Why is that? In Mediterranean lands summers are rainless. The annual drought turns the land straw-colored. The earth seems to burn up. Californians know this pattern. Everywhere, summer's heat is a danger to the heart. Statistics show that heat, more than any other factor, is responsible for weather-related deaths. A hymn text fits this paradox: "Even in the midst of life, death has us surrounded."

It's not a coincidence that on August 10, in the heat of summer, the church celebrates the fiery martyrdom of Rome's beloved deacon, Lawrence, who the stories say was burnt on a gridiron. A liturgical antiphon reminds us of the legend that Lawrence told his executioners, as if he were grilled meat, "Turn me over, I'm done on this side." Lawrence's feast day became an occasion to laugh at death by hosting a barbecue. Supposedly, heaven itself mourns the martyr's death in the annual Perseid meteor shower, called "Saint Lawrence's tears," which reaches its peak during the nights following the feast.

The name of the other great deacon-martyr, Stephen, is the Greek version of the Latin Lawrence. Both names mean "leafy laurel crown," in reference to the victory wreaths worn by those who kept their eyes on the prize. Think about this association whenever you decorate anything with a wreath.

*J*ohn the Baptist: The late-summer 40 days include the memorial of the martyrdom of John the Baptist (August 29), which is an important fast day in Eastern churches. John the Baptist, one of whose emblems is the summer sun, has been our mystical companion during the summer. On June 24, at the time of the solstice, we celebrated his birth. On August 29, as the days rapidly begin to shorten, we celebrate his death. On September 23, the Eastern churches remember John's conception—John's death linking arms, so to speak, with his conception. We'll take a closer look at this story beginning on page 75, when we unfold something of the mystery of the autumn equinox.

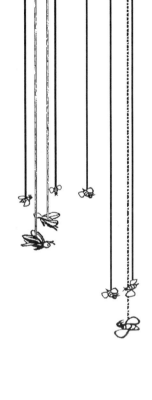

Like the story of the martyrdom of Lawrence, the story of John's murder is one of great violence, and, oddly, the only gospel account of a birthday celebration—wicked King Herod's. (The Bible's few other accounts of birthdays are equally nasty.)

Does the classroom have a statue or picture or other image of John the Baptist? That's a useful thing to have in place all year long. One of the most important images found in Byzantine churches is a triptych called "deisis": Christ is central; on one side stands Mary, her arms upraised in receptivity; on the other stands John the Baptist, pointing to Christ. (The image is available from most printers of icons, or can be downloaded from the Internet.) The three-part image shows the church's theology of Christian formation. In our relationship with Christ, in our transformation into Christ, we are like Mary, open to receiving the Word that transfigures our flesh and blood, and we are like John, humble fools, giving witness to the dominion of God by "decreasing" like John "so that Christ may increase" (John 3:30).

This 40-day period also includes Mary's most important festival, the Assumption, August 15, as well as the feast of her Nativity, September 8. Like the death and conception of John the Baptist, the death and birth of Mary are linked on the liturgical calendar.

In times past and in Eastern churches to this day, the Assumption (especially its vigil) is observed as a wake and funeral for the virgin Mother of God. The entire church, the children of Mary, gather to give witness to the "passover" of their mother. For something of the sense of the all-embracing power of this event, listen to John Tavener's 1991 piece, "The Last Sleep of the Virgin." Surround an image of Mary with August herbs, flowers and fruits. Keep watch in silence and contemplate the passover of the mother of us all.

Traditional iconography of the death of Mary (her "dormition"—her "falling asleep") shows two images of the Blessed Virgin, one on top of the other. In the lower image Mary is very old, pale, withered in the tremendous beauty of old age, on her deathbed. But above this scene she is also shown as if she were a baby in the arms of her son Jesus. She is wrapped in swaddling cloths, newborn. Around her gather the disciples, giving witness with us to the mystery of the church, that in baptism we too are newly born in Christ, our old age cherished and made beautiful, our youth renewed.

Assumption Day has long been an occasion to give thanks to God for the bounty of the earth and sea and sky. Folks in coastal areas bless the creatures of the sea. In mountainous regions, sheep and goats are blessed. A widespread custom on Assumption Day is the blessing of herbs, vegetables and flowers. A text can be found in *Catholic Household Blessings and Prayers,* Revised Edition, published in 2007 by the United States Catholic Conference of Catholic Bishops. It includes these splendid words that allude to the Magnificat, Mary's song of praise:

All powerful God, . . .
fill the hearts of your people with gratitude
that from the earth's fertility
the hungry may be filled with good things
and the poor and needy proclaim
the glory of your name. (page 172)

*R*esource Idea

*C*alling the earth our mother is an identification made in ancient times, nearly universal in the human race. In the chapter on the Assumption in her marvelous book *To Dance with God* (Mahwah, NJ: Paulist Press, 1986), Gertrud Mueller Nelson underscores the linguistic link between the words "matter" and "mother." The mystery of the virgin Mother of God is wrapped up in the mystery of the sanctity of matter.

August 14 and 15 is also the anniversary of the end of the Second World War. In 1950, with Pope Pius XII's declaration of the dogma of the Assumption, the ancient festival was given new emphasis as an occasion to honor the holiness of created things, especially the human body. War demonstrates that flesh is destined for destruction. On Assumption Day we rejoice that our flesh is destined for glory.

The preface of the eucharistic prayer for Assumption Day includes these moving words:

Today the virgin Mother of God
was taken up into heaven
to be the beginning and the pattern
of the Church in its perfection,
and a sign of hope and comfort
for your people on their pilgrim way.

Mary's Month— and It's Not May!

Two natural focal points for decoration as the school year begins are Mary's shrine and the classroom cross. Make a good start by giving extra attention to these year-round features in the classroom.

$\mathcal{A}$ late summer counterpart to (or substitute for) a "May shrine" would be especially appropriate from August 15 to September 15: August 15 is the solemnity of the Assumption of Mary; August 22 (the octave of the Assumption)

is the memorial of the Queenship of Mary. September 8 is the feast of Mary's birth. September 15, the day after Holy Cross Day, is the memorial of the Sorrows of Mary.

The church has several "seasons" for special devotion to Mary. These late summer weeks are an ancient and beautiful time for such devotion. So are the seasons of Advent and Christmas, as well as the Pentecost novena. Compared to these times, which have the weight of biblical tradition behind them, devotion to Mary during May and October are newcomers to the calendar.

$\mathcal{T}$he psalm for Assumption Day speaks of the queen arrayed in gold, and it's hard to think of a better day to crown an image of Mary. Throughout these weeks gold, yellow, rose, deep blue and other rich, royal colors can be used as bunting around Mary's statue, which can also be decorated with baskets of nectarines or eggplants and bunches of dill, Queen Anne's lace and sunflowers.

Apples are mentioned often in the scriptures and so are grapes. Both ripen at this season and both have become emblems of Mary. In many of Europe's great vineyards, September 8, the feast of the Nativity of Mary, is the occasion for blessing the grape harvest, one of the merriest times of the year. The assembling of harvesters who dedicate themselves to a common purpose, everyone working together for the common good, is a customary symbol not only of the church but of the school community at the start of the academic year.

*T*wo colors in particular are associated with Mary: blue and red. Blue, as the color of the sea and sky, represents the mortal, created world. Red, the color of fire, represents the divine and the immortal. In traditional Byzantine iconography, Mary is often shown wearing blue clothing but wrapped in a red mantel. This pattern signifies that, in Mary, heaven has embraced earth. The mortal is wrapped in immortality.

In her pregnancy Mary yearned to hold God as a child in her arms. So, too, as a member of the church, she longs for the fullness of time, when Christ will be all in all. The church is like the expectant Mary, always living as if it were Advent, always waiting in joyful hope.

Mary is also shown veiled in deep blue fabric that is studded with stars. This color, the color of night, is a sign of Mary's night watch with the church for the dawning of the eternal day. Other signs of expectation, such as eggs or sprouting flower bulbs and seeds, or the blossoming branches of fruit trees have a long association with Mary. Several flowers, such as lavender, marigolds and roses, and several insects, such as ladybugs and honeybees, are associated with Mary. The garden itself is one of Mary's key images.

*T*hroughout the year the area around the statue of Mary in the classroom makes a great site for certain small-scale and richly symbolic images. In autumn you might accumulate tokens of the harvest there. A November shrine in remembrance of the dead might go nearby. Some people veil Mary's statue in deep blue during Advent and then remove the veil and add an image of the infant Jesus at Christmas. During Lent she can be ornamented as the Mother of Sorrows, veiled in purple with a handsome model sword nearby as a reminder of Simeon's prophecy.

In each season *School Year, Church Year* will suggest other appropriate and traditional ways to give attention to Mary's image.

Beginning the School Year

In the excitement of the first days of the academic year we celebrate the dignity and destiny of our flesh and blood.

*L*ike the preface for the Assumption of the Blessed Virgin Mary, the preface for the Transfiguration of the Lord puts into perspective the Church's high regard for the human body as it speaks of Christ:

His glory shone from a body like our own,
to show that the Church,
which is the body of Christ,
would one day share his glory.

*P*rayer Corner Idea

*E*ven amid August's stories of death and martyrdom, the value of life is trumpeted. The festivals of late summer are like a pep rally against violence, like a cry for justice. These days speak to the issues of a school year lived in mutual respect, in decency, in safety, in productivity, in loving care for one another and for the neighborhood. The prayer corner or other spots in school, under the "patronage" of late summer saints—such as Rose of Lima, Monica, Augustine, John the Baptist, Gregory the Great and the Blessed Virgin Mary— can feature a display about the ways we show how we value one another, about methods of resolving conflicts, about handling anger, and about the ways the school community works together to keep everyone safe.

Like Labor Day (by lovely coincidence in the United States and Canada also celebrated within these 40 days), these late summer days are occasions to lift up before God the things that "earth has given and human hands have made." In addition to the Assumption Day blessings, traditional seasonal blessings include that of fruit on Transfiguration Day, of an outdoor barbecue on Saint Lawrence's Day, of flocks and herds on Saint Bartholomew's Day, of the grape harvest and of herds on the feast of the Nativity of Mary, and of the cross on Holy Cross Day.

$\mathcal{A}$t the beginning of the school year what's needed, of course, is a blessing of the school, of the classroom, perhaps also of the very earth on which the school campus rests. The beginning of the school year may not be the time to bless "the work of human hands," but instead to bless the bright promise of your coming efforts. Bless the hands! Bless the promises they hold!

$\mathcal{A}$ctivity Idea

$\mathcal{R}$esource Idea

A fine order of service for the blessing of the school and also for a blessing of the classroom cross are found in the autumn section of Elizabeth Jeep's *Blessings and Prayers through the Year* (LTP). The book suggests a ritual, texts, and songs.

$\mathcal{B}$egin by cleaning. That's what we do at home before a festival day. It's not satisfying to decorate a mess. Let students join in the work if possible. That way they better "own" the material things around them. Knowing what you know about these 40 days, make a special point to clean the classroom cross, Mary's shrine and any nameplates or signs, including the classroom number. Clean doorways top to bottom. These are sacred sites.

Maybe you also can do something about cleaning any outdoor signs, too, and any sacred statuary on school property. Students might freshen up the landscaping or at least pick up the litter. There's hardly any point in cleaning the classroom as an emblem of new beginnings if the view out the windows is a mess.

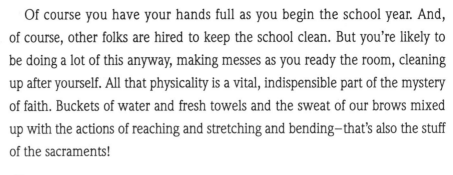

Of course you have your hands full as you begin the school year. And, of course, other folks are hired to keep the school clean. But you're likely to be doing a lot of this anyway, making messes as you ready the room, cleaning up after yourself. All that physicality is a vital, indispensible part of the mystery of faith. Buckets of water and fresh towels and the sweat of our brows mixed up with the actions of reaching and stretching and bending—that's also the stuff of the sacraments!

*S*et a date for the blessing of the classroom and send out the invitations. Students will need time to get ready for the event. A very fine choice each year is September 14, Holy Cross Day, at the close of the late summer days of transition. (And if that falls on a weekend, do it on the final school day beforehand.) Be sure to invite parents. Also, invite the janitorial staff to your classroom blessing. Have students bring in homegrown flowers for them. Pitch in for a box of chocolates to give them. The janitorial staff members are your allies throughout the year and may now need a "pre-apology" for the messes you're sure to make.

*D*ream up a way to involve as many neighbors as possible in the blessing of the new school year. At least invite the parish community. Even folks with no direct ties to students and the school year are sure to be participating in spirit in the reconvening of classes after summer vacation. Your neighbors see the schoolyard filling. They see all the back-to-school paraphernalia in the shops. Commuters again find themselves maneuvering alongside buses each morning. They see, and they remember their own days as students.

In some cultures the start of school is a community-wide event. Special honey cookies in alphabet shapes are sold in bakeries—an edible wish for a sweet new year of learning. With the same wish, students bring flowers and fruit to teachers. We have a lovely vestige of that wish for a fruitful and sweet year in the custom of bringing an apple for the teacher. What other ways can you "eat the alphabet" and get the school year off to a sweet start?

*T*he apple has become a great symbol of the start of the school year and might be used liberally in decorations. You might reverse the direction of such gifts from home to school and have the school itself sponsor the giving of apples to parishioners and neighbors along with a wish for a good year for all. Students can craft "Happy New School Year" signs ornamented with paper

 *A*ctivity Idea

apples or paper pencils or rulers that are given to neighbors or parishioners to display on their front doors.

Blessings and Prayers through the Year includes a Blessing of Food for Sharing in Part Three, Prayers for Special Times. This would be the perfect prayer to bless the fruit you distribute. Use handsome baskets to hold the fruit, and you might ornament the place if possible with a few branches from plants that are similar to the ones on which they grew, such as branches from apple trees or grapevines. If you have guests, hang a welcome sign over the classroom door and supplement the sign with a hearty handshake, too. Ornament school property with windsocks and flags or even balloons.

*D*isplay Idea

In some places it might be possible to have a safe procession around the school or a procession in neighboring streets. Perhaps during the procession you can leave apples and good wishes by neighbors' doorways. Processional banners and streamers on poles are sure to make the event more festive. Random handbells and percussion instruments can make good "traveling music." The litany of the saints is a Catholic classic for processions because the litany is an invitation for the entire company of heaven to join us in our efforts.

*A*ctivity Idea

*T*ake time to discuss the need for students to be good neighbors. We're good neighbors when we don't litter, when we hold down the noise, when we treat one another with charity and treat guests with hospitality. We're good neighbors when we respect property, when we don't cut through yards on our way to and from the school, when we volunteer time to help the elderly or organize a cleanup. Many schools already have programs that give students an opportunity to be good neighbors. The blessing of the year can be the annual kickoff to these programs, so in your intercessions that day be sure to ask God to assist these efforts.

September

Entering into the Mystery
of September

*T*raditionally, in monasteries, September 14, Holy Cross Day, marks the end of the warm season and the beginning of the cold season. Schedules and wardrobes and meals are adjusted to accommodate the chilly weather and decreasing hours of daylight. A half-year later, on Good Friday, it's back to the warm season regimen.

The new school year means that our schedules shift. Our clothing changes. Even our meals are affected. Folks with no connection to school may develop the urge to buy pencils, erasers and a box of foil stars. It's in our blood.

*A*utumn can seem like the year's grand finale, but it also feels like a fresh start. The first chilly mornings get energies into high gear. We hang Indian corn on the front door, we clean, we bake a sweet potato pie, we may discover within ourselves a streak of nostalgia as the days shorten, as the agricultural year reaches fulfillment. This, too, is in our blood.

In Mediterranean countries the first autumn rains after the rainless summers bring the earth to life, like a second spring. Perhaps that's why the Jewish people begin the year at this season. The Jewish New Year, Rosh Hashanah, is coincident with the new moon that marks not the first but the seventh month of the Jewish calendar. (The first month falls in spring.) The ancient Roman calendar also began the count of the months in spring, which is why "September" means "seventh month." Like the Jewish calendar, the Byzantine Christian calendar begins the year in the "seventh month," in September.

*I*n the old Roman Catholic calendar, following Holy Cross Day was the week of the autumn ember days, a fast in thanksgiving for the new season. (Imagine that—fasting as an act of thanksgiving!) The ember days were a kind of New Year celebration marking the arrival of the equinox.

Jewish and Christian poets imagined that the first day, when God set the world's clock, must have been an equinox, when day and night are equally long, when the sun rises due east and sets due west. After all, back "in the beginning," God certainly must have made everything in balance. (It's more than coincidence that, at the autumn equinox, the sun enters the zodiacal constellation of Libra, the scales.)

But which equinox? Some folks argued that spring is the logical choice as the anniversary of creation. Doesn't everything seem to resuscitate in spring? But some people said autumn is the better choice. Surely, they thought, in the beginning God made everything fruitful and ripe. Eventually, the mystical poets reached a compromise so that both equinoxes came to be regarded as equally fitting candidates for the anniversary of the creation of the world.

September

3 Memorial of Gregory the Great, pope, religious, doctor of the church

8 **Feast of the Nativity of the Virgin Mary**

9 Memorial of Peter Claver, presbyter, religious, missionary

13 Memorial of John Chrysostom, bishop, doctor of the church

14 **Feast of the Exaltation of the Holy Cross**

15 Memorial of Our Lady of Sorrows

16 Memorial of Cornelius, pope, martyr, and Cyprian, bishop, martyr

17 Optional memorial of Robert Bellarmine, bishop, religious, doctor of the church

19 Optional memorial of Januarius, bishop, martyr

20 Memorial of Andrew Kim Taegŏn, presbyter, martyr, Paul Chŏng Hasang, catechist, martyr, and their companions, martyrs

21 **Feast of Matthew, apostle, evangelist**

26 Optional memorial of Cosmas and Damian, martyrs

27 Memorial of Vincent de Paul, presbyter, religious founder

28 Optional memorial of Wenceslaus, ruler, martyr

Optional memorial of Lawrence Ruiz, married man, martyr, and his companions, martyrs

29 **Feast of Michael, Gabriel and Raphael, archangels**

30 Memorial of Jerome, hermit, presbyter, doctor of the church

First Monday: Labor Day in the U.S.A. and Canada

On the Jewish calendar the festivals of Pesach (Passover), and Rosh Hashanah (the New Year), are both considered anniversaries of creation. Passover falls in the middle of the first Jewish month, close to the time of the vernal equinox. Rosh Hashanah begins the seventh month—the holy month—at the time of the autumnal equinox. Yom Kippur (the Day of Atonement), ten days after Rosh Hashanah, also employs the imagery of the equinox as a "day of balance," when heaven and earth are made "at one," when God's people are re-created and made new.

In Short, in September

- Begin the autumn-long gathering of signs of the harvest that will reach a crescendo on All Saints Day.

- Use September 8, the feast of the Nativity of Mary, as a time to renew the classroom shrine of the Blessed Virgin Mary.

- Use September 14, the feast of the Exaltation of the Holy Cross, as a time to renew, decorate and bless the classroom cross.

- Gather images of the angels and have fun on September 29, the feast of the archangels Michael, Gabriel and Raphael.

- Somewhere in the classroom you might want to set up an almost permanent coil of grapevine or suspended tree branch or a "cloud" of Dacron® filler, or some other attractive contrivance for displaying small, hung ornaments. On this branch or vine or "cloud" hang images of angels, then on Saint Francis's Day hang images of animals. In November, hang images of ancestors, and so on. The display might be cumulative, with more and more things hung on it throughout autumn.

September Ordinary Time
- Seasonal vesture color: *green*
- Some complementary colors: *gold, orange, rose, blue, teal*

*I*n the Christian calendar, Good Friday and Holy Cross Day are considered anniversaries of creation. The cross itself, with its base plunged into the earth and its top touching heaven, with its arms seeming to reach from one horizon to the other, is an emblem of God's embrace of creation. Even among some non-Christian peoples an equal-armed cross or a cross set into a circle represents "all that is." The astronomical symbol of the planet earth is a cross.

*S*everal important festivals on the church's calendar are set to coincide with the equinoxes and solstices. Luke tells us that angel Gabriel appeared to the priest Zechariah in the midst of a cloud of burning incense. The angel told Zechariah that his wife, Elizabeth, had conceived a child, John the Baptist. Christian poets imagined that Zechariah wasn't just an ordinary priest but the high priest, and that it wasn't just an ordinary day but the holiest day, Yom Kippur, the Day of Atonement.

Yom Kippur also derives its significance from the equinox, the time of "at-one-ment," when day and night are equal, when creation is imagined to return to the "original goodness" that God saw in it back "in the beginning." In announcing Elizabeth's conception of John, Gabriel quoted the prophet Malachi and said that, in the ministry of John, parents would be at one with their children, heaven's justice and peace would break out on earth.

Since Luke tells us that Gabriel appeared to Mary six months after the appearance to Zechariah, if John's conception took place at Yom Kippur, at the time of the autumnal equinox, then Jesus' conception took place at the time of the vernal equinox. That's why we celebrate Annunciation Day at the vernal equinox, the Nativity of John the Baptist at the summer solstice, and the Nativity of the Lord at the winter solstice.

Remember this if someone asks you why we keep Christmas in December!

$\mathcal{A}$ Celestial Calendar for the School Year

The school year begins with the days close to the autumn equinox. Midyear falls at the time of the winter solstice, when days are shortest. The second half of the school year passes from winter to spring, from the darkest days of the year to the brightest.

$\mathcal{F}$rom day to day in September be sure to ask students to pay attention to the rapid shift in the point along the horizon that the sun rises or sets. On the days surrounding the equinox, ask students to notice how the sun sets due west. (Of course, sunrise and sunset happen when class isn't in session.)

Bring in an almanac and chart the length of the days. You'll notice that a 12-hour day and 12-hour night doesn't exactly correspond to the day of the equinox. That's because "night" is measured from the moment the sun disappears below the horizon to the moment the sun reappears at dawn, not from when the sun is bisected by the horizon.

$\mathcal{A}$t the start of the school year you may want to set up a chart—a celestial clock—to keep a yearlong record of the sun's journey through the seasons. You can do that by regularly marking the position of the shadow that an object casts. See the box on the next page for instructions.

$\mathcal{A}$ctivity Idea

According to the book of Genesis God placed the stars, moon and sun in the sky to measure the "seasons, days and years." In as many ways as possible, keep track of the celestial mechanics that govern the calendar. Hans Augusto Rey's 1976 book *The Stars: A New Way to See Them* is a classic that deserves a place in any classroom library, if only to open up this aspect of the basic "language" of the Catholic way of life.

Making a Celestial Clock

Indoors

Find a south-facing window. Place an object in the window that will cast a shadow on the wall or floor at noon. This object might be a sun-catcher or even a circle of thick paper taped onto a pane. Just be sure that the object will stay in position throughout the year.

Outdoors

Find a south-facing wall. In the ground poke a stick that casts a noon-time shadow on the wall. Perhaps a ball can be hung in the limb of a well-placed deciduous tree or shrub to use as a shadow-caster. If an outdoor wall isn't suitable, the stick or ball can be positioned to cast a shadow on a plywood surface set into the ground. Just make sure everything stays put!

Indoors or Outdoors

Once each month at one in the afternoon during Daylight Savings Time and at noon during Standard Time, mark the floor or wall where the shadow falls. Figure out an acceptable way to mark the surface, a way that doesn't damage it and yet will stay in place. The mark can be something as simple as a circle of paper with the date written on it that's affixed to the surface with masking tape.

Bringing in the Sheaves

"Harvest moon" is the full moon closest to the autumnal equinox. At this time of year, moonlight helps harvesters stay in the fields to complete their work. Because a full moon rises just as the sun sets and sets as the sun rises, it shines all night. In a way, a full moon gives us a foretaste of heaven's eternal light.

Several cultures have a major festival at the time of the harvest moon—demonstrating once again that great minds think alike. Of course, food is most plentiful at harvest time. Once the harvest is gathered, the bulk of the year's work is done. The Chinese in particular make much out of this occasion. In a few pages we'll take a good look at the Jewish harvest-moon festival of Sukkot.

For Christians the harvest is a powerful scriptural image of the paschal mystery. Saint Paul told us that Jesus Christ is the first fruits of the dead. Jesus is the first of God's holy harvest. And soon all who have died will be gathered into heaven, each reaped "in proper order" (1 Corinthians 15:23). The ingathering began on Calvary, as Jesus breathed forth the life-giving Spirit. The harvest will be completed on the final day.

Because Christian peoples live in so many different climates and regions, the timing of harvest celebrations varies. Among Catholics in Europe and the Middle East, depending on the climate, one or more of the days between Pentecost and All Saints is kept as a harvest celebration. Catholics in the United States failed to adapt the liturgical calendar to include a harvest festival, and the civic observance of Thanksgiving Day has come to fill the gap. In most places, however, late November is well past the season of harvesting. We may associate the harvest with autumn, but it takes place in spring and summer, too.

*S*ummer and fall are marked by successive harvests. In the north, strawberries ripen in June, cherries in July. Wheat and rye, depending on the place, are cut in July or August. Peaches and sweet corn are abundant later in summer. September and October bring the grape harvest. In California, olives and nuts ripen in late fall and may be gathered throughout the winter months.

So, too, in the liturgical year there is a progressive "harvest." Between Pentecost and Advent a process unfolds that echoes the harvest and that is completed in the liturgy at Christmas and Epiphany, as the year grows old and is renewed. Let's take a moment to explore this process. It's a key to unlocking the mystery of this time of year.

*T*he church's harvest time begins with the Fifty Days of Easter and reaches completion at Epiphany. Pentecost is called the "day of first fruits" and is tra-

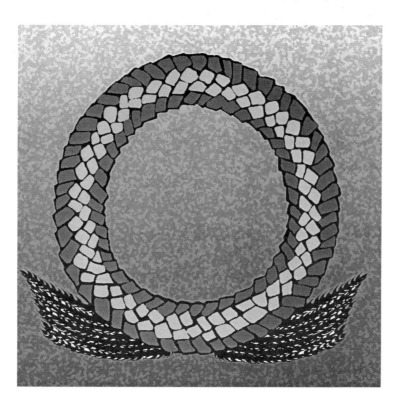

ditionally celebrated with a hearty helping of the first produce of the land. Pentecost is the first of many harvest festivals. Throughout the summer and autumn we rejoice in the metamorphosis brought about by warmth and sunlight and rain.

At the end of June, the festival of Saints Peter and Paul—whose work began the "harvest of the kingdom"— is observed in several cultures as the start of the wheat harvest. Of course, where wheat ripens later the harvest festival is later. On page 58 we mentioned Lammas Day, August 1, the Celtic grain harvest festival. In wheat-growing cultures this harvest—the most important of the year, the one that garners "our daily bread"—is surrounded by folk traditions. (Some are discussed in connection with Christmas, beginning on page 176.)

The English call any grain "corn," a term no doubt confusing to Americans. Keep this term in mind when researching European harvest customs, such as "corn dollies," which are rich symbols of the harvest made from woven wheat. The word "dolly" means "effigy." A corn dolly can look like a crown, scepter, wreath or other geometric shape. The tradition of weaving corn dollies is enjoying a revival. Is there a practitioner in the neighborhood who can show the class how it's done?

*W*hat looks more "right" in the fall than a scarecrow? There's the practical reason for creating one—to chase away marauding birds—but that's never been particularly effective. There's another reason, an ancient one. The figures represent the "spirit of the harvest." In many places an effigy of a human being was created from the portion of the harvest that would be used as the seed-source for the next year. This figure was called the "grandparent" and received the affectionate care that this title implies. Unlike a scarecrow, the effigy of the harvest was carried inside and placed somewhere dry and safe, kept free of vermin, and watched over through the winter. Of course, the seed became the parent of all future harvests—and its safekeeping a matter of life or death!

Think about this if you gather seeds from garden flowers to save for the following year. These too need careful storage and bear something of the stamp of the "parent of future generations." You might explain the custom to students, perhaps ask them to bring seed from their gardens (cosmos, cleome and four-o'clocks are good flower seeds to save). Keep the seeds somewhere dry and safe through the winter, and then distribute them to students next spring.

In times past, sometimes two harvest effigies were made, a grandmother and a grandfather. They were crowned queen and king and were set in thrones as if to preside over the harvest festivities. Crowns and scepters were created from grain woven into these shapes. Hanging a "harvest crown" (a wreath of grain) outside a home or inn was a sign of welcome to any traveler to come join in the plenty—and to help with the work.

You might want to create a scarecrow-like figure crowned with a wreath as a symbol of the abundance of the harvest. It can go inside or out. The entire school might have a contest to see which class can create the finest one. Your "harvest grandparents" can look like anything or anyone as long as they are created from grain and other natural materials, and are treated with respect and affection as symbols of God's generosity and providential care. They also are signs of the hospitality we owe one another as God's children, of the great expectations placed on those to whom great things have been given.

*D*isplay Idea

Throughout the fall, out of natural materials such as corn husks, one classroom creates figures of the saints, especially the harvest-season saints famous for their care of those in need—for example, Peter Claver, Vincent de Paul, Francis

*D*isplay Idea

of Assisi, Hedwig, Anthony Mary Claret, Martin de Porres, Martin of Tours, Frances Xavier Cabrini, Margaret of Scotland, Elizabeth of Hungary, Rose Duchesne. As each figure is fashioned and joins the others, the stories of the saints are told. The figures are hung from a grapevine that fills the room throughout the fall with bright foliage, bittersweet vines and bundles of miniature corn. Underneath donations of food are collected for food banks.

*T*hroughout late summer and autumn the colors used in the classroom can reflect the season's liveliness, employing countless shades of purples, blues, yellows, golds and greens. Hang a wreath of strawflowers, gomphrena, statice or dried herbs around the classroom cross. In the prayer corner a seasonal icon such as the birth of Mary, the exaltation of the cross, the victory of Saint Michael or the gathering of all saints around the paschal lamb can be honored with flowers and herbs.

Take advantage of the abundance of roadside garden stands and farmer's markets. Student gardeners can contribute some of their backyard bounty. Who cares if a spider or beetle tags along for the ride? But don't let good food go to waste. Send it home with someone before it begins to deteriorate.

Some craft stores and florists sell edible waxes that can be sprayed on vegetables and fruits to keep them from shriveling quickly. To this end, rutabagas, turnips and parsnips often are dipped in melted beeswax.

Gourds and pumpkins won't last longer if shellacked, although some people think these look prettier when shiny. The fungus that causes the fruits to decompose is a transmittable disease. If you get gourds and pumpkins from a disease-free source, they can last all winter. Some people suggest washing the fruit with a solution of bleach and water or a garden fungicide to kill spores, but if the fruit is already infected this does no good.

It's best to assume that a pumpkin will decompose and to place it on a moisture proof surface, and then to check it on a regular basis. A pumpkin can decompose over a weekend and the juice will stain carpet. Be especially careful about using a pumpkin near artificially colored oak leaves because any seepage and the dye in the foliage are a nasty combination.

$\mathcal{A}$t this time of year many field flowers and grasses dry naturally. So instead of putting these in water, arrange them in a pot of dry sand or perlite. (Do this one stalk at a time, which is the only way to achieve a billowy effect.) Some materials need to dry upside down if they are to stay looking good, so before making an arrangement with them, bundle them with raffia or a rubber band and hang them upside down a week or so to dry.

Achoo!

As a rule of thumb, most colorful flowers, such as goldenrod and asters, are bee-pollinated. The pollen is sticky and heavy and is not likely to get up noses and cause allergic reactions. It's just not true that goldenrod aggravates seasonal allergies. The culprit is ragweed, which blooms at the same time as goldenrod and has inconspicuous, wind-pollinated flowers. Most grasses pollinate in spring and early summer, so by the time you gather the seed plumes, pollinating season is long past.

Some people use hairspray to keep dried materials from decomposing. This won't work with certain materials, such as cattails, which make a merry and even explosive mess when they fall apart. ("Petting" a dried cattail and watching the seedheads burst out and float away is great fun—outdoors.) In general, the trick to keeping dried flowers intact is not to touch them and to keep them away from open windows and air vents.

Sing a Song of Harvest Home

Transfiguration marks a turning point in the year. The imagery of the harvest intensifies: On this day, at the seeming height of the land's productivity, we climb the holy mountain with Jesus. We witness the metamorphosis of the Lord, and, like Peter, we shout, "How good it is to be here!"

And then, like Peter, we ask if we should build booths. A strange question! The gospels tell us that he suggested building the booths, "not knowing what he said" (Luke 9:33). But we know.

Peter is talking about *sukkot,* the rickety shelters built to celebrate the Jewish festival called by that name, Sukkot. This festival begins two weeks after the Jewish New Year and five days after the holiest of holy days, Yom Kippur. Sukkot sets the seal on the new year. Since the Jewish year begins at a new moon, two weeks afterward is a full moon, a harvest moon.

A *sukkah* (*sukkot* is the Hebrew plural) is built from branches and decorated with fruits. It calls to mind the shacks, the "harvest homes," that harvesters used to set up in fields during the busy days when it was too much of an interruption to head home. According to tradition, the roof of a *sukkah* is left partly undone to allow the sun and moon to shine in, to let the wind enter and the rain fall through. To stand in a *sukkah* is to be surrounded by creation.

But on the mountain Peter never built *sukkot.* God's shining cloud enveloped the scene and then vanished. The disciples looked up, and Jesus was alone. It's as if the gospel writers are telling us that a *sukkah* has already been built. There's no need for another. This dwelling is the transfigured body of Christ, our true home that will wrap us in life—and how we long to enter it! (See 2 Corinthians 5:1–5.)

*I*n the mystery of the Christian year, soon after Transfiguration Day, the Blessed Virgin Mary (August 15) and John the Baptist (August 29) are the first to be gathered into Christ's *sukkah.* Its main support beam, the holy cross (September 14), bolsters the booth against autumn storms. Then, "in proper order," all the angels (September 29) and saints (November 1) are harvested into this shelter. Finally at Epiphany the whole of creation is wrapped in the *sukkah* as the fullness of Christ fills all in all. The stars themselves shout the good news!

When at Christmas we talk about building a nativity scene you'll be reminded of the *sukkah.* Although Eastern Christians usually depict Jesus' birthplace as a tomblike cave, Western Christians often depict it as a rickety *sukkah* filled to the rafters with emblems of creation.

*A*ctivity Idea

At the festival of Sukkot a class trip to a synagogue or Jewish center may be in order. One of the hallmarks of the holiday is hospitality. Perhaps you'll have a chance to see the *lulav* (bundle of palm, willow and myrtle branches) and *etrog* (a citron fruit) that are held in the hand and waved while psalms are sung. One of these psalms you might know well—Psalm 118, with its joyous cries of "hosanna" and "hallelujah," and its words, "This is the day the Lord has made."

Piling It On

The process of "liturgical ingathering" from August 6 to January 6 gives us a strong clue about how we might decorate the classroom through these months—cumulatively! For instance, if at the end of September you use images of angels to celebrate Michaelmas (see page 95), leave them in place during October, and add images of the saints for All Saints Day. Throughout these weeks accumulate harvest decorations and have them build in beauty and plentifulness. Use these again, della Robbia–style, when you fashion the nativity scene at Christmas. (Ideas for doing that are found beginning on page 171.)

*D*isplay Idea

*F*rom summer through fall and winter, emphasize the gradual transfiguration of materials. For instance, in June, at the end of the school year, you might bring into the classroom a few stalks of newly sprouted field corn (supposedly "knee high by the Fourth of July"). As the new school year begins you might have a few stalks of green, tassled corn, or fresh ears of sweet corn. In November you might ornament the room with whole sheaves of frosted, brown corn, the ears now dry and brittle. The harvested corn is a traditional emblem at the Advent feast of Our Lady of Guadalupe, and the stalks make a traditional Central American way to enclose a nativity scene.

*I*n whatever you do, try to make it appear that All Saints Day and then Christmas and Epiphany really are goalposts in the church's year. They are crescendos to which autumn leads. They are festivals of fulfillment.

Hail, Holy Cross!

The Roman emperor Constantine built Christian shrines over the sites of Jesus' crucifixion and burial. In mid-September in the year 335 the shrines were opened and dedicated. Afterward, each year on September 14 Christian pilgrims came to Jerusalem to celebrate the anniversary of the dedication of the shrines.

In Byzantine tradition September 14, Holy Cross Day, is a major fast day and is considered Good Friday's mirror image. The cross is set up in church and honored with kisses. Ethiopian Christians in particular have enormous affection for the day. Besides the ceremonies in church, at home a cross is set up outdoors and ornamented almost like a Christmas tree or a *sukkah.* At night the cross is illuminated, while songs are sung around it, dances danced and stories told.

*H*oly Cross Day is the most important church festival in September. It deserves special celebration. The color of the day is red, as on Good Friday. Everyone in school can wear reds and purples that day.

Activity Idea

Be sure to wear a cross around your neck if you have one. The feast is an occasion to speak about our regard for the holy cross. This means that any cross worn on the body is more than jewelry; indeed, it is worn as a sign of faith, reverently, and never in a way that would hurt someone else's feelings. The cross is to be a sign of unity, not division.

In a sense, Holy Cross Day is Good Friday clad in the garments of late summer. Fragrant basil (which means "royalty") is associated with this day: According to legend, the herb covered the site where Helen found Jesus' cross.

Because of its rapid growth, basil is a sign of resurrection. Its leaves emerge from the stem in a cruciform pattern (like other members of the mint family), and its unique aroma gives a nostalgic quality to the feast. Basil and other herbs and September flowers are used to carpet the floor under the cross this day.

*B*less the classroom cross on Holy Cross Day. *Blessings and Prayers through the Year* includes a way to do that. First, if possible, take down the classroom cross and clean it. Clean the wall, too. Even if the classroom cross is chipped or ugly, think of all the people who have occupied this room before you. In mystery, in the body of Christ, they are represented by this cross.

Perhaps you can arrange to have the cross repaired, if needed. If the classroom doesn't have a cross, use a simple one made of two branches lashed together. This can be left in place through the year. Eventually the class might commission an artist to fashion a cross on behalf of a former student or teacher—perhaps someone who has died—as a gift to the school, or else a beautiful one can be found and bought. Especially if you have a new cross, you'll want to bless it according to the rite in the *Book of Blessings.* (This book should either be in the sacristy of the church or in the rectory office. It would be a good idea for the school office to have a copy, too.)

*R*esource Idea

*F*or the feast day, and perhaps for the entire autumn season, drape the wall behind the cross with a bright cloth of reds, purples, oranges or other royal colors. Set flowers nearby. A spray of ornamental grasses and long-lasting flowers such as hydrangea might be used to weave into a garland or wreath to surround the cross. Goldenrod, statice, peacock blue, helichrysum and other strawflowers will dry naturally and last a long time, although it's best to work with them when they're fresh and supple. A farmer's market is a great place to buy these in quantity.

Show students how basil and other members of the mint family (such as oregano, thyme, lemon balm, coleus, salvia and marjoram) have foliage that

Prayer of Blessing for the Cross

Blessed are you, Lord God, Father all-holy,
for your boundless love.
The tree, once the source of shame and death for humankind,
has become the cross of our redemption and life.

When his hour had come to return to you in glory,
the Lord Jesus,
our King, our Priest, and our Teacher,
freely mounted the scaffold of the cross
and made it his royal throne,
his altar of sacrifice,
his pulpit of truth.

On the cross,
lifted above the earth,
he triumphed over our age-old enemy.
Cloaked in his own blood,
he drew all things to himself.

On the cross,
he opened out his arms
and offered you his life:
the sacrifice of the New Law
that gives to the sacraments their saving power.

On the cross,
he proved what he had prophesied:
the grain of wheat must die
to bring forth an abundant harvest.

Father,
we honor this cross
as the sign of our redemption.
May we reap the harvest of salvation
planted in pain by Christ Jesus.

May our sins be nailed to his cross,
the power of life released,
pride conquered,
and weakness turned to strength.

May the cross be our comfort in trouble,
our refuge in the face of danger,
our safeguard on life's journey,
until you welcome us to our heavenly home.
Grant this through Christ our Lord. Amen.

emerges crosswise from the stem. Perhaps students can bring various kinds of herbs from home, and you can collect them in a basket under the cross. Fragrant herbs remind us of these words of Paul from his second letter to the Corinthians: "Thanks be to God, who in Christ always leads us in triumphal procession, and through us spreads in every place the fragrance that comes from knowing him. For we are the aroma of Christ" (2:14–15).

Thorny roses and gladioluses also might be used this day and the next, the memorial of Our Lady of Sorrows. *Gladius* is Latin for "sword." The shape of the leaf can remind us of Simeon's prophecy that a sword of sorrow would pierce Mary's heart and would open the hearts of all who encounter Christ.

*Y*ou too might have a triumphal (and aromatic) procession on Holy Cross Day. Arrange for the class to carry the cross outdoors, perhaps around the school. Everyone can also carry herbs, bells and banners. A Jewish autumn tradition in celebration of the scriptures is to poke a bright pennant into an apple for each child to carry in a parade that honors the Torah as a "tree of life" that nourishes the people. Christians call the holy cross of Jesus their tree of life. Carrying fruits and branches and pennants of all kinds is a universal sign of celebration.

*A*ctivity Idea

Another option is to make simple crosses, perhaps of small leafy twigs, each poked into an apple or other seasonal fruit, so that everyone can hold a cross during the blessing. Another tradition is to bake cross-shaped cookies that are brilliantly decorated. Before the apple or cookie is eaten everyone says these words from an ancient song for the cross, *Crux fidelis* ("Faithful cross"): *Dulce lignum, dulce clavos, dulce pondus sustinet* ("Sweet the wood and sweet the nails, laden with so sweet a load").

*P*erhaps students can bring their crosses from home to church that day for a blessing. You'll need to arrange a beautiful place to put the crosses during the

Bulletin Board
for September
Hail, Holy Cross!

It's not easy getting into the spirit of September 14, Holy Cross Day, without feeling enormous affection for the cross. This love for the cross undergirds a fantastic number of ancient songs, poems, liturgical antiphons and writings that speak of the cross as if it were the most precious thing on earth—something so beloved that you kiss it the way you kiss a parent or child.

The cross represents everything mentioned in the Bible that's made from wood—the tree of life, Noah's ark, the wood Isaac carried up the hill, Moses' staff, Aaron's blossoming rod, the wood that was thrown into salty water to make it fit to drink, the ark of the covenant. And all these wonderful things represent Christ and the church—who gives us life, who preserves us, who sustains us.

Holy Cross Day, in the church's tradition, marks the turning of summer to autumn—in a similar way Good Friday marks a traditional turning from winter to spring. It would fit tradition to spend a bit of time on September 14 to "autumnize" the classroom.

Cover bulletin boards with autumn-colored paper. From other autumn-colored materials each student can prepare a cross with the student's name on it. One classroom prepared crosses out of dried flowers and grasses, another out pressed, dried leaves. The crosses can be placed in interlocking patterns over the background paper. Research into traditional shapes for the cross will reveal a fabulous range of designs. In the library or on the Internet, search for Ethiopian patterns—intricate metal filigree—and Lithuanian patterns—usually of wood.

Of course, the crosses don't need to go onto a bulletin board. If the papers are sturdy and won't curl, the crosses can be hung from the light fixtures or be gathered on branches or be used to create a kind of halo around the classroom's crucifix. The crosses can stay in place this autumn and be the backdrop for photos and other mementos of the dead in November.

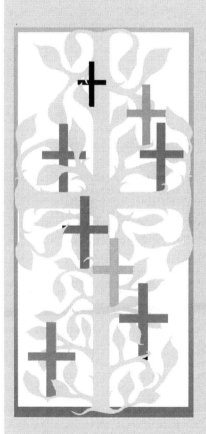

blessing. (The altar is not an appropriate spot for them.) Perhaps spread a table with handsome fabric that is scattered with fruit and flowers. Set it in the main aisle in church or in another place that doesn't compete for attention with the altar. If the weather's good, you might do this outdoors.

You might also bless any jewelry crosses that the students are wearing, but they're too delicate to take off during the blessing. Instead, ask students to touch their jewelry crosses while the blessing is chanted.

When back in the classroom, before putting the cross back on the wall, everyone can kiss it. Lay the cross on a handsome brocade pillow and allow everyone to take time to come forward reverently to offer the cross some sign of affection. This takes time. Any herbs or fruits or flowers or small wooden crosses or pennants that were carried in procession can be placed around the principal cross during the veneration. Some of this ornamentation might be left in place throughout the fall, which is why it seems best to use decoration that fits the flavor of autumn.

*I*n one parish school, early in September, students create beautiful cardboard crosses that are blessed at Mass and handed out to everyone on Holy Cross Day. They photocopy onto white card stock a cross with a geometric Celtic design (see page 93). The crosses are cut out from the card stock, colored so that no two are alike, and plastic jewels and sequins are glued onto them. They're then gathered in a basket and blessed and distributed at the end of Mass.

Or, alternatively, the crosses could be hung with ribbons from a bare tree set up in a classroom or in the school foyer or in the church vestibule. If you do this, leave it up throughout the fall and add additional ornaments as the season progresses. If space is tight you might suspend a tree branch from the ceiling, or suspend a coiled grapevine, which can be left in place through the year to hold various kinds of seasonal ornaments.

A tree is a key scriptural image on Holy Cross Day. In the beginning God planted a garden, but we only succeeded in getting ourselves kicked out of it. In overwhelming generosity, once again God plants a garden for us. In the middle, as a new tree of life, God sets the holy cross. Eden's tree brought us death, but the tree of the cross brings us life. From the holy cross God welcomes us home to paradise.

Besides the story of the crucifixion and the story of Adam and Eve, several other Bible stories are associated with this festival. The first reading at Mass tells of the time the people were saved from poisonous serpents by lifting an image of a bronze serpent on a wooden pole. Any Bible story that mentions wood, such as the story of Noah's ark, is understood by Christians to be wrapped up in the mystery of the holy cross. It's hardly surprising that we have such high regard for wood and for carpenters!

Angels Watching over Me

Those are the first words of a spiritual:
"All night, all day, angels watching over
me, my Lord. All night, all day, angels
watching over me."

*T*he Greek word *angelos* simply means "messenger," as does the Hebrew word for angel, *malakh.* (That's where the name of the prophet Malachi comes from.) God's angels are messengers. That's what their wings signify—messengers need a reliable way to get around.

The scriptures have no trouble identifying anyone or anything that carries out God's will as an "angel." Saint Matthew, whose feast falls on September 21, is depicted as a winged messenger. Matthew's gospel begins with accounts of angels appearing in Joseph's and the magi's dreams. Two days later, on September 23, the Eastern churches celebrate the appearance of the angel Gabriel to Zechariah, who was told that his wife Elizabeth was pregnant and that the baby was to be named John—John the Baptist! (That's how Luke's gospel begins.) In Byzantine icons John the Baptist is sometimes shown with wings because he too is identified as God's messenger.

*I*n the book of Tobit the angel Raphael identified himself as one of the seven who stand before God's throne. Biblical books mention the angels Michael, Gabriel and Raphael by name. Folklore supplies many, many names for other angels. But speculation about angels is risky conjecture. In Saint Paul's day the Colossians worried that eating certain foods on certain days would make angels angry. Paul told the Colossians that Christ is so far superior to any angel that, in proper perspective, angels are unimportant. Making too much of angels and devils is a form of superstition that denies the power of Christ.

The strange, apocalyptic books of Esdras, which are known by the church but not considered part of the Bible, mention the archangel Uriel, whose name means "God's light." The names of angels (and of most of the early martyrs) describe important virtues. Michael means "God's likeness," Gabriel means "God's hero," and Raphael means "God's healing power." You can see how these would make good names for anyone.

September 29 is the feast day of the archangels Michael, Gabriel and Raphael. In some places the feast is called "Saint Michael and All Angels" or "Michaelmas" (which rhymes with "picklepuss"). The day's liturgy is a celebration of the company of heaven. But the company is far from placid. We recall the "great war in heaven" described in the book of Revelation. Michael routed the angels who wanted to be God's rivals. The "tipping of the year" (in the northern hemisphere) toward darkness is an image of the unbalancing of heaven and the overthrowing of Lucifer.

A few days later, on October 2, the church remembers the guardian angels. In the liturgical year, as nights grow longer than days, it's as if the angels of light are sent to keep watch over us.

The feast of the angels calls for a celebration! Michaelmas is a great occasion for going all out and really having some fun with decorations.

Begin by gathering together as many images of angels as you can find. Avoid trite ones. Owing especially to commercial hype the past few years, finding beautiful images of angels has become relatively easy. Look for reproductions of some of the classic artwork depicting angels. Add angel-wing seashells, angel food cake, angel-trumpet flowers (although these are poisonous)—anything that reminds you of angels.

Figure out a way to gather the images in one spot. A useful way to do that is to hang them from a tree or a branch or a vine. That way lots of different things can be arranged attractively and tidily.

Another way to display lots of different objects—a way that fits the festival—is to create a "heaven." If you have a dropped ceiling in the classroom made of styrofoam, you can attach each object to a thread, tie the thread to a straight pin, and then poke the pin into the ceiling. You also can cut white Dacron® padding into cloud shapes and attach these to the ceiling or to the overhead lights and then attach the objects to the padding. Or simply suspend your angelic images from the light fixtures.

Borrowing from traditions for "All Angels Day," you might add depictions of any of God's winged creatures. Butterflies, bees, bugs, birds, bats—anything that flies is a symbol of the link between earth and heaven. You might go all out and have everyone design wings for themselves to attach to their clothing.

Display Idea

*I*n addition to wings, halos also are features of angels. The word "halo" has an interesting lineage. It's related to the words "holy," "whole," "all," "well," and even the words "healthy" and "wealthy." These are rooted in the Greek word *kala,* meaning both "beautiful" and "good."

There are different kinds of halos. Much classical art shows a circle of light radiating from the heads of angels and saints. Sometimes a halo is more like a crown or victory wreath—all these circular things are signs of fullfillment and completion, signs of wholeness and perfection.

That's why so many festival traditions employ the shape of the circle, such as the eating of circular breads and pastries. The angels and saints are imagined to dance in circles, too, emblematic of the fullfillment they enjoy in heaven. Many traditional festival dances, such as the Romanian *kolo* and the Israeli *hora,* are circle dances, foretastes of heaven's eternal dance.

A kind of halo seen in Christian art is the almond shape formed when two circles begin to intersect. The intersection represents the meeting of heaven and earth. The shape is commonly seen in Byzantine art, and is called a *mandorla* or *mandula* (meaning "almond"). The shape also is seen surrounding the figure of Christ positioned over the doorways of medieval churches.

Thanks in part to this "heavenly significance," almonds themselves and almond-rich desserts have become especially meaningful holiday fare.

*M*ichaelmas, as a harvest-time holiday, is a day for rich foods. Is anything in the works in the school cafeteria? Foods stuffed into other foods—such as stuffed peppers and stuffed cabbage and stuffed grape leaves—are especially associated with harvest time, and among Christians represent the overflowing fullness of the heavenly city.

Ornamentation that surprises us by opening up to reveal even more ornamentation also carries the significance of heavenly fulfillment. That's why the autumn and winter holidays have long been occasions for overdoing it with a bit of festival excess. We're trying to anticipate the surprises that await us in God's dominion.

Asters are autumn-flowering perennials particularly associated with this feast. They're native to North America and brighten roadsides with their purple or white blooms, although Europeans grow them too and call them "Michaelmas daisies." Asters and daylilies are great "companion plants" with spring flowering bulbs, since in early summer as the bulbs go dormant (never remove the foliage until it dies naturally), the daylilies and asters hide the dying bulb foliage and provide summer and autumn flowers.

Flower Bulb Planting Time

Now's the time to bless and plant crocus, daffodil and tulip bulbs. (*Blessings and Prayers through the Year* has a ritual for this.) Few flowers are more guaranteed of successful flowering as long as you plant them in a sunny spot that won't ever get flooded or waterlogged. It's hard to imagine a more wonderful way to bring to students a grand image of their own efforts in school than by planting bulbs in early autumn, close to the start of the school year, that will bloom in spring, close to the conclusion. Anything worth waiting for has a season of gestation, when efforts stay hidden, when wonderful things happen in secret. It's worth the effort to find a protected spot outdoors to plant bulbs.

Crocuses and other small bulbs, such as anemones, chionodoxa, scilla and pushkinia (a flower named after the beloved Russian poet Pushkin) tend to bloom and multiply in a garden year after year. Tulips are fussier and some varieties bloom well only the first year after planting. Some climates are unsuited to crocuses and tulips. Southerners can plant jonquils and zephyranthes. People on the West Coast can grow ranunculus and freesias.

Bulletin Board for September

Ye Watchers and Ye Holy Ones

For a bulletin board for late September, in celebration of the angels, cover the board with gold or russet paper. Have every student create a set of wings (or even entire angels) from a limited palette of papers or other materials (perhaps, for instance, papers in shades of yellow and orange and purple, or perhaps various shades of foil; limiting the palette results in a classy and harmonious final design). The wings can be bird wings, bat wings, even pterodactyl wings—or what students imagine to be angel wings. (One student used wing-shaped seashells.) Research is needed, along with care and creativity. Artfully, attractively, students can add their own names to their wings, perhaps using a pen with gold ink. (When students produce anything for public display, it has to be done well so it doesn't turn into a testimonial to carelessness or indifference.)

Overlap the wings across the bulletin board. Then tell biblical stories of angels. (We mention a few on these pages.) Over the wings, add well-crafted depictions of the scriptural stories. In finding or creating images of angels, remember that angels aren't necessarily Caucasian. Why would their skin color be like any human skin color? And who's to say angels have skin? Ezekiel's depiction is downright creepy, with angels more like balls of fire than people with wings. In creating the image of an angel, the goal isn't to be bizarre; the goal is to depict God's strength, wisdom, care, and even God's knack for surprising us.

Perhaps around your bulletin board might be placed other celestial signs—sun, moon, planets, comets and stars. Or else circle the board with these words from Psalm 148: "Praise the LORD! // Praise him, all his angels; / praise him, all his host!" September 29 is the feast of the angels, and on October 2 we remember the angelic guardians of humanity. The bulletin board might remain in place through the fall, with saints added in November among the angels.

*I*n celebration of the feast of the angels, search for or create depictions of heaven. These can range from visions of shining clouds and the saints streaming through the pearly gates (images found in the Bible's book of Revelation) to unusual images, such as portraits of heaven from the American South as the foggy land across the river, or as a cotton field ready for picking, or as a church supper with abundant foods to eat.

An image of heaven from Germany looks like a kitchen crammed with *Äpfel, Nuß und Mandelkern*—apples, walnuts and almonds. An African image depicts heaven to be like the yam harvest.

A wonderful Finnish custom is to weave rye and wheat into a trellis, then to set the trellis horizontally on four poles (creating a kind of Jewish *sukkah*) or else to suspend the trellis horizontally from the ceiling. This "roof" is hung with foil stars and is simply called, "heaven."

In one class each student brings in a picture of herself or himself, or else a picture of the entire family. These are attached to stars cut out of posterboard. The stars are hung with monofilament (fishing line) from the light fixtures, along with all sorts of depictions of angels. The photo-stars can be made more exciting by tucking each photo into a star-shaped matte made from two stars placed on top of each other, one of which has a "window" cut out to show the photo. The photo-stars are saved to use again at Christmas over the nativity scene.

*B*iblical descriptions of the heavenly hosts are anything but saccharine. None of them are cute, some are horrifying, and many are beautiful and thrilling. Read the tenth chapter of the book of the prophet Ezekiel. Do you know the giddy spiritual "Ezekiel saw the wheel way up in the middle of the air"? Angels can be weird! Ezekiel's cherubs are not plump and cuddly but fiery and fierce. You wouldn't want one to show up at school. Even in the familiar stories of angels in the gospels, notice how the writers fail to offer descriptions.

But we do hear that angels find it necessary to begin by undoing the fear their appearance arouses.

Some classic images of angels are strongly militaristic, such as the depiction of Michael destroying hell's satanic dragon. Angel guardians are figures of skill and power. The books of Exodus and Psalms imagine God as an eagle grasping people in its talons and carrying them up to the heights—not to devour but to safeguard them within its nest. This image comes close to much angelic imagery. Imagine being God's eaglets!

As a teacher you may be uncomfortable with militaristic iconography, or with such clearly mythological themes as demons and dragons. But before you banish these from the classroom, consider what would be lost: Cultures from England to India to China have tales of dragons. A person has to wonder what in the human psyche, the world around, invents this image. (Another oddball image that has counterparts all around the world is the phoenix, the firebird.) The stories about these creatures, in all their incarnations, tell of the cosmic conflict between opposing forces, between light and darkness, between warmth and cold, between energy and lethargy.

In Christian stories, too, the theme of conflict is strong, and the strongest story, the one with biblical roots, is the tale in the book of Revelation about the war in heaven, when Michael defeated Lucifer. The story's springtime counterpart in Christian iconography is the tale of George battling the dragon, a story modeled on the Greek story of the hero Perseus, who struggled against a sea monster on behalf of his beloved Andromeda. In triumph the couple rode off on the winged horse Pegasus. (The characters of this legend, even Pegasus and the sea monster Cetus—in the form of constellations—grace the skies on autumn evenings, so be sure to have a look.)

George is a patron of springtime. Michael is autumn's patron, and the image of Michael battling Lucifer might have a place in the classroom throughout the fall. Of course, in telling the stories of George or Michael (and of the other dragon-battling saints such as Margaret of Antioch), we're telling about the death, burial and resurrection of the Lord. We're telling about the paschal mystery. The Easter sequence (a gospel hymn) includes the powerful line *Mors et Vita duello conflixere mirando* ("Death and Life fought a wondrous conflict"). In spring Life wins. In autumn the outcome of the battle is not so certain. Death seems to gain the upper hand.

*A*utumn is our annual encounter with darkness. Images of angels used in the classroom during early autumn might stay in place throughout the season and be the foundation on which other images are added at All Saints Day. At All Souls and in November we'll hear more about Michael. Another of the archangel's traditional roles is to guide the dead into paradise. That's why Michael is sometimes shown carrying scales to "weigh" the good and bad deeds of the dead.

Raphael, too, as the healer and guide in the book of Tobit, has been a beloved companion at this time of year. His feast day on the former Catholic calendar fell late in October. Clearly, as winter looms, all of us are in need of the protection of a healer.

Gabriel is more associated with Advent and the springtime solemnity of the Annunciation, but Gabriel's trumpet (or, more precisely, the *shofar,* a ram's horn), which will one day awaken the dead, is a strong autumnal image. A real ram's horn can cost hundreds of dollars, but perhaps someone in the school community will think it a fine investment. An autumn class trip to a synagogue might include the sounding of the *shofar.*

*W*e almost could call autumn a season of angels, at least in folklore. The failing light of autumn can make doomsday seem close at hand. The lengthening night may make it easier to imagine death's dragon lurking in the shadows. How fitting that, as autumn begins, Uriel descends to bring light to our eyes. Michael rallies us to battle against evil and to protect us from our own selfishness. Gabriel lifts the horn and lets out a sound loud enough to wake the dead. Raphael takes us by the hand and guides us home.

Winged Watchers

The first words of the familiar and beloved hymn "Ye watchers and ye holy ones" (the melody was originally an Easter carol, which accounts for the multiplicity of alleluias) refer to angels—"watchers." A great word! *Angelos* in Greek means "messenger," and in ancient times the archetypal messenger was Hermes or Mercury, the mythical god with wings on his feet. Borrowing Roman imagery, Christians drew wings on their depictions of anyone regarded as God's messenger, not just the angels. And they didn't just draw two birdlike wings. There might be two, four, even dozens of wings formed from all sorts of materials, sprouting from most any part of the body.

 *A*ctivity Idea

October

Entering into the Mystery of October
Francis of Assisi and the Blessing of Pets
Let's Break a Bad Habit: October Is Not a Month-Long Halloween

Entering into the Mystery
of *October*

*L*iturgically speaking, October is an "in between month." September was rich in festival days. November will be even richer. October falls in between.

For many, October is the last chance to finish outdoor work before winter sets in. We wash windows, paint, fix up the landscaping. This is a month of "cocooning," of "feathering our nests." In the classroom the intention usually is to make October productive, with extra attention to work.

*O*ctober is a month of ingathering. Migratory birds gather in noisy flocks before departing. Gnats form vapory clouds. An old term for this time of year is "goose summer" because geese are in such evidence, honking high overhead. "Goose summer" gives us the word "gossamer," which once meant "spiderwebs." In mid-autumn, spiders and many other creature are busily laying the eggs of next summer's generation. In the garden the webs are everywhere. (Think about this term when you see a homeowner covering the house with artificial spider webs for Halloween.)

Since the end of June the length of the day has been decreasing, gradually at first, now rapidly. The

loss hits home when clocks are turned back on the last Sunday of October—just in time for Halloween and the days of the dead. There's an autumnal "passover" taking place, the opposite of spring's. Within a few days, so it seems, leaves color and fall. One morning we wake up and the garden is frosted. This, of course, is more than an image of death: It's death staring us in the face.

*M*uch of autumn evokes nostalgia, a lovely word that means "a desire for homecoming," our yearning to be where we belong. Christian nostalgia has a distinctive character because the home we yearn for is not in our past but in our future, within the reign of God. For us the "good old days" are still to come.

The root of the Hebrew word "jubilee" also means "homecoming." To yearn for the days of jubilee is to yearn for God's ways to become our ways. In the words of the Jewish prayer called the Kaddish, "Lord, you make peace in heaven. Make peace on earth." Much of autumn and contiuing through Advent is occupied in the liturgy with thoughts of the "last things," in Greek, *eschata:* death, judgment, God's reign. On autumn Sundays we hear in the gospel readings the final passages from the year's evangelist that precede the account of Jesus' passion. These passages contain Jesus' most intense warnings about the end of the world and the arrival of Judgment Day. We'll hear these in November. In October we hear many parables of the coming kingdom.

*T*he ingathering of the harvest becomes, in the liturgy, an important image of what heaven's homecoming will be like. The psalms associated with autumn blend these images: In Psalm 126 we sing that those who sow in tears will reap in joy. In Psalm 65 we shout, "You crown the year with your bounty!" In Psalm 146 we sing that the Lord gives food to the hungry, justice to the oppressed and watchful protection to the wayfarer. In Psalm 122,

*O*ctober

1 Memorial of Thérèse of the Child Jesus, virgin, religious

2 Memorial of the Guardian Angels

4 Memorial of Francis of Assisi, religious founder

6 Optional memorial of Bruno, presbyter, hermit, religious founder

Optional memorial of Marie-Rose Durocher, virgin, religious founder

7 Memorial of Our Lady of the Rosary

9 Optional memorial of Denis, bishop, martyr, and his companions, martyrs

Optional memorial of John Leonardi, presbyter, religious founder

14 Optional memorial of Callistus I, pope, martyr

15 Memorial of Teresa of Jesus, virgin, religious, doctor of the church

16 Optional memorial of Hedwig, married woman, religious

Optional memorial of Margaret Mary Alacoque, virgin, religious

17 Memorial of Ignatius of Antioch, bishop, martyr

18 **Feast of Luke, evangelist**

19 Memorial of Isaac Jogues and John de Brebéuf, presbyters, religious, missionaries, martyrs, and their companions, martyrs

20 Optional memorial of Paul of the Cross, presbyter, religious founder

23 Optional memorial of John of Capistrano, presbyter, religious, missionary

24 Optional memorial of Anthony Mary Claret, bishop, religious founder

28 **Feast of Simon and Jude, apostles**

Second Monday: Thanksgiving Day in Canada

with pilgrims of every time and place, we rejoice to enter Jerusalem, our final home, the city of peace and endless jubilee.

Nostalgia has an added spark in autumn. The earlier nightfalls get some of us indoors earlier, and the chilly weather certainly has us scrambling for shelter and togetherness. Add to that the bounty of markets

In Short, in October

- October has an "in-between" character since it falls between the September festivals that surround the autumn equinox and the festivals that fall in November. Use October to prepare for November and for Advent.

- Keep up the harvest time décor and make sure that it clearly builds in intensity toward All Hallows. Suggestions for this décor are found beginning on page 79.

- Don't turn Halloween into October's month-long "theme." Make decisions about how you will decorate for All Hallows and not just for All Hallows Eve.

- You may want to host a blessing of animals on October 4, Saint Francis's Day. In many places October's great beauty lends itself to our praise of God in creation.

- Many autumn saints are known for their care for those in need. You may want to maintain a site in the classroom for the gathering of gifts for the needy.

October Ordinary Time
- Seasonal vesture color: *green*
- Some complementary colors: *gold, orange, violet, burgundy, brown*

at this season, and we have the fixings for an extended feast of reminiscing and storytelling.

*N*ights of remembrance are an antidote to fear, which hides in autumn's shadows. October has many such antidotes—for instance, the Guardian Angels (October 2). In the mystery of the memorials of the saints, the month brings us into some mighty fine company. Thérèse of Lisieux (October 1), the "little flower," promises to spend eternity doing good on earth. Francis of Assisi (October 4) urges people to work together to protect God's creatures. Teresa of Jesus (October 15) teaches us to rely on our wits. Princess Hedwig (October 16), in self-sacrificing compassion, demonstrates the virtue of *noblesse oblige.*

The evangelist Luke (October 18) tells stories of angels who urge us not to fear. Legends say that the martyr Ursula (October 21) and her friends lead heaven's dance. A month from Saint Ursula's Day is Saint Cecilia's Day (November 22)—we need these patrons of music and dance as the weather turns mean and drives us indoors.

Folklore tells us that the apostles Simon and Jude (October 28) remind us that no cause is lost. Hope springs eternal. Even tulip bulbs planted in October tell us that the time of darkness will end, the winter will pass, spring will return. In Christ, human flesh has its planting, its rest, its rising:

> *My flesh shall slumber in the ground*
> *till the last trumpet's joyful sound;*
> *then burst the chains with sweet surprise,*
> *and in my Savior's image rise.*

(from an early American hymn by William Billings, in *The Psalm Singer's Amusement,* 1781)

Francis of Assisi and the Blessing of Pets

A saint for our times! Francis seems the perfect patron for anyone who is confused, who has grown disgusted with the insipid values of the world, who seeks to be filled with true joy even in the midst of emptiness.

*I*n his splendid "Canticle of the Sun," Francis addressed God's creatures as sisters and brothers. Francis is now considered the patron saint of ecologists. He also can be considered a patron of dispossession, a saint who refused to give in to the materialism of his upbringing. He owned a single garment. He chose to associate himself with the "have-nots" of his time.

Francis was tireless in negotiating peace, and his times were filled with war. Not only were European Christians going on crusades to slaughter Jews, Muslims and Middle Eastern Christians, neighboring towns in Italy battled one another the way city gangs prey on one another nowadays.

Page 149 in *Companion to the Calendar* offers a fine, further introduction to Francis, and this popular saint is featured in a hundred other books. Take time on his feast day to read about Francis, if only to tell once again the marvelous tale from *The Little Flowers of Saint Francis* about his befriending and making a good Christian out of the "fierce wolf of Gubbio."

*R*esource Idea

*I*t's easy to find all sorts of images of Francis, most emphasizing his regard for the interconnectedness of living things. If you don't have a statue or other depiction of Francis to grace the classroom perhaps one can be borrowed for the day. Or download an image off the Internet, print it on photo-quality paper, and then frame it. Or search the library for a book that includes

a picture of Francis and leave it open on a fine book stand, with some autumn flowers placed nearby.

A custom building in popularity for Saint Francis's Day is the blessing of animals, pets in particular. The rite of blessing for animals in the *Book of Blessings* and in *Catholic Household Blessings and Prayers* may be appropriate for farm animals, but for pets, the "Blessing of Pets" for October 4 in *Blessings and Prayers through the Year* will serve better.

In some places the blessing of pets takes place in the church itself or in the parking lot or school yard, either after school or on the weekend close to Saint Francis's Day. Allow time for students to get home to prepare their pets for the journey. A local vet may have literature about the best ways to transport animals. Usually the safest way is to use a proper carrier.

Be sure to bless any classroom pets, such as fish or lizards or even tarantulas. (And while we're on the subject—are the resident classroom animals treated with respect and affection, cared for faithfully, kept in health and in safety from year to year for as long as they live? The treatment of animals in the school may be many students' only lesson on the lasting responsibility we embrace when we take on the care of an animal.)

*T*he first consideration in blessing pets is the safety of the animals. While it can be glorious to gather pets together in the church itself—which is one more reason to leave churches uncarpeted—some pets won't tolerate the trip, or shouldn't be subjected to it.

An alternative to transporting a pet is to bring a photo of the pet to church. A good place for that is a table in the main aisle or somewhere apart from the altar. Find some fun fabric printed with all sorts of animals to use as a table covering. Gather on the table all sorts of other images of animals. Any zoo store likely is busting at the seams with folk-art depictions of animals, and with picture books and craft books filled with designs for animal-oriented art projects.

In your decoration for the blessing of animals, try to include representations of indigenous critters. Even Central Park in New York is home to an amazing array of creatures. It wouldn't be far-fetched to have students design animal masks to wear to the blessing. You also might bag and distribute edible treats for the pets at the blessing.

Among the decorations, you might want to add depictions of animals to the images of angels you put up for September 29. A classic biblical image joining a pet and an angel is of Raphael and the dog that accompanied Tobiah on their journeys. (The suggestion in this book is to keep adding to this display through-out the fall, so that it reaches a crescendo at All Saints.)

*M*any of the saints are associated with animal companions. Cistercian writer David Bell has gathered stories of these companions from Jewish, Christian and Muslim traditions: *Wholly Animals: A Book of Beastly Tales* (Kalamazoo: Cistercian Publications, 1992). This is a great book!

Jesus' 40-day fast in the wilderness, where, according to Mark's gospel, he lived with wild beasts, is a scriptural foundation for the stories of the animal companions of the saints. Like Jesus in the desert, the saints are also returning to paradise, to the peaceable kingdom that was our first home and that, God willing, will be our home when time is fulfilled. Living in harmony with animals in our homes offers us a glimpse into Eden.

*I*f you establish a birdfeeder on school grounds, be sure to maintain it, even over weekends and holidays. Birds come to rely on the feeder. A supply of fresh, clean water should be nearby. Specific kinds of birdseed attract specific species of bird. The birdfeeder will also attract vermin and predators.

Autumn Gardening

Plants deserve their due, too. October is an important gardening month. Some schools have discovered the benefit of maintaining a school-yard garden, a place to escape a bit and think, a living labora-tory. Of course, it's lovely to keep a statue of Saint Francis there.

Successful school-yard gardens often make use of native plant materials—these species are survivors. Also, students do much of the work, even through the summer, so that they "own" the results. Now's the time of year to plant spring-flowering bulbs, to prepare the beds and to plant certain perennials and woody plants. Since in most places autumns are dry, watering is crucial.

In the United States a spell of warmish weather that follows the first freeze is called "Indian summer." In Europe late-season warm spells may be named after the closest saint's day, for instance, "Saint Luke's little summer." If you manage to protect the garden from frost, supposedly Luke helps you out and ripens a few more of the unripe vegetables. In others words, "God helps those who help themselves."

Let's Break a Bad Habit: October Is Not a Month-Long Halloween

From infancy many of us have been raised to think of each month in terms of a holiday celebrated during the month. For example, February is the month of Saint Valentine's Day. March is the month of Saint Patrick's Day. Preschool calendars that teach children the names of months inevitably add hearts to February and shamrocks to March. We're surrounded by this kind of thinking and the appeal lies in its simplicity.

The October calendar almost always is ornamented with signs of Halloween. In all sorts of venues, Halloween has become October's theme. Throughout the month some people surround themselves with Halloween's ghosties and ghoulies and long-legged beasties. In a similar way in the United States, Thanksgiving has become November's theme, and Christmas is December's. The observances of these holidays has become stretched backward for a month.

Catholics in love with their way of life ought to have trouble with this sort of thinking. It doesn't square with what we hold dear. It isn't helpful to our imaginations. It puts the emphasis where it doesn't belong.

To the Catholic way of thinking, Halloween is the eve of All Saints Day. It is not October's running theme. Halloween isn't even an actual day. Instead,

it's a vigil, begun at nightfall. Halloween is the "opening movement" of the festival of All Saints. Describing Halloween not as a vigil but as a holiday in itself leads to some peculiar and foundationless thinking that gives Halloween too much weight. Halloween gets bent out of shape when we imagine it as a day or even a month that is separated from All Saints.

An example of peculiar thinking is that some people say that "Halloween celebrates evil the way All Saints celebrates goodness." As another example, some writers—Catholic writers—have described Halloween as part of a "triduum" (a three-day observance) along with November 1 and 2, and that October 31 "is about the souls in hell" the way that November 1 "is about the souls in heaven" and that November 2 "is about the souls in purgatory."

Such notions keep reappearing especially in articles for teachers and at first seem to make sense—but they don't square with Catholic attitudes about the bonds of grace and love that link earth and heaven within the communion of saints. Thomas Aquinas wrote, "Since all the faithful form one body, the good of each is communicated to the others." Catholic faith is loath to admit that the love of Christ has failed, that members of the body of Christ need amputation. There may be a roster of saints (with never any suggestion that the roster is complete), but the church has no roster of the damned and certainly wouldn't observe a day to celebrate them.

In October we are getting ready for a great festival. We don't jump the gun on it. We make ready. And the anticipation is sweet.

That's part of the spirit of October in the Catholic classroom—anticipation, preparation. It's harvest time. We keep up and increase the harvest decorations. It's fall planting time, too, time to make outside and inside ready for the upcoming winter. And, in a gradually increasing manner, it's time to make ready for the great festival of All Saints and then the Commemoration of the Faithful Departed. Make sure that an emphasis goes on November 1 and 2, with October 31 understood as the time to enter into the festival.

The saints' days late in October—for instance, Saint Luke (October 18) and Saint Ursula (October 21)—are customary occasions to begin in earnest the cooking and cleaning and decorating for All Saints. An old English custom on October 28, the feast of Saints Simon and Jude, is to parade from door to door in a neighborhood and to beg for the fixings of the All Saints dinner. This sounds a lot like trick or treat! You might take a cue from this practice and

Bulletin Board
for October
All Creatures
of Our God
and King

The well-known hymn tune "Lasst uns erfreuen herzlich sehr" can get a workout each fall. To this tune, on the feasts of Mary and the angels and the saints, you can sing "Ye watchers and ye holy ones." (The first verse is about angels, the second about Mary, the third about the saints in heaven—and the fourth about us!) On Saint Francis's Day, October 4, to the same tune you can sing "All creatures of our God and king." The words are based on Francis's "Canticle of the Sun." They're great words praising the Lord in communion with every creature God has made.

Francis's words are a lot like the song of Shadrach, Meshach and Abednego in the fiery furnace. In that place of death, they asked everything everywhere to praise the Lord. Amazingly, Francis asked death to join the song.

Cover a bulletin board with paper autumn leaves. (Rubber cement is helpful, or even staples if the board is covered in cork.) Real leaves can be used too, if you choose a non-curling kind, such as white oak and its kin (these are oaks with rounded, not pointed, leaves). Any real leaf will curl a bit, but that adds a beautiful texture. You will need a lot of leaves. They're probably still green in early October but will dry in muted shades of olive and tan.

Read or, better, sing Saint Francis's canticle and also the Benedicite (named from its first word in Latin)—the song of Shadrach, Meshach and Abednego. (In some Bibles this song is found in Daniel 3:52–90, and in some Bibles in the apocrypha, where it is called "The Prayer of Azariah" or "The Song of the Three Young Men.") Students can depict the many creatures named in these songs, and the depictions can overlay the autumn leaves. In the center you can place a picture of Saint Francis or else a picture of the three young men. (Don't forget to add the angel, who joined the song and whose wings beat out the flames of the furnace.)

When finished you'll have a bulletin board with angels and stars, earth and heaven, rain and snow, clouds and lightning, seas and rivers, as well as animals of the sea, sky and land—and people, too, of every kind. You might encircle the board with the hymn's first words: "All creatures of our God and king, lift up your voice and with us sing: 'Alleluia!'"

Wondrously, what you'll have is perfect to keep in place through Thanksgiving Day. In the spirit of the liturgy, all of autumn is an occasion to sing "thank you" to the Lord of heaven and earth.

All creatures of our God & King

lift up your voice & with us sing

observe a moratorium on Halloween images until, say, a week before All Saints. Holding off will make the decorations more welcome, less taken for granted.

*R*ead over the material in this book about All Saints Day (pages 121–28) and a classroom shrine for the dead (pages 129–33). Choose and then use decorations that can have a place in the classroom throughout the month of November, the church's month for remembering ancestors and praying for the dead. Make connections between any spooky decorations and the strengthening anticipation of Judgment Day, an anticipation that, in the liturgy of November and of Advent, mirrors our anticipation of Christmas and the renewal of the year.

A number of spooky images—images with scriptural roots, such as skeletons, tombstones, dragons, bats and harvester's tools, along with the glorious images of the saints in bright robes carrying palm branches—surface in the liturgy throughout the autumn, and then intensify in November and on into Advent. These images don't suddenly appear and then disappear on October 31. We've already received a healthy helping of them on September's feast day of the angels. As we move through October, nights continue to get longer and spookier. And the end of October doesn't put an end to the process. The darkness intensifies through November and December.

*D*isplay Idea

The deepening darkness suggests that in the classroom, as in the liturgical year, many of the images associated with Halloween accumulate throughout the fall, and that some remain throughout November and on into Advent. This pattern also suggests that we make a dedicated effort to create or find appropriate images and not simply settle for all of the Halloween decorations that are available (although many of these are useful in the Catholic classroom).

*N*o doubt in storage you already have a number of decorations for Halloween. Figure out which sorts of decorations are appropriate and which aren't. For instance, store-bought or handcrafted images of skeletons, ghosts, graveyard scenes, nighttime creatures such as bats—these are traditional decorations used as *memento mori*. They're perfect for celebrating All Saints, All Souls and the entire month of November.

Other store-bought Halloween materials—Frankenstein's monster, Dracula, Egyptian mummies—as fun as these might be, are far-fetched. You may want to retire them. Some people would say that most images of witches ought to be retired, too. They have a checkered history among Christians. They symbolize

Christian disdain for pre-Christian religions, religions whose rituals were dismissed as "witchcraft."

*I*t may strike us a bit odd to use spooky images to celebrate All Saints and All Souls, but in fact these images have a long history in Catholic cultures. We've taken a shine to them and have seen fit to ornament our churches with grinning gargoyles and grotesques. In Latin America and Europe it's difficult to find a church or clocktower without at least a few skeletons in evidence. Traditionally, the back wall of a church—the last thing you see when exiting the building—is decorated with a depiction of the Last Judgment, complete with graves opening and the dead rising, with a heaven filled with angels and a hell filled with devils.

Images of demons have a special place in Christian iconography. Almost always they are shown cowering in fear or stuck behind locked doors or else being trampled underfoot by Christ and the powers of heaven. (That's what's happening in the depiction of Saint Michael battling Satan.) The demons aren't happy with what's happening to them. They hiss and spit in anger. And almost always, even in their hideousness, they are made to look comical. God's mighty laughter strips them of power.

The same dynamic is afoot when Christians dress up as demons, when Christians use images of hell in celebration of the reign of heaven. That's what's going on at All Saints and All Souls. The spooky decorations are meant to evoke a hearty laugh, a laugh in the face of death. We spend a lot of time poking fun at death, because death and injustice and the other sorrows of the world often seem to have the upper hand. But we know that in Christ we will have the last laugh. The "divine comedy" is guaranteed a happy ending.

November

Entering into the Mystery of November
All Hallows: A Harvest Homecoming in Heaven!
A Shrine for the Dead
Other November Observances

Entering into the Mystery
of November

In every season the church celebrates the paschal mystery—the Easter mystery—the mystery of the life that is stronger than death. Throughout the year within the liturgy we make use of signs of this transcendent life, the life that is ours in Christ.

However, in November, with winter settling in, evidence of Easter is hard to come by. The signs in nature seem to point in the wrong direction, away from Easter. The bright glory of autumn foliage and flowers with which the month begins quickly disintegrates under the influence of the increasing darkness and cold. On the liturgical calendar, November begins with a glorious festival, but the month ends in a far more somber mood, as Advent arrives.

In many places, November is the dreariest, cloudiest, least sunny month of the year. In the north the first snows fall. In the south trees drop their foliage. Migrating birds depart. Frost puts a slimy end to the gardening year. All this dying and departure, this fogginess and gloom set many hearts to imagining what lies beyond the grave.

November begins the "dark quarter" of the year. This quarter is bracketed by Hallowmas (an old name for All Saints Day, November 1) and Candlemas (an old name for the feast of the Presentation of the Lord, February 2).

The dark quarter has long been the season of fears, and chief among these is the primordial fear of the dark. Nowadays, with a flick of a switch, we are able to hold some of the darkness at bay. We're also able, if we're fortunate, to insulate ourselves from a number of other fears that preoccupied our ancestors—the fear of hunger, of starvation, of running out of winter fuel, of disease.

However, the insulation is thin. Even with light, food, fuel and medicine, the old fears are with us still. They hide in the shadows. They weigh on the soul. We may have managed to make ourselves more comfortable, but we can't keep death away.

Around the world, the late autumn and winter festivals include customs clearly intended to drive the age-old fears away. We light lamps, gather around a fire, prepare extra-hearty meals, gain a few pounds, seek out companionship, share hospitality more freely, sing and dance, reminisce, tell tall tales, dream about the future, and even escape into the refreshment of imagination and fantasy.

Here's one way to think about the liturgical spirit of the days from November through February: Throughout these days we face our fears, and we help one another transcend and not become crippled by them. In the words of an Irish sea chanty: "We all join hands and form a chain, till the leaves of springtime come again."

In November, if the harvest has been good, pantries are full. All through the fall we have been harvesting things, bringing them indoors, and putting them into storage. In November, as winter weather arrives, it's our own turn to come inside, to seek out the warmth and dryness and safety of our homes.

Naturally, concern for the welfare of others is a hallmark of late autumn and winter. None of us can rest securely in our homes until all people have a place to call home. November is particularly rich in memorials of saints who were known for their care for the poor, the sick, the disenfranchised: Martin de Porres (November 3), Martin of Tours (November 11), Frances Xavier Cabrini (November 13) and Elizabeth of Hungary (November 17).

Not only the fruits of the earth are harvested, but animals as well. An ancient term for November

November

1 **Solemnity of All Saints**

2 **Commemoration of All the Faithful Departed (All Souls)**

3 Optional memorial of Martin de Porres, religious

4 Memorial of Charles Borromeo, bishop

9 **Feast of the Dedication of the Lateran Basilica in Rome**

10 Memorial of Leo the Great, pope, doctor of the church

11 Memorial of Martin of Tours, bishop

12 Memorial of Josaphat, bishop, martyr

13 Memorial of Frances Xavier Cabrini, virgin, religious founder

15 Optional memorial of Albert the Great, bishop, religious, doctor of the church

16 Optional memorial of Margaret of Scotland, married woman, queen

Optional memorial of Gertrude the Great, virgin, religious

17 Memorial of Elizabeth of Hungary, married woman, religious

18 Optional memorial of the Dedication of the Basilicas of the Apostles Peter and Paul in Rome

Optional memorial of Rose Philippine Duchesne, virgin, religious, missionary

21 Memorial of the Presentation of the Virgin Mary

22 Memorial of Cecilia, virgin, martyr

23 Optional memorial of Clement I, pope, martyr

Optional memorial of Columban, abbot, missionary

Optional memorial of Miguel Augustín Pro, presbyter, religious, martyr

24 Memorial of Andrew Dung-Lac, presbyter, martyr, and his companions, martyrs

30 **Feast of Andrew, apostle**

Fourth Thursday: Thanksgiving Day in the U.S.A.

Last Sunday in Ordinary Time: **Solemnity of Christ the King**

was "Blood Month." Summer-fattened animals were slaughtered. This event meant a time of hearty feasting within a community. A beautiful 1978 Italian film, "Tree of the Wooden Clogs," includes an authentic and powerful scene of the November slaughter of a pig. The impression is not of violence

In Short, in November

- The liturgical ingathering that has taken place throughout the autumn reaches a crescendo. Visuals in the classroom can mirror this crescendo as images of the saints and mementos of the dead are added to the autumn décor.

- Reflecting the deepening darkness and the increasing cold, the mood of November shifts from the brightness of All Saints to the more somber, wintry and mystical atmosphere of Advent.

- Choose appropriate decorations for All Saints and All Souls that can stay in place at least through the first weeks of November.

- In your celebrations, do not separate Halloween from All Saints and All Souls. Think of Halloween as "November Eve" and you'll be on the right track.

- Set up a shrine for the dead. Gather pictures and other mementos, and add signs of the harvest. Leave this up through the month. It wouldn't be inappropriate to leave it up during Advent as well.

- Face death squarely. Talk about it. Study it. Distinguish a holy death from the unwholesome images offered by the entertainment industry.

- Set up (if you haven't already) a place to collect donations for those in need.

- In the United States, during the second half of the month, add a few images of the saints.

November Ordinary Time
- Seasonal vesture color: *green*
- Some complementary colors: *gold, orange, rose, blue, teal*

but of reverence, respect, collaboration. The entire community joins in the work. The church sees in such cooperative work an image of itself.

For Christians, the annual November slaughter—death that leads to an abundance of life—like the harvest of fruits and grains, became an image of the paschal mystery, of the life that is stronger than death. And, of course, the plentiful food offers a foretaste of the everlasting banquet of the saints.

The entire month of November (and indeed the entire autumn, including Advent) weaves together these key themes: harvest ingathering and thanksgiving, a taste of heaven's abundance, the sharing of charity, homecoming in the new Jerusalem, the inevitability of death and judgment, the arrival of God's glorious reign. Those themes echo loudly through the month and are never separated.

For a taste of the spirit of November, just for fun, play for the class the final movement of Gustav Mahler's fourth symphony. The movement is a German poem set to music, a delightful vision of heaven where Saint Peter fries fish, Luke slaughters an ox, Martha serves asparagus, Ursula dances and Cecilia sings. For something else in the same vein, sing the folk song "Jerusalem, my happy home" and the spiritual "Oh, what a beautiful city."

Sing also the grand hymn "Come, ye thankful people, come" with its marvelous words "all is safely gathered in, ere the winter storms begin." That's what's happening in the liturgy of November—the Lord of the harvest gathers us into the safety of heaven. We march into the holy city, and we take our seats at the supper of the Lamb.

All Hallows: A Harvest Homecoming in Heaven!

Some people claim that All Saints Day (November 1) is a celebration of the saints whose names are unknown to us. You often hear that said, but it's not a helpful way to think about the day. When you think about the festival of All Saints, don't focus first on the word "saints." Think instead of heaven. Think instead of what God's holy city might be like.

The preface of the eucharistic prayer for All Saints Day calls it "the festival of God's holy city, the heavenly Jerusalem, our mother." (Saint Paul called Jerusalem "mother.") All Saints Day is a homecoming festival in Jerusalem— a family reunion with Mom and Dad—and you don't have to be dead to be invited.

Originally in the church in Rome (and still to this day in the Eastern churches) the All Saints festival took place soon after Easter, to underscore the connection. After all, the resurrection and ascension of the Lord is a prelude to Judgment Day, the day of homecoming, the day of Jesus' arrival in glory. The festival of All Saints became an occasion to make a pilgrimage. The entire process of a pilgrimage—making a journey and reaching a destination—was a symbol of achieving homecoming in heaven.

The All Saints pilgrimages became tremendously popular, and Rome soon discovered that you need plenty of food to accommodate pilgrims. So the festival

of All Saints was transferred from springtime to November 1, to a time of year that fell after the harvest had been gathered and food (and spare time) were more likely to be plentiful.

*T*he All Saints pilgrimages are with us still, but they have taken on some extraordinary guises: Trick or treat is a neighborhood pilgrimage, a first cousin to the tradition of caroling from door to door at Christmas. A few generations ago, the visiting of neighbors house to house was a hallmark of the eve of almost all important days. Decorating and illuminating an entryway and throwing doors wide open to guests is the customary first act in many Catholic festivals. "A guest in the home is Christ in the home"—so says a proverb—and you can't have a Christian festival unless Christ is invited inside!

What do classroom and school doorways and windows look like at All Saints? What guests will you be inviting? What kind of pilgrimage can you embark upon to celebrate the festival?

Not too long ago in schools the eve of All Saints was the occasion for parades—another kind of pilgrimage. Marching around a building represents the longing of the saints to enter God's holy city, who "compass about and hem the golden gates of Jerusalem." Some schools still host Halloween parades, and if you do this, perhaps you can safely march around the school and church, or perhaps begin in school and march into church. A parade needs a destination. Noisemakers are supposed to be part of the fun, and this noisy parade—complete with scary masks and costumes—is an ancient way to chase death, hell and the devil out of town.

*W*hat about Halloween costumes? A Portuguese custom at All Souls is to dress up like the dead "to make them more comfortable when they come home to visit." Dressed like the dead, people take musical instruments into the cemeteries to serenade their ancestors and to escort them home to keep the days of the dead. Here we have one origin of Halloween costumes—to blur the distinctions between the living and the dead. (Dressing like saints is a new-fangled notion in Catholic schools and can be grand fun, especially when coupled with the homework to discover the stories of the saints' lives. However, our ancestors probably would have thought that pretending to be saints is presumptuous.)

All sorts of old-fashioned traditions during November and on through the winter—although most of them never made it to North America—involve dressing up as creepy creatures and trying to scare friends and neighbors. (Saint

Nicholas's brimstone-covered companion is one of these traditions.) The customs are rehearsals for Judgment Day. When the spooky visitors depart, we're let go with a warning—this time. Next time, the judge may not be so lenient.

Here we have another reason for dressing up at Halloween: We're rehearsing doomsday. We're imagining what it's like to live the beatitudes. Like trick-or-treaters dressed every which way, the company of heaven will be a ragtag lot— the poor in spirit, the meek, the mourning. One day, God willing, we will be welcomed into God's own house. Safe at home, our true home, we will take off our masks—the sins and sorrows of this world—and be overwhelmed by God's generous and amazing grace.

$\mathcal{N}$ovember 1 had been, on the ancient Roman calendar, a festival of the final gathering of the earth's fruits. The harvest is a key image of Judgment Day. The book of Revelation tells of God sending out the angels to "harvest the earth." The gathering up and storage of the harvest is compared to God's ingathering of all things on the day of resurrection. Like a harvest festival, heaven will be a place of abundance, of hospitality, of fulfillment.

The first reading at Mass on All Saints Day, from the book of Revelation, describes a Sukkot procession in heaven, complete with the bright garments and palm branches of the Jewish harvest festival. (Sukkot is described beginning on page 84.) The festival is celebrated by waving leafy branches, including palms, fragrant myrtle and willows, which suggests that we celebrate All Saints Day with an abundance of autumn foliage. Oak foliage in particular is long lasting and dries beautifully.

All Saints Day, like Sukkot, is a harvest festival, a time to anticipate Judgment Day—that "great getting-up morning" when Gabriel will sound the trumpet, when the dead will rise, when all peoples will stand before their Judge.

The association with the harvest accounts for the season's traditions of bobbing for apples, carving pumpkins, as well as other traditions that make use of nuts, fruits and vegetables—especially the sweet treats that run the spectrum from sugar skulls to candy corn. This bright bounty is a backdrop of All Saints and All Souls.

What's a good sign of the harvest in your own neck of the woods? In some Mexican towns, marigold flowers are essential decorations at this time of year. The pungent aroma of the foliage is said to aid memory. In some Italian towns, beans are used as the harvest-time emblem to celebrate the occasion. Beans are tossed at windows during the night, and it's claimed that the rattling sounds are the dead trying to enter. Pots of bean stew are called "the bones of the dead." Yum!

*J*ack-o'-lanterns have become for many North Americans one of the primary signs of the season, a sign that joins the harvest with remembrance of the dead. The tradition has an interesting history. Pumpkins were unknown in Europe before Columbus's expeditions brought the vegetables back from the West Indies. In the old days Europeans carved white turnips into the shape of skulls, hollowed them out, added a candle and used these as lanterns to welcome the dead into the home. These lamps were called "death's heads." Schoolchildren in some parts of central Europe still make *rebenslichter,* turnip lamps, and have splendid evening parades with them during All Hallowstide — regarded as the days from Halloween until November 11, the feast of Saint Martin of Tours.

*Y*ou might use other fruits and vegetables in addition to pumpkins to make lanterns. Of course, pumpkins are hollow and easier to turn into lanterns than turnips. Among Catholic immigrants to America pumpkins became the vegetable of choice for the All Hallows lamps. Setting a lantern by the entryway to the home is a way to welcome anyone, living or dead, to come share in the feast.

(Although there are several stories about the "Jack" who supposedly lent his name to the jack-o'-lantern, the stories are not very old. The word "jack" once meant "effigy of a human being." A "jack-o'-lantern" is a lamp made in the shape of a person.)

Harvest Games

A number of games employing nuts and fruits traditionally were played at this season — a season that lasted until the new year.

Peel an apple or orange into a single spiral strip. Toss the peel backward over your shoulder. What letter does it form, and what might this letter signify?

Crack open a nut or acorn: a mealy or wormy nutmeat bodes poorly, a fresh and full one bodes well.

*S*upposedly, at All Saints summer and winter bump together. Whenever two seasons touch, as they do on many of our festival days, it was imagined

that time cracked a bit, allowing eternity to seep through. On festival days heaven's timelessness was thought to be especially near at hand. This kind of thinking remains true to the liturgical spirit. In the liturgy we enter into the *hodie,* God's endless "today" in which the past, present and future are rolled up into one grand *now.*

In powerful ways the festivals of late autumn and winter stir up memories of the past and hopes for the future. To a heart open to wonder, these days are especially laden with mystery.

*H*alloween is a problem for some people. Some communities have banned it. Some continue the celebration but endure a steady barrage of criticism.

Let's take a look at some reasons for the problem. The most serious reason is that, in American culture, Halloween became secularized and wrenched from its mooring as the eve of All Saints Day. Imagine if Christmas Eve came to be separated from Christmas. That's what happened to Halloween.

It's a mistake to separate Halloween and All Saints. In Catholic schools it takes a return to tradition (which is especially difficult because it entails new ways of thinking) to restore Halloween to its rightful place as the eve of All Saints. That's the only place for Halloween in a Catholic institution.

Missing this mooring, some people claim that Halloween is satanic. The entertainment industry bolsters the claim by using the holiday as an excuse to show everything vile. A lot of bent and goofy values get taught in the process, along with a number of weird and unorthodox religious beliefs.

Among liturgically minded Christians, certain scary decorations were a way of laughing at death. The job for us nowadays is to make sure the laughter is there—and the reverence, and the mystery, and the good news of Jesus Christ. Our culture has turned death into profitable entertainment. That's not what All Hallows should do.

*S*ome resources for teachers make the claim that Halloween is a "pagan" festival, a leftover in our culture from pre-Christian peoples. The resources are telling a half-truth. To find the origins of most Halloween traditions in the United States, we don't have to look much earlier than the twentieth century.

Before the Civil War, the majority of Americans, true to their Calvinist roots, did not keep Easter, Christmas or other liturgical observances. Mostly in the past hundred years, public schools and some Protestant Sunday schools began to celebrate a few of the liturgical days, although these were largely shorn of their liturgical framework. So the public schools kept All Hallows Eve, but not

All Hallows Day. They kept Christmas, but not Advent or Epiphany. National observances such as Thanksgiving and Mother's Day had the same weight as Christmas and Easter.

Because holidays were geared to children, over time a child was expected to "grow out of" holidays, not "grow into" them. Difficult and complex holidays, such as Easter, were simplified. To craft the school celebrations for Halloween, bits of Catholic (mostly Irish) tradition were put together piecemeal. Of course, nowadays the public school holidays are going through another evolution in an effort to take seriously the separation of church and state.

The irony here is that Catholic schools simply latched onto the public school holidays. October, November and December in some Catholic schools look a lot like these months in the public schools.

*I*t's true that the pagan Celts held a festival of the dead and of the harvest at this season. So did other peoples. So did Christians. After all, the lengthening nights spark remembrance of the past. It's a wholesome and holy thought, especially when the weather turns mean, to imagine our ancestors not lying dead in their graves but instead alive inside our homes, curled up warm and cozy by the fire.

Many of the traditions at All Saints and All Souls are geared toward welcoming the dead into our thoughts, even into the warmth of our homes, companions at our tables. This is good Catholic thinking. We know all about sitting down to supper with our ancestors. We are called to do it every Sunday. Every eucharist is a holy communion of the living and the dead, where that terrible barrier called "time" is removed, where we enjoy a foretaste of the wedding feast of the Lamb, where Christ sits us down to supper.

A provincial French custom, similar to Christmas stockings, is to leave children bedside treats as gifts from the dead. Children wake up on All Souls Day to find small presents and candy given in the name of departed relatives and friends. This is a wonderful custom—and certainly the dead would approve of being remembered this way.

*A*nother customary way to remember the dead includes planting trees in their name. Planting tulip bulbs is a wonderful All Souls Day tradition that gets the earth beneath our fingernails and that has us burying something seemingly dead in the glorious hope of resurrection.

Donations of charity or the funding of a gift that is bequeathed in the name of the dead are also longstanding traditions. Throughout November, near the classroom shrine of the dead, keep a hamper to receive gifts of canned goods, clothing and other donations for the needy. The instinct here is that one of the best ways to remember the dead is by keeping a watchful eye on the welfare of the living.

A Shrine for the Dead

Catholics are shrine-builders. From Guatemala to Germany, Ireland to India, Catholic cultures know the art of creating shrines. A shrine is an assemblage of all sorts of materials, displayed reverently, purposefully, affectionately. A shrine helps focus prayer. It stirs the imagination. It sparks remembrance.

For some strange reason, many Catholics in the United States have gotten out of practice in the art of shrine-building. We may have trouble with something that came naturally to our ancestors.

Even still, apparently the art of shrine-building remains in our bones, deep down. When a tragedy strikes, the natural response is to build a shrine. We heap flowers and candles and messages of good will at the site of a tragedy. We sign a book to express our feelings, to make our prayers visible. We leave oddball things, too—balloons, food, stuffed animals.

In time for All Souls Day—and kept up through the month of November—it's traditional in Catholic circles to create a shrine to memorialize the dead. It's difficult to imagine something that is not appropriate in such a shrine. Done well, a shrine for the dead becomes a delightful hodgepodge that transcends boundaries of taste when the choices are sparked by a good heart.

The objects gathered in such a shrine usually are of four kinds: photos and other memorabilia; foods and other "gifts" for the dead; emblems of autumn and of the harvest; emblems of life and of the divine life that is stronger than death. Everyone contributes.

To begin, clear a spot, something larger than the usual prayer corner. (You may have dedicated an area in September for festival displays, and perhaps you already have hanging branches or vines or some other contraption for hanging or receiving and displaying a multiplicity of objects.)

Add a beautiful blank book for the names of the dead. Set it on a handsome book stand. Ornament it with colorful leaves. During the weeks before All Souls Day students can write down in this book the names of people they know who have died. You might also add names from the news. Photos can be added to the book. Names can be written in the book at any time. There's no cutoff point. You might even want to keep this book in a special place in the classroom all year.

Building a Shrine for the Dead

1. Clear a spot, something larger than the usual prayer corner, but near the classroom cross.
2. Add a beautiful blank book for all to write in the names of the dead.
3. Decorate the shrine according to the ethnic customs and imaginations of your students.
4. "Gifts" for the dead have a place in such shrines.
5. After you have built the shrine, use it in prayer.
6. Instead of dismantling the shrine when Advent begins, transfigure it.

Nearby, a cornucopia can overflow with fruits, nuts, gourds, grains. Add candles or hanging lamps, if this can be done safely. Add celestial signs, too, perhaps—clouds, stars, sun, planets, moon. Add images of the angels and saints (if these haven't been gathered at this site throughout the autumn). Saint Michael, in particular, is regarded in folklore as the "ferryman" of the dead, protecting them and guiding them into paradise.

*C*onnect the site to the classroom cross—perhaps by locating the shrine nearby, perhaps by stringing bright autumn-colored ribbons from the cross to the shrine. Ornament the cross with autumn flowers and foliage.

Also, in some manner, visually connect the shrine of the dead to Mary's shrine. When we bury the dead, within the mystery of the liturgy, it's as if we are enfolding them in the arms of their mother. The earth is a premier symbol of our Blessed Mother. In her, the mortal gave flesh to the immortal. In her, the earth became full of the grace of heaven.

Invite students to bring from home pictures and other objects that call to mind the dead. Photos and other mementos of the dead may be too precious to leave unguarded. Perhaps these can be scanned into a computer's photo reproduction program and copies printed to use in the shrine, with the originals given back to their owners.

Pay special attention to including mementos of those who have died in the past year. Some parishes and parish schools produce small booklets for each November that include pictures of those who have died in the past year; also included are their survivors' recollections of them.

A shrine to the dead is made bright with emblems of life. Traditional signs of life include winged creatures. Migratory birds especially are understood by many as emblems of the dead, who depart from us and yet whose return we eagerly await. The queer and yet magical sound of geese flying high overhead at night, often steering their course by the moon—is there a lovelier and more evocative image during autumn?

In parts of Mexico the arrival of migratory ducks is an All Souls Day spectacle that is said to offer a foretaste of Resurrection Day, the day of our homecoming in heaven. Candy images of turkeys and other birds are used to ornament shrines of the dead and also are left on graves. Anything with feathers is said to help fan the flames of memory and to help prayers fly to heaven. Think about that when ornamenting the classroom in November with gorgeously feathered fowl!

The shrine might also include the phoenix, the firebird that rises from its own ashes, an emblem beloved by the first generations of Christians.

A particularly marvelous Mexican and Central American approach to remembering the dead is to create playful depictions of the dead interacting with the living. A tremendous amount of folk art for All Souls Day is now available from these regions, and some of these can serve as models for classroom art projects that borrow the spirit of the originals. Most of this art is a hoot: Skeletal surgeons botch the surgery while the patient tries to put herself back together. A funeral cortege is shown in which the mourners are skeletons that attempt to bury the living. A wedding party of skeletons emerges from a church, and the rice tossed on the bridal couple trickles through their fleshless ribs.

Is this too grisly? It certainly isn't gory. The artisans make it clear that the dead are having great fun. This sense of playfulness is present in much Christian art and lore in which the dead are described. For instance, a German folktale tells of the time the dead made off with the moon, sneaking it away sliver by sliver. They were tired of waiting for the eternal light promised to them on Resurrection Day. Saint Peter eventually convinced them that the wait is worthwhile. He talked (and bored) them to sleep, and then set the moon back in place. This literature, as does the liturgy itself, blurs the divisions between the living and the dead, and celebrates the communion of saints.

The depictions of the dead meddling in the affairs of the living aren't always courteous. One strong Mexican tradition is to depict living people as skeletons in order to poke barbed fun at them. This same spirit comes through in the Halloween and Mardi Gras customs of dressing up as living people and then parodying them.

*G*ifts for the dead have a place in such shrines. Offerings such as candy and other delicious things to eat that have been added to the shrine eventually are shared among the living—because the dead are a generous lot. This tradition at heart is the origin of the sharing of Halloween treats. The sharing of sweet foods embodies Psalm 34, in which all are invited to taste and see the goodness of the Lord.

The shrine also is the perfect place to gather donations for the needy. Giving gifts of charity made in the name of those who have died is an important part of the Catholic way of life.

*A*fter you have built the shrine, use it in prayer. All month long you might choose to end classroom prayer by facing the shrine and adding an intercession for the dead to your morning prayer. Candles might be lit there during prayer. Each week flowers might be freshened. Be sure to add images of the saints as their memorials arrive.

All Souls Day, November 2, and its octave day, November 9 (the feast of the anniversary of the dedication of the Lateran Basilica, which is the cathedral of Rome and the "mother church" of Roman Catholicism), are special days for focusing prayer at the classroom shrine of the dead.

Several other school activities during November can complement your remembrance of and prayer for the dead. One school has the pastor, a few of the parish's ministers of care, and the director of a funeral home spend a few hours answering students' questions and leading a discussion about death and dying. November's a great month for a science project on the skeletal system, for a history project on the founding fathers and mothers of the town, for a music project exploring, say, the use of the funeral chant *Dies irae* by great composers. This is a month to learn about and give honor to native peoples, the peoples whose burial grounds are the earth we walk upon. This is a month to make grave rubbings, to have a field trip to a historical society, to go see a museum's mummies. You get the idea!

*I*nstead of dismantling the shrine when Advent begins, transfigure it. As November heads into Advent, mirror what is happening in nature. Tone down the autumn colors. Add touches of winter. Simplify the shrine and the rest of the room. Add images of the late November saints and then the Advent saints.

Advent shares many images in common with November, including remembrance of the dead. Read the text of the song "O come, O come, Emmanuel." It's hard to find lovelier words of prayer for the dead. Advent continues and intensifies the autumn-long "procession" that leads to the coming of Christ, the arrival we await throughout our lives, an arrival symbolized and anticipated by the festivals of All Saints, Christmas and Epiphany.

In the liturgy Christ is always arriving. In the words of Cardinal Jean Danielou, "there is always an Advent going on."

*O*ther November Observances

The month is amazingly rich in just the right saints for this time of year. A number of them are known for their care and kindness for the sick and poor. Martin de Porres (November 3), who was poor himself, and Elizabeth of Hungary (November 17), born into wealth, both cared for the sick. We need such patrons as the weather turns ugly.

*F*rances Xavier Cabrini (November 13) and Rose Philippine Duchesne (November 18) are saints on the American calendar, and both were educators. Frances was known for her work among city folk, Rose among country folk. Like Elizabeth, Rose was born into a prestigious family.

*N*ovember has a number of peacemaker saints: Pope Leo (November 10) stood face to face with Attila the Hun. In eastern Europe, Josaphat (November 12) sought to reconcile Roman Catholics, Byzantine Catholics and the Orthodox. Dorothy Day (November 29) became a journalist for the homeless and for the cause of peace.

First among equals of the November saints are Martin of Tours (November 11) and Cecilia (November 22). In a sense, these saints have come to represent the spirit of November, even if much of what we tell about them is holy legend.

*C*ecilia is the patron of musicians, although nothing we know about her offers a reason for this association. It seems that the onset of wintry weather simply needs a patron of the arts!

Toward the end of Saint Matthew's gospel, just before we hear about the passion, death and resurrection of the Lord, we hear about Jesus foretelling the end of time and the coming of the timeless reign of heaven. Jesus told a parable about five wise and five foolish bridesmaids whose job it was to await the arrival of the bridegroom at the home of the bride, so that the wedding could begin. The foolish women let their lamps burn out. The wise women made ready for their long wait by acquiring ample oil for their lamps. (An oil lamp, especially something that looks like Aladdin's lamp, makes a fine symbol for this time of year.)

Display Idea

The women martyrs are compared to these wise bridesmaids. The martyrs help us keep watch wisely for the arrival of the groom and the start of the wedding—in other words, for the arrival of Christ and of the reign of God, which will be as marvelous as a wedding.

Certain saints in late autumn and early winter have been identified in folklore as "five wise bridesmaids." The list is inexact. One scheme includes Ursula (October 21), Cecilia (November 22), Lucy (December 13), Agnes (January 21), and Agatha (February 5). They surround the Christmastime coming of Christ like bridesmaids holding high their lamps.

*I*n folklore Martin of Tours is sometimes imagined as Old Man Winter, ruddy-faced, clad in furs, arriving on the scene gruffly and irresistibly. Like Bishop Nicholas in December, Bishop Martin also visits the earth, enters homes, passes judgment and dispenses small punishments and treats—a foretaste of Judgment Day.

Martin's most famous legend tells of the days before he became a Christian, when he was a Roman soldier. He was riding his horse during the first snowfall of the season, and he came upon a shivering, crippled beggar. Martin cut his own cloak in half and then gave half to the beggar. That night in a dream the beggar appeared to Martin and identified himself as Christ the Lord.

Martin was born in the Roman province of Pannonia, what is now Hungary. He was made bishop of Tours in Gaul, what is now France. No wonder people of many nations consider him a favorite—the perfect bishop. Martin was the first person not martyred to be acclaimed a saint.

Bulletin Board for November
Jerusalem, My Happy Home

Three distinct motifs fill the month of November—thanksgiving at the end of the agricultural year, remembrance of ancestors, and longing for heaven. The liturgy blends all three motifs, and so might classroom décor. That means blending some of the decorative themes of Halloween and Thanksgiving, and not being rigid about having one holiday's signs come down when the next holiday's signs go up. It also means expanding our image-world at this time of year to include the liturgy's marvelous language about the holy city, harvesting angels, hissing demons, and throngs of bright-robed saints, waving palms to give glory to the Lamb and to welcome the Bride.

A bulletin board with paper Pilgrims and the words "We give thanks" just won't do in a Catholic classroom. Something richer is required. The other suggestions for autumn bulletin boards (pages 91 and 113) gave ideas for backgrounds and designs that might largely stay in place until November. Added to these this month might be images of the saints, of the Lamb, and of the dead. Carrying over designs from one autumn month to the next is a lovely way to express the season's motif of ingathering and harvesting.

It's not far-fetched to mix images of saints with images (such as photos) of relatives and friends who have died. Signs of the harvest, autumn foliage and flowers might also be added. Our ancestors are God's holy harvest. However, you may want to separate images of the saints from mementos of the dead so that it won't appear we are canonizing all who have died.

One way to blend images is to construct on a bulletin board the depiction of God's holy city surrounded by a 12-sided wall, with 12 jewelled gates. (See Revelation 21 and 22. All the many kinds of precious stones used for the gates can be imitated by bright cellophanes or plastic jewels. The Lamb stands in the center of the city and should be especially well crafted. Notice how Revelation describes the Lamb—shining more brightly than the sun. A river flows from the Lamb through the city and waters the tree of life, which has 12 kinds of fruit. The leaves of the tree are for "the healing of the nations" and might be inscribed with the names of countries and cultures.

Within the walls you might include images of the saints giving praise to the Lamb. Students can create depictions of their patrons and namesake saints. Outside the walls, eager to enter the gates, might be images of the dead, such as photos brought from home. (Copies of these might be made if the photos are irreplaceable.) The border, mirroring the tree of life, might be made from images of fruits, vegetables, autumn flowers and foliage.

Saint Martin's Day became a kind of Thanksgiving Day at the end of the agricultural year. Roast goose is traditional on Saint Martin's Day, and a goose is often shown as Martin's companion. Although the Pilgrim settlers in New England were not Catholic and had abandoned the observance of saints' days, they remembered the Martinmas feast and modeled their Thanksgiving observance on this feast, as well as on the Jewish festival of Sukkot.

In 1918, Saint Martin's Day—the eleventh day of the eleventh month—was chosen as the day for the armistice that ended World War I. Martin had been a symbol of European unity and of the abandonment of war in favor of peace.

*T*hanksgiving Day is a civic holiday in the United States and is a relative newcomer to the November calendar. Even newer is the solemnity of Christ the King, which before 1969 was observed on the Sunday before All Saints Day, and has only been around since 1925. Many people who think a lot about the liturgy have mixed feelings about the appropriateness of the placement of both of these days on the calendar.

Some argue that late November is too late for a harvest festival. Some argue that Christ the King duplicates the themes of Palm Sunday, Ascension, All Saints and Epiphany. On the one hand, the church's liturgy has a longstanding tradition that precedes Advent with the gloomy images derived from the eschatological books of Daniel and Revelation. The images don't jibe with turkey and pumpkin pie. On the other hand, both Thanksgiving and Christ the King echo many of the images that overflow earlier in November.

As these days draw near and November comes to a conclusion, in the midst of your shrine for the dead, in the midst of your memorial images of the saints, in the midst of the signs of the harvest, add just a few more images for Thanksgiving Day. Tell the complex tales of the encounters of the native peoples of the Americas with immigrant settlers.

In keeping with the November-long remembrance of the ancestors, students can contribute items that represent their ethnic heritages: a bit of Irish lace, Guatemalan pottery, a Filipino lantern, Iroquois beadwork. The adding of emblems to the classroom décor can be accompanied by students' reports on their heritages. A map of the world will come in handy in sharing the reports.

The Season of Advent

Entering into the Mystery of Advent
The Church's Winter
The Advent Wreath
Advent Is Jam-Packed
The Final Week of Advent

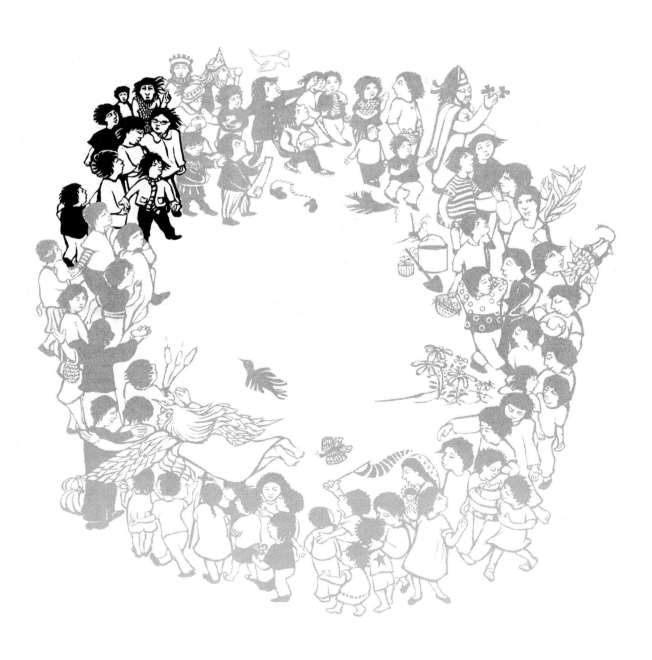

Entering into the Mystery
of Advent

We all fade like a leaf,
and our iniquities, like the wind, take us away,
for you have hidden your face from us.

—Isaiah 64:6c, 7c

*T*he season of Advent begins on the fourth Sunday before Christmas. Or, more precisely, it begins the evening before that Sunday, at sunset on Saturday night, when it's traditional to light the first candle of the Advent wreath. When Advent ends on Christmas Eve, the season of Christmas begins, which lasts until the feast of the Baptism of the Lord, well into January. At Christmas we will welcome the coming of Christ. During Advent we do what we can to make ready for Christ's coming.

In preparation for Christmas we invite others to feast with us. We write cards to keep in touch. We clean house. We shop. We attend rehearsals. And every so often we try to focus on why we're doing all the work: Perhaps, while we pray, we light the candles of the wreath or open the little doors on an Advent calendar, or we take a moment in the morning to appreciate the beauty of dawn, or else in the evening we sit quietly in the darkness.

*T*he liturgical calendar doesn't mix Advent, the season of preparation, with Christmas, the season of play, but the work and the play both bring joy. **The anticipation during Advent is sweet.** Our preparations can be emblems of the yearlong work we must do, in reflection of the season's scriptures, to "beat swords into plowshares," to clothe one another in "the garments of justice and mercy," to wait patiently for the Lord's peaceable kingdom. In this kingdom, according to the prophet Isaiah, the wolf will be the guest of the lamb, a baby will play safely with a cobra, the ox will share its hay with the lion—and the lion will be completely contented with its vegetarian meal!

Would you like to get yourself knee-deep into the spirit of Advent as quickly as possible? Take a late autumn walk in a cemetery. The warm-season birds have fled. Jays and crows, the least lyrical of the birds, remain, like shrieking spirits among the stones. In the middle of the graveyard, surrounded by the dead, surrounded by death, sing this verse of "O come, O come, Emmanuel":

O come, O Dayspring, from on high,
and cheer us by your drawing nigh;
disperse the gloomy clouds of night,
and death's dark shadow put to flight.

Advent is the church's name for the turning of autumn into winter. Throughout the autumn our eyes may have been distracted from the death underlying the beauty of the season. Fat pumpkins, bright chrysanthemums, a fiery sugar maple—these lively signs turned our gaze from death. But now, as November ends, pumpkins are frozen mush, maple trees are bare. Death is unmasked. Our Easter faith is put to the test.

In speaking of the destruction of his nation, the prophet Jeremiah drew on a frightening image—that once the autumn is past, there will be no new harvest until the next year. When he speaks of the "fountain of tears," Jeremiah also makes use of the imagery of rain during winter, the only season of reliable rain in lands around the Mediterranean Sea.

The harvest is past, the summer is ended,
*   and we are not saved.*

Is there no balm in Gilead?
Is there no physician there?
Why then has the health of my poor people
*   not been restored?*
O that my head were a spring of water,
*   and my eyes a fountain of tears,*
so that I might weep day and night
for the slain of my poor people.

—Jeremiah 8:20, 22—9:1

The passage from summer to winter (and the images of Advent) have been unfolding in the liturgy for months now. In the northern hemisphere, since late June, days have been growing shorter. Since late July the climatic thermostat has been slipping downward. The world grew ripe, then overripe, then began rotting. Then, in places, the freezing weather set in, putting an end to the growing season.

The church calendar reflects this autumnal process, with celebrations of fruitfulness in August and September, and then, at the beginning of November, with a major celebration coincident in many places with the breathtaking coloration of foliage, with the gathering and departure of birds, with the most autumnal of autumn weather. But soon afterward, ready or not—wham! Winter arrives.

Liturgically speaking, Advent arrives in stages, like leaves falling from a tree. Advent is a slow process that began, some would say, at Ascension, at the height of spring, when the disciples stared eagerly into the heavens in anticipation of Jesus' return, but then were told—by two citizens of heaven—to quit cloudgazing and to get about their business.

In the liturgy, Advent also arrives suddenly, as if a switch has been thrown, like a frost that lays waste the garden, like a sudden snowfall that transfigures the landscape. The scriptures describe the Lord arriving "like a thief in the night," "when we least expect." "Be on guard" is the Lord's own warning. "Be on guard."

As an antidote to the darkness, during Advent the members of the church name and face their fears. With God's help, we look beyond them. Perhaps we even laugh at them. Like neighbors helping one another survive the winter, we link arms to face our fears together, as the church. That's what the seasons of Advent and Christmas are, the church united in joyful hope, facing its fears, marching through the

In Short, during Advent

- Advent is short and can easily become overstuffed. In whatever you do during Advent, keep the season in perspective with the ways you keep other seasons.

- Simplify and pack away anything nonessential. With many things put away, give the room a thorough cleaning.

- Ornament Mary's shrine in a manner appropriate to Advent. Be sure to include an image of John the Baptist. Mary and John might be called the patron saints of the season.

- In most places around the country, it seems best to ornament the classroom during Advent with wintry colors and emblems. Celestial signs also seem to fit the season.

- There is no one right way to build an Advent wreath. If you have a wreath, the most important thing is prayer around it.

- Advent calendars have become a beautiful way to count down the days until Christmas. (However, "counting up" the days of Lent and of the Easter season is a far more ancient tradition.) Again, there is no one right way to count the days as long as the count is kept. Creativity is in order here.

- The first part of Advent, until sunset on December 17, is the tail end of autumn. Leave some signs of the harvest and of late autumn. The second part, from the evening of December 17 until Christmas Eve, corresponds to the "Halcyon Days," the days of the solstice. This final week of the season has a unique character and is the time to prepare the classroom for Christmas.

- The gospel's nativity stories and the characters from those stories don't appear on the liturgical scene until the final week of Advent.

Advent

- Seasonal vesture color: *violet (rose on the third Sunday)*
- Other seasonal vesture colors from the tradition: *deep blue, light blue, black*
- Some complementary colors: *silver, white, gray, brown, forest green*

darkness toward the light. Imagine the members of your classroom, a microcosm of the church, naming their problems and then transcending them. Imagine them linking arms in a mighty procession.

Our fears are formidable and legitimate. Those who are teachers of the mystery of Advent do the young and old a disservice by disguising fears beneath a heap of tinsel, by sugarcoating the season's delicious bitterness, by letting jolly Christmas carols drown out the songs of Advent, by turning on Christmas lights too soon and blinding eyes to the beauty of the night.

Holding off on Christmas isn't a discipline for discipline's sake imposed on Catholic Christians. Holding off on Christmas in order to allow Advent to be expressed is simply the right and respectful way to treat one another as fellow members of the church. We need Advent to become who we truly are, a people who are waiting—waiting for heaven's own justice to break forth on earth, waiting for God's festival to begin, a festival that will last forever and always.

*W*inter can be a scary season. It was especially scary only a few generations ago, still within the memories of some of the living, before penicillin, before rural electrification. Muddy, rutted roads made transportation difficult. In November some people said goodbye to people they wouldn't see until spring. A baby's cough knotted the stomachs of the child's parents. The mouse seen in the corncrib or the blight on the stored vegetables were regarded as precursors to disaster. Such signs demanded immediate action.

Nowadays we perhaps preserve food as a hobby, but not too long ago canned and dried foodstores were a household's primary supply. Families could run out of food or fuel during winter. And it was a communal concern. To survive winter the cooperation of one's neighbors was essential, a matter of life or death.

Students might take time in late autumn and winter to visit historical societies and other groups that show how people lived in the past. They might ask grandparents for their recollections (and their recollections of recollections) about day-to-day life, and then gather these remembrances into a book. They might research how the ancient fears of hunger, illness and exposure to the cold still preoccupy many in the world today. Civil or economic unrest or natural disasters bring these troubles to the fore—and reveal how thin our insulation against these problems really is.

*F*amiliar customs of the season—the Yule log, the Advent wreath, the coal and switches borne by Saint Nicholas—have their roots in rituals surrounding the winter fuel supply and in winter's increased need for light. These rituals aren't fun and games! They're a matter of life trying with all its might to stay stronger than death.

Just when we may have thought that winter's deadliness has been largely surmounted, medical studies are telling us something we never should have forgotten, that long nights can cause depression and push some of us over the edge, into despair. Something chemical is going on inside our brains. Those of us who are most vulnerable need help to make it through the season of darkness.

In the spirit of the old-fashioned customs surrounding winter fuel and light and health, what new rituals can be devised in school? How can the old rituals be adapted? Perhaps this is a good year to hold a blessing of the school furnace and the overhead lights, or of the annual flu shots, or of the donations gathered and then sent off to a food pantry.

*A*n upbeat response to lengthening nights is called "cocooning" in some quarters. Perhaps it's in our blood to eat extra heartily, to fill pantries, to feather our nests when the weather turns wild.

We keep in the classroom spare caps and pairs of mittens for the times that a student is in need of these. Perhaps at home we keep on the shelf a few too many cans of baked beans or corned-beef hash—just in case. And who can focus on daily tasks when the snow or rain falls fiercely, when winds howl? Such events just about demand hot chocolate.

Baking a fruitcake or stollen or minced pie—or another of those seasonal foods that seem to jam as

much goodness as possible into one dish—is a traditional way of laughing in the face of the gaunt and hideous spirit of starvation. When you know what it is to be hungry, you know that a fruitcake is not funny. It represents life in its fullness.

The tradition of Advent is to prepare certain baked goods and then to set them aside to ripen until Christmas. This ripening—the development of full flavor and texture—is an image of Advent. All sorts of "forbidden fruits" may accumulate during the season, and the "game" of Advent (like any game, involving self-imposed discipline) is to hold off on the sharing and eating until all of us together can sing "Christ is born." The feasting of Christmas becomes a return to paradise, except this time the fruit is no longer forbidden.

On Saint Nicholas's Day, December 6, it's customary in some places to enjoy a small helping of Christmas's baked goods, which are then locked away during the remainder of Advent. In other places the feast of Our Lady of Guadalupe is an occasion to enjoy a foretaste of Christmas. Many of Advent's other customs also offer a small taste of Christmas. Such foretastes make sense only in their meagerness and rarity compared to the full delights of the season to come. For instance, the evergreens within the Advent wreath (and only within the

wreath) give us a whiff of the headier aromas that await us at Christmas, when we set up the tree and deck the halls with an abundance of evergreens. The few candles in the wreath are meant to be enjoyed in

darkness—at Christmas the multiplicity of lights will outdazzle the wreath.

*P*erhaps the loveliest image of Advent is pregnancy. We keep Advent in the company of the Blessed Virgin Mary. During Advent we remember her expectation, when she waited for the birth of her child. Through the message of the archangel Gabriel, she heard God's word and kept it. She was filled with the Holy Spirit, and in her body the body of Christ came to be.

Waiting for the birth of a child is a bit like waiting for Christmas. During a pregnancy there's a strange and wonderful mix of happiness and nervousness, of contentment and fear. Those are good words to describe Advent.

*A*dvent is a season of waiting. Keeping Advent well is rehearsal for all the other times in our lives when we must wait. In chapter 25, the book of Isaiah says that we await the day that God will remove the veil that separates people from one another. When that happens, we shall see things as they really are. God will wipe the blinding tears from our eyes. We'll be welcome to God's groaning board, a table big enough for everyone and everything. On that day we'll shout:

> *This is the LORD for whom we have waited;*
> *let us be glad and rejoice.*

> —Isaiah 25:9

*A*nother of our Advent companions is John the Baptist. Your classroom really should have a fine image of John. He prepared the way for Jesus. He lived in the wilderness, and people were so beguiled by him that they went out into the wilderness to hear him speak. You might ornament the image in Advent with signs of the wilderness (signs that can be returned during Lent).

John told people things they didn't want to hear. He told them what was wrong with them and what was wrong with their leaders, and two of the leaders, King Herod and Queen Herodias, became so angry with John that they put him to death. Imagine John preaching in a shopping mall during December. What might he say to us?

Cantankerous John had a sweet tooth, eating "locusts and honey." Scripture scholars point out that one form of "locust"—grasshoppers—are permitted by Jewish food laws and are a good source of nourishment. Another "locust"—the fruit of the carob tree—is found throughout the lands of the Mediterranean and tastes a lot like chocolate. It ripens in autumn and is often found in grocery stores before Christmas. Another name for carob is "Saint John's bread." Search for it!

Honey seems a miraculous substance. How do bees convert flower nectars into that golden gooey goodness? Because honey's high sugar content tends to prevent it from spoiling, it was used as a preservative and became a symbol of deathlessness. That's exactly what the honey-based drinks ambrosia and nectar mean—"deathless." At one time the newly baptized were given a taste of milk mixed with honey as a sign that they had passed over from the land of exile into the Promised Land, the place that scripture says is "flowing with milk and honey." Think about this at Christmas when you toast the season with eggnog!

*E*ach year advertisers begin the Christmas celebration earlier and earlier. In the 1950s stores were decorated just after Thanksgiving. Nowadays some stores are decorated soon after Labor Day. Most everyone's in gear by Halloween.

Marketers have manipulated language to put us in the mood to spend money. The terms "holiday season" and "the holidays" were generally understood in the 1950s to mean the days from December

*N*ovember

30 **Feast of Andrew, apostle**

*D*ecember

3 Memorial of Frances Xavier, presbyter, religious, missionary

4 Optional memorial of John of Damascus, presbyter, religious, doctor of the church

6 Optional memorial of Nicholas, bishop, wonderworker

7 Memorial of Ambrose, bishop, doctor of the church

8 **Solemnity of the Immaculate Conception of the Virgin Mary**

9 Optional memorial of Juan Diego, hermit

11 Optional memorial of Damasus I, pope

12 **Feast of Our Lady of Guadalupe**

13 Memorial of Lucy, virgin, martyr

14 Memorial of John of the Cross, presbyter, religious, doctor of the church

21 Optional memorial of Peter Canisius, presbyter, religious, doctor of the church

23 Optional memorial of John of Kanty, presbyter

25 to January 1. The terms have come to mean the "shopping days before Christmas." That shift in meaning, brought about by marketers beginning in the 1960s, is a successful effort to get us to buy and consume Christmas-related products for an entire month before December 25. The defunct term "shopping days before" speaks of preparation. We're buying things for an upcoming event. The term "holiday season" instead speaks of celebration. We're buying things to consume immediately.

A new term, "holiday," is being used more and more frequently by marketers, and the word "Christmas" is used less and less: "holiday cards," "holiday tree," "holiday songs." Folks who want to see Christ put back into Christmas first need to see Christmas put back into Christmas!

don't know that Advent and Christmas are two different seasons—and why should they? For generations now almost every parish and parish school have filled Advent with Christmas parties and pageants. The excuse sometimes offered for jumping the gun on Christmas is that the days between Christmas Day and Epiphany are a school vacation, and catechetical programs go on vacation, too. But if we jump the gun on Christmas we lose Advent, and that would be a terrible loss.

Keeping Advent makes a person an oddball in a world that begins Christmas early in November. But, when we look around, we Advent-keepers aren't the only oddballs. Anyone who isn't a Christian also may be struggling with the way our nation keeps November and December. Liturgical Christians are learning about this struggle. It's tough.

Harder than keeping Advent is keeping Christmas when it finally arrives—celebrating around the tree and singing carols and enjoying get-togethers when the shopping malls and radio stations and many of our neighbors have called it quits.

One generation after another has learned from the stores, and not from the liturgy, how and when to keep Christmas. A few generations ago we learned to begin "the holidays" at Thanksgiving. Now we're learning to begin once Halloween is done. Our Catholic way of life has something to say about the "how" and "when" of the seasons. The season of Christmas begins on the eve of December 25 and lasts for several weeks afterward. Before Christmas comes Advent. Advent has its own joys.

*F*irst Advent, then Christmas—that's something basic to our calendar. And this basic information is something we probably need to spell out clearly because it's not common knowledge. Ask around. Many of us hear the word "Advent" as the ecclesiastical term for "holiday season." Many Catholics simply

*H*ere are a few practical reasons for keeping the seasons of Advent and Christmas according to the Catholic calendar. The seasons are part of our Catholic identity. We don't just keep the seasons. They keep us as well. They help us be who we are.

A December spent in preparation and anticipation and a January spent in celebration make the winter pass more pleasantly. A large part of the liturgical mystery of a Catholic winter has to do with very human needs for warmth, light, camaraderie and mental stimulation. Christmas and its "sister season," Carnival, when celebrated with gusto, are able to drive away the blues.

Advent is a brief season of preparation for a winter of celebration. In the quiet of Advent we make ready to hear angel songs. In the darkness we prepare to be dazzled anew by the star of Bethlehem.

The Church's Winter

Nights now are as long as they get. The weather grows dreary. Travel can get difficult. This is a season that stirs many people's fears and dreams and heartfelt prayers.

Late autumn slipsliding into winter can remind us of our need for a **Savior,** who comes with life and health and peace, who comes not only for ourselves but for all in the world who are hungry or homeless, for all who long for justice and freedom. No wonder Advent's color is a somber purple, its songs plaintive, its prayers filled with yearning! And no wonder the Advent scriptures are so filled with hope, encouragement and a summons to vigilance! Advent is rich with images and words, melodies and moods that we use to show solidarity with all who wait for the reign of God.

Decorations can reflect this spirit and make use of many colors and signs of winter. For instance, nearly every paper-goods store has a supply of tissue or foil snowflakes and icicles. Or these can be crafted by hand. If you have bare branches or vines or some other contraption for hanging ornaments (good to have year-round), during Advent it can be hung with paper snowflakes, clear icicles, glittery frost.

Make a point to keep wintry images true to where you live. Winter in your own neck of the woods might conjure up images of rain and mud and even fragrant orange blossoms. Use these signs in service of the season.

Bulletin boards can be prepared in Advent's traditional violet and rose (which isn't pink but a deep and dusky color). Add to that grays, blues, purples, silver and white, and you have a handsome mix. A person can make a good case for claiming that black is the handsomest and most fitting Advent color—and in ancient times some churches felt likewise and used black for vesture before Christmas. The color of the night sky conjures up something at the heart of the season. Early in Advent you might make a point to avoid most green, red and gold, which are strongly associated with Christmas. Then add these colors to the classroom during the final days of Advent.

We're at the tail end of autumn. Don't be too quick about getting rid of signs of the harvest. Perhaps tone down any bright golds and oranges and replace these with darker russet, brown and purple colors. Pine cones, brown leaves, seedpods and dried grasses are perfect during Advent, but the only evergreens or lights traditionally used during the season are in the Advent wreath, which is meant to give us a small foretaste of the many lights and greenery used at Christmas. (Traditionally speaking, the use of greenery and flowers at Christmas is meant to drive winter away and even hasten the springtime. For more about that, see pages 174–75.)

Advent decorations can offer us a foretaste, a hint of the blessings in store for us—but not the full dose. The classroom in Advent can stay fairly simple. A lot of clutter can come down right before the start of the season. Let the bareness be a visual surprise on the first school day of Advent. That will make it a bit easier to give the room a good cleaning—sparkling windows allow the pale winter sunlight to fill the room as much as it can.

Advent's restraint isn't meant to be morose. Instead, it's meant to whet the appetite. Think of Advent in practical terms: Before we can keep a festival, we have invitations to send, rooms to clean, decorations to get into shape. One

reason we hold off on Christmas during Advent is that we're so busy with all the hard work of getting ready for the festival.

*F*or folks in the United States, most years the First Sunday of Advent falls during Thanksgiving weekend. So the beginning of Advent is coincident with the full-fledged push of advertisers to convince us that the "holiday season" has arrived. For students and teachers, Thanksgiving means a three-day school week, and since activities are directed at the upcoming holiday, there's little room for preparation for Advent. If you will be talking to students about the effects of commercialization and about the ways we keep Advent and then Christmas, you will need to take time earlier in November to do this. In the unusual years that Thanksgiving falls after the solemnity of Christ the King, you can use the post-Thanksgiving and pre-Advent week to make the transition.

No matter how you prepare for Advent, the first school days of the season will require some time reserved for decorating the classroom, especially if you use fresh evergreens in the wreath, so schedule accordingly.

*N*ot all of Advent is a preparation for Christmas. Advent is divided into two parts, before December 17 and after. Before December 17 the liturgy aims toward our preparation for the coming of the reign of God, announced by John the Baptist and all the prophets.

This first part of Advent, along with the rest of late fall, is our annual opportunity to immerse ourselves in a number of fascinating, intense and even scary subjects—death, judgment, heaven and hell. In some places in the world, Advent's decorations look a lot like Halloween's! All Saints Day begins a time filled with spooky images, images that appeal to the mystical imagination, images that set the soul stirring in wonder.

A bit of that spirit can be brought into the classroom. For example, students can create a depiction of the Last Judgment, or some wonderful art of this scene can be put on display. (A customary location for this scene is over a doorway.)

*T*here are all sorts of masks from the Americas, Europe and Africa that Christians have used at this time of year as a kind of playful warning to each other about the coming of doomsday. One parish school, in conjunction with the art department, has several occasions from Halloween through Mardi Gras when students make masks. The masks are then used to act out stories: in November the parable in Matthew's gospel about the wise and foolish bridesmaids; in January the story of the coming of the magi and the slaughter of the

Holy Innocents and then the Holy Family's flight into Egypt; and at Carnival time the story of Queen Esther, probably the Bible's craziest story.

During early Advent, a class, with the help of masks and costumes, may want to depict one of the medieval mystery plays about doomsday, or perhaps tell the gospel stories about John the Baptist, or else tell the wonderful legends of Saint Nicholas. Later in Advent tell Luke's gospel stories of the angel Gabriel's annunciations to Zechariah and to Mary. Also, tell other biblical stories of conceptions and births—of Ishmael, Isaac, Samson and Samuel. These passages about births are included among the passages for December 19 in LTP's *An Advent Sourcebook.*

esource Idea

Using spooky images and masks in celebration of Advent and other winter occasions might be unfamiliar to us, but in much of Europe even dear Bishop Nicholas's and the martyr Lucy's customary roles have been to offer a good measure of stern finger-pointing in an attempt to scare sense into us. (Saints are allowed to do that!) Like John the Baptist, another of Advent's curmudgeons, Nicholas and Lucy warn us to amend our lives before Judgment Day.

The treats—emblems of God's generous grace—left behind by the saints are richly symbolic. Nicholas's citrus fruits (such as tangerines) and Lucy's swirled saffron pastries ("Lucy cats," said to resemble a cat's tail) are signs of the sun, meant to cheer us during these sun-starved days. Candy canes represent

Nicholas's crosier. Honeycakes remind us of one of John's favorite foods. (More about such visits from the saints is found beginning on page 156.)

If you created a shrine for the dead during November (page 129), it seems appropriate to leave it in place during Advent, but to modify it to make it more wintry looking. It can be replaced on December 17 with the empty manger.

$\mathcal{A}$dvent is perfect for celestial signs—stars, comets, whirling planets. As the darkness deepens, so does our preoccupation with mystery. The season begins with the gospel's description of the dimming of the sun and moon and the falling of the stars, the signs of the end of time.

One of the prophet Isaiah's images of the eschatological "day of the Lord" is that the sun and moon will be equals, astronomically impossible but poetically intriguing. During Advent the sun rides lowest in the sky and the full moon rides the highest it gets all year (just as in June the sun rides highest and the moon lowest). That means that, in earth's northern hemisphere, in Advent the sun is dimmest and the full moon brightest—a small foretaste of Isaiah's vision. Keep an eye out for this phenomenon. Offer a lesson on the stars visible during the evening on winter nights. They happen to be

Icy Beauty

Advent seems the right time for using stars and snowflakes designed from clear, silver, blue, purple and white materials, and these look magical swirling over windows, hung from the ceiling, festooned on bare branches. (Ice crystals, including snowflakes, have six sides, with almost no exceptions despite all the many forms that snowflakes take.) If you want the entire school to take on an "Advent look," the use of icy colors and images might be a good way to go.

the most brilliant of the year's stars, a brilliance complemented by the clarity of the air of winter's cloudless, frigid nights.

*A*dvent and Christmas are fine seasons to visit a planetarium. An astronomy lesson on the solstice is a perfect adjunct to lessons about the liturgical year. You might also gather pictures and information about architectural or archeological sites used by various cultures to measure the movement of the sun and to keep track of seasons.

Many European churches include observatories for the study of astronomy. Although history teaches us the scandals of the church's opposition to science and to new ways of thinking, the complete picture of history would show far more instances of the church's fostering of science and learning and the arts— from the Irish monks who preserved much of the classical knowledge of ancient Greece and Rome, to the work of the priest Nicholas Copernicus in the early 1500s, to Pope Gregory XIII's reform of the calendar in 1582 (imagine the work of getting politicians to agree on something as momentous as a calendar change!), to the founding of the science of genetics in the mid-1800s by the priest Gregor Mendel.

Take advantage of the exciting possibilities that open up in the school when the teachers of religion, the sciences, mathematics, history, literature and the other arts work together in observance of the seasons.

The Advent Wreath

The tradition of the Advent wreath probably comes from a time when wooden wheels were hung indoors during winter to keep them from warping in the frosty weather. Most traditional seasonal customs—such as Yule logs, the lenten fast and Easter eggs—stem from some essential and ordinary seasonal happening to which people gave a mystical interpretation.

*T*he word "yule" itself is derived from the same root word as "wheel." Yuletide is the turning of the year. The fact that wheels were hung high is an important aspect of the tradition of the Advent wreath. By suspending a wheel you can look up into the circle and imagine that it's like a crown, or like the turning wheel of time, or perhaps it's even a hole to peek into heaven! This image of a hole into heaven (the word "hole" is also related to "wheel") is a common architectural device in sacred spaces.

An Advent wreath can be any ring of greenery with four candles. The four candles are for the four Sundays—the "brightest lights"—of the season. The wreath can be beautiful on a table, but if possible try to hang it. The hardest part will be putting a hook into the ceiling, although sturdy ceiling light fixtures ought to be able to hold the wreath. For hanging an Advent wreath without a hook and without fastening the candles to the wreath (the two hardest parts about making an Advent wreath), see the box on page 154.

*I*t's really difficult to make a wreath from scratch. You'll need what seems like a mountain of twigs and miles of wire. Already made, fresh wreaths usually show up in stores before Advent begins. Wreaths come double- or single-sided, and the double-sided ones not only look good from any angle, but when they dry they don't curl as much as a single-sided wreath. But they cost more.

A straw or grapevine wreath can be used over and over and can be studded with fresh greenery each year. In keeping with the custom's purported origins, you might even use a wagon wheel festooned with pine garland!

Candles can be fastened to the wreath with the aid of special candle holders available in German import stores, or a woodworker can make them. Basically, they look like a candleholder with a nail poking out the bottom. The nail is used to nestle the candleholder into the wreath and keep it upright. Lemons or apples can be carved out to use as candleholders, with a long nail poked through them. The fruit is beautiful but needs refreshing once a week.

The candles aren't essential. The prayer that makes use of the wreath is what really matters.

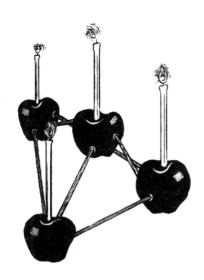

A Simple Advent Wreath

Supplies

Four strips of eight-inch-wide fabric cut into three-yard strips

A roll of florist's wire

A double-sided balsam wreath

Four macramé plant hangers

Four glass globes

A box of eight-hour vigil lights

Tie four strips of fabric to the florescent fixtures in the classroom using florists' wire. Suspend a fresh double-sided balsam wreath from the strips, tying the ends with florist wire.

Instead of attaching candles to the wreath and trying to get them to stand straight, as a safer and easier alternative, four fishbowl-like (but prettier) glass globes can be placed into the macramé plant hangers and also suspended from the florescent lights. Each morning the proper number of eight-hour vigil candles are put into vigil-light cups, which are put into the globes and left to burn throughout the school day.

The central Europeans who first concocted the notion of counting the weeks of Advent using a wreath also came up with all sorts of other contraptions for counting the weeks or days of the season, as well as for counting the days of the Christmas season, the days of Lent, and the days of the Easter season. Judging from centuries of tradition, there is no one right way to make or use an Advent wreath.

The primary image is the circle, the window out of time and into eternity. This primordial symbol calls to mind other circular symbols, especially a wedding ring and a royal crown. Secondary images are the evergreens, the counting of the weeks, and the colors employed. Austrians use red or white candles. The use of purple- and rose-colored candles is rather recent, from the mid-1900s in America. (In any case, a central European farm family wasn't likely to find an array of specially colored candles and would make do with what was available.)

*A*s Christmas nears you might add ornaments to the wreath. Cranberries can be strung (dental floss is strong enough for this task!) and looped over the wreath. In some places it's traditional to suspend a star each day from the wreath. In one classroom the "Advent stars" hold small pictures of the students. In another classroom the Advent wreath gradually gets hung with tagboard snowflakes that get taken home and decorated with pictures of Bible stories. (The task at home is to read the story and then to illustrate it.) A variation would be for each household to illustrate the star or snowflake with a seasonal custom that is kept at home.

Traditionally, the Advent wreath is hung over the spot where the Christmas tree and nativity scene will go. Nestling the nativity scene at the base of the tree is a way of indicating that all creatures (represented by the tree's ornaments) have come together to rejoice in the birth of the Savior, and that the birth of Christ turns the earth into Eden. At Christmas, if it's hung high enough, the wreath can be left in place to form a "crown" suspended over the tree and nativity scene.

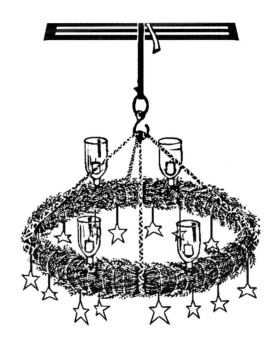

Advent Is Jam-Packed

Even without jumping the gun on Christmas parties and pageants, Advent's calendar is full of special days and once-a-year customs.

*T*here may be special celebrations for Saint Nicholas (December 6), Immaculate Conception (December 8), Our Lady of Guadalupe (December 12) and Saint Lucy (December 13)—and all those wonderful Advent feasts fall within an eight-day stretch! That's too much of a good thing. Pick the special occasions of the season with an eye toward the whole. Let the ones you keep in the classroom complement and not overwhelm Advent.

Saint Nicholas (December 6) is the patron of children. Saint Lucy (December 13) was herself a child. Saint John the Baptist is our Advent companion especially on the second and third Sundays. And at Mass on December 19, December 23 and December 24 we hear about John's conception and birth. The Virgin Mary is celebrated on December 8, December 12 and during the final week of the season. Images of these saints and their symbols can grace the room throughout the season. And on their days, with some outside help, the class might have a "celestial visit" from the saints.

*S*uch visits take traditional forms. Someone dresses up as the saint, and then is offered, in the name of the saint, respect and affection. When done well and in proper form, these visits are meant to appeal to people of all ages, not just to small children. The notion isn't to trick us into believing that the person in disguise is actually the saint. The notion is for everyone to suspend disbelief and to enter into the mystery of the company of heaven—and that's good liturgy!

In one school Saint Nicholas (whose name means "victor" in Greek) enters each classroom with his helpmate and alter ego, a demon redeemed from sin. The demon (who takes one of several forms, depending on the tradition) reminds the witnesses of the fate of the unrepentant (or perhaps reminds us that God's grace knows no limits). Nicholas is dressed in Byzantine ecclesiastical robes and a crown, and carries a walking staff, his shepherd's crook. The demon is sooty with burnt pitch, wears rags and drags chains.

When the pair enters a classroom they interrupt whatever is happening in the room. The demon snaps and snarls and causes disturbances, but Nicholas himself remains dignified. He talks about his homeland in what is now the nation of Turkey. He also talks about the use of the Greek language by the first generations of Christians—because it's helpful to know some Greek in order to comprehend the meaning of the words that we use. For instance, Nicholas points out that the word *diaconos,* "deacon," means "servant," that *presbyteros,*

A Bulletin Board for Advent
John the Baptist

Here's a design based on traditional images in Christian art. Much of it can stay in place during the Christmas season, too.

Cover the board with deep purple—or another good, wintry color you can leave in place until Lent. Overlay the top third with a shade of sky blue, your "sky." Have flowing through the bottom two-thirds a blue or aqua S-curve as your "Jordan River." The sky can include clouds (from which God's voice will be heard when Jesus is baptized), and the river include fishes and other underwater creatures. Some ancient images of the Jordan show a many-headed sea dragon, Leviathan, the embodiment of chaos, lurking beneath the water!

A simple or complex depiction of Saint John the Baptist can be standing knee-deep in the river. The gospels tell us he wore a camel-hair garment bound with a leather belt. His hair and beard are usually shown disheveled and wild, a reference to his living in the wilderness and also to his fiery preaching. So, too, his eyes are most always shown fiery and wide. John can have one arm raised high, holding a seashell from which water flows.

Since the gospels tell us that John ate locusts and honey, you might add a repeated pattern of grasshoppers and bees as a border around the bulletin board, or else feature the insects in a corner of the scene.

A tree with an ax at its base can be located on the riverbank. John used this image—"even now the ax is lying at the root of the trees" (Matthew 3:10)—as a sign of the imminence of the kingdom of heaven. In that kingdom any tree that fails to bear fruit will be hacked into firewood. The riverbanks also might have aquatic irises (signs of the Holy Trinity because of the three-part flowers) and cattails, which are ancient signs of resurrection, perhaps because they seem indestructible.

Why the reference to the Holy Trinity and to Easter? In the Christmas season the Baptism of the Lord is celebrated as the first revelation of the Trinity—Father, Son and Holy Spirit—and a foretaste of the paschal mystery. Baptism is a ceremony for sinners, which is why John protested to Jesus that this baptism made no sense: Jesus was free of sin. But Jesus told John that his baptism was meant to be a sign. In baptism Jesus took on the form of a servant. In this humility God the Father called Jesus his own beloved Son. Many images of the baptism of the Lord show angels on the riverbank, with veiled hands in a customary gesture of adoration. The angels give witness to the divinity of Christ.

During the Christmas season, add a depiction of Jesus being baptized by John. (If you have a sea monster in the water, Jesus should be standing on it.) Add a dove over Jesus' head.

"priest," means "elder," and that *episkopos,* "bishop," means "overseer" and is related to the more familiar word "periscope."

Lastly, the holy bishop offers something between a pep talk and an exhortation about the demands of discipleship in these troubled times. He may even castigate the behavior of students—or the teacher—and call them to account for anything that transpired the past few months that did not reflect gospel values. When he exits, his helpmate leaves behind candy canes, emblems of Nicholas's shepherd's crook. The emphasis is on the visitation, not on the treats.

Students should be prepared for the visit by recounting the legends of the holy bishop. A marvelous musical setting of those legends, spelled "Saint Nicolas," was composed by Benjamin Britten.

*T*he Blessed Virgin Mary is close to our hearts during Advent. Her statue can receive attention, perhaps with a swath of dark blue and silver fabric wrapped around it. Nearby, emblems of the sun, moon and 12 stars can call to mind the words of Revelation 12:1.

During Advent your year-round statue of Mary might be replaced with or complemented by an image of the Immaculate Conception (December 8) or of Our Lady of Guadalupe (December 12). Both images show Mary wrapped in the sash once worn by pregnant women. It's a custom during Advent in some places to veil Mary's statue (especially to veil statues that depict Mary holding the infant Jesus) and to remove the veil at Christmas.

The image of Our Lady of Guadalupe may be surrounded by ears of corn and dried corn shocks. On the Advent feasts of Mary, out-of-season roses (or other flowers) may be used to ornament Mary's shrine. Roses and other flowers that are coaxed into bloom during winter are traditional signs of Gabriel's words to Mary: ". . . for nothing is impossible with God." In Catholic tradition, Mary's symbols include the flowers and fruits of the earth, since she represents the full perfection of God's creatures. Within the womb of Mary the "divinization" of the universe began, a divinization that will be completed when Christ is all in all.

A "Barbara branch": A custom for Saint Andrew's Day (November 30) or Saint Barbara's Day (December 4) is to put a freshly cut twig of cherry, plum or forsythia into a vase of water so that, with luck, it will sprout in time for the new year. This is called a "Barbara branch" and makes a lovely sign of expectation. Along the same line, some people sprout wheat seed during Advent, although this custom seems more fitting during Lent (see page 218).

Paperwhite narcissus started at the beginning of Advent will come into bloom by the end. To bloom by Christmas, an amaryllis needs to be started around All Saints Day.

*T*he "tree of Jesse" is a medieval image based on phrases from the book of the prophet Isaiah. A tree branch rises out of the loins of Jesse, the father of King David. (Earthy stuff here!) According to the medieval image, the fruits hanging on the tree are the kings of Israel. The Virgin Mary is the fairest fruit, and in her lap sits the child Jesus. The tree emphasizes the royal lineage of Jesus rather than the ancestors that predate Jesse.

Although the image of the tree of Jesse is scriptural, the practice of setting up a "Jesse tree" during Advent is newfangled. In the final days of Advent, the church proclaims Matthew's account of the genealogy of Jesus. In celebration of this account, some people create a tree that gets hung with symbols of Jesus' spiritual ancestors. A lovely and simple kit for doing this was prepared by Carolyn Altstadt and published by Abbey Press (Saint Meinrad, Indiana 47577; 1-800-962-4760).

*H*owever, the custom of the Jesse tree can get misinterpreted when we misinterpret Advent itself: Something we may have been taught (and may be teaching others) is that Advent is a time to imagine we are like the people of the Old Testament waiting for the Messiah. The problem with this thinking is that during Advent we aren't just pretending to wait. We are waiting, and we wait in spirit with Isaiah and Mary and Nicholas and Lucy and with every person of any generation who has yearned for God's reign.

Actually, telling the wonderful Old Testament stories—such as creation and the great flood and the exodus—is just what the church does in the liturgy during Lent, in preparation for Easter, and not during Advent (see pages 238–42). And decorating a tree is what we do for Christmas, not for Advent. It doesn't make much sense to set up some sort of separate "Advent tree."

Traditional decorations on a Christmas tree—for instance, apples, acorns and birds—represent Bible stories, scriptural virtues, as well as all the creatures God made. In the final week of Advent you can decorate a kind of "Jesse tree" by hanging symbols of the O Antiphons (and all sorts of other decorations, too) on the classroom or school Christmas tree, which can be put up on December 17. That way the decoration of the tree is one of our final preparations for Christmas. (Save the lighting of the tree until the Christmas season.)

Countdown to Christmas

Many folks count the days of Advent with the help of an Advent calendar. LTP has a beautiful one with an accompanying prayer book. The calendar deserves a beautiful location in the room near a window or other source of light so the calendar windows can shine.

Although Advent calendars come in all sorts of oddball designs, religious and nonreligious, traditional designs reveal the nativity scene only on Christmas Eve. You can create your own Advent calendar. It's as simple as having a series of images, one for each day of Advent, that are gradually revealed. One classroom uses their classroom window panes to count down the days to Christmas. Translucent cellophane images are taped to the panes. Another hangs beautiful stars from the ceiling lights, one for each day.

The nativity of Christ doesn't really enter the liturgical scene until the final days of Advent (see the discussion beginning on page 163). Advent calendars that are geared totally toward the nativity are missing the mark.

Giving trees: In some classrooms it's become the practice to set up a Christmas tree in Advent and to gather gifts around it for the needy for distribution at Christmas. These are called "giving trees." However, setting up a Christmas tree that is decorated and lit during Advent is not traditional. It's not a Catholic thing to do. Think of another spot to collect gifts during Advent.

Collecting gifts for those in need is a year-round Christian practice, appropriate to every season. Sharing gifts with those in need—and sharing other forms of hospitality—is essential before a festival. We simply have no right to keep a festival if we haven't done our best to help others keep it too.

$\mathcal{A}$ Christmas tree represents the tree of life in paradise. The gifts gathered around it (and, in olden times, on its branches, including the edible ornaments that at one time were very popular) represent the tree's fruits. When our first parents grabbed the forbidden fruit from the tree of the knowledge of good and evil, God grew fearful that they soon would eat the fruit of the tree of life and become like God.

At Christmas we stand around this new tree of life, and we take its fruit. In fact, the fruit is freely offered to us by God—that's the notion behind offering one another gifts. They echo God's own generosity.

The meaning of the tree lies in its use according to the calendar. If we wait until Christmas to stand before the tree and to "taste" its fruits, we are making a claim about what we believe Christ has come to accomplish: In the words of the saints, in Christ God has become human so that humans might become God. In Christ we are re-created in God's own image and likeness.

The Final Week of Advent

If Advent is like the nighttime, these last days are like the hours before dawn. All nature is waiting for the sunrise. If Advent is like a courtship, the final week of the season is the betrothal. Christmas is the wedding. If Advent is like a mother's pregnancy, now the baby is kicking in her womb. Soon the child will be born.

The intensity of a child's anticipation of Christmas is very close to the mood of the liturgy during the final week of Advent, which are the days that wrap around the winter solstice. On December 17 (but not before) the liturgy turns toward Bethlehem. Suddenly, during the final week of Advent, onto the scene marches Zechariah and Elizabeth, Mary and Joseph—as the church proclaims the gospels of Matthew and Luke about the events leading up to the birth of Jesus.

From Matthew we hear of Joseph's dream of an angel. From Luke we hear about the angel Gabriel's annunciation to Zechariah and then to Mary, about Mary's visit to Elizabeth, and about the birth of John. What with all the wonderful Christmas books that come out every year, it's easy to find lovely art depicting some of these gospel stories to be set this out on easels and book stands.

The final week of Advent is the time to move decorations toward Christmas. Perhaps during this week you set up the stable with the cow and empty manger, perhaps you move the statues of Mary, Joseph and the donkey closer and closer each day to your "Bethlehem." That word in Hebrew means "house of bread," the place that satisfies hunger. (This partly accounts for Christians' affection for ornaments made from wheat straw and bread dough.)

The O Antiphon art printed here can be photocopied without permission for use in the classroom.

Your Bethlehem scene is the perfect site to gather donations for a food and clothing drive.

Especially if students help in this, just before Christmas vacation, all of you can decorate the classroom for Christmas. (Or, if you do that yourself, you can put up decorations during the break.) That way the festive finery will be in place when students return in the new year.

*M*oving the statues toward the stable is a little like the Central American custom of *Las Posadas,* "lodgings," which begins on the evening of December 16, nine days, a "novena," before Christmas Day. The number nine evokes the months of a pregnancy. It also reminds us of the days that the disciples waited in the upper room, following the ascension of the Lord, for the coming of the gift of the Spirit. This waiting was itself a spiritual pregnancy.

Of course in North America we hear mostly about the Mexican and New Mexican customs during the Advent novena. But similar customs exist throughout Latin America, the Philippines, Spain, Italy and other Mediterranean countries. In fact, the observance of the pre-Christmas novena was once nearly universal among Christians as an outgrowth of the ceremonies surrounding the solstice during the week before Christmas Day. The image of the search of Mary and Joseph for lodgings becomes an image of the church itself, a stranger in a strange land, forever seeking shelter on the journey toward the fullness of time. Almost every Christian culture has a few songs that tell of the journey to Bethlehem, and these carols are perfect for this time.

"Advent caroling" (with Advent songs) during these final days of the season and then Christmas caroling during the upcoming 12 days of Christmas are a way to take goodwill and hospitality into the streets and from door to door. Since charity begins at home, concoct a way for each classroom to serenade the others. Organize something of the *Las Posadas* processions by carrying (safely) the statues of Mary, Joseph and the donkey from room to room. The essence of *Las Posadas* is hospitality toward people different from ourselves. That spirit would be part of the way you organize any card or gift-giving in the classroom.

*D*uring the last week of Advent, the church sings the O Antiphons at Evening Prayer. There is an antiphon for each evening from December 17 to December 23. They are called O Antiphons because each one begins with the word "O." The antiphons include many of the biblical titles of Christ, such as "Lord," "Lawgiver," "Sun of Justice" and "Cornerstone." The custom of the "Jesse tree" (page 160) calls to mind one of these titles, "Flower of the root of Jesse." (Jesse was King David's father.)

The familiar song "O come, O come, Emmanuel" is a metrical version of the O Antiphons that many people know and love. LTP's *Companion to the Calendar* gives each day's antiphon and the corresponding verse of the song. In addition, LTP's *An Advent Sourcebook* gives the scriptures from which the antiphons were drawn, as well as related poetry and prose.

*R*esource Idea

The Season of Christmas

Entering into the Mystery of Christmas
The Nativity Scene
Christmas Customs
The Epiphany of the Lord
The Baptism of the Lord

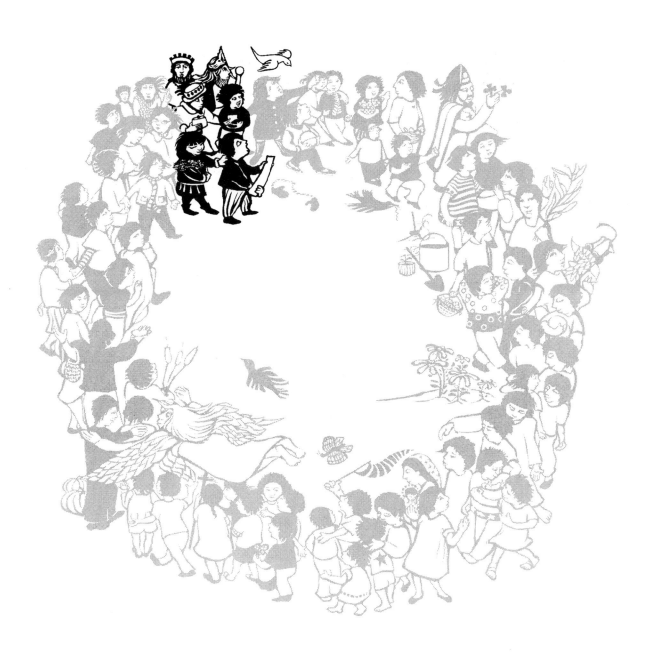

Entering into the Mystery
of *Christmas*

*T*he year is filled with sacred signs. Chief among these is the length of day and night, a sign that, in the northern hemisphere, strongly governs the winter quarter of the Catholic calendar. According to this calendar, the days before the winter solstice—the days of deepening darkness—are a time of quiet expectation. We call the time "Advent." We take time to settle into the darkness, perhaps even to befriend it.

Then, if we lead our lives according to the Catholic calendar, we keep the days following the solstice as a festival of the Light that no darkness can extinguish, a time of heaven-on-earth—the season we call "Christmas," "Christ's feast." The Christmas season lasts well into the new year, and these glorious days are followed by the time of Carnival, which lasts until Lent, joy following upon joy. (We Catholics know how to drive away the winter blues!)

During the season of Advent we were called to do the hard work of making the world ready for Christ. Whether or not we have done this work, whether or not we are ready for it, the Christmas festival comes like a surprise, like an unexpected gift, like the undeserved but abundant grace that God bestows so lavishly on this sinful world. Christmas brings us into company with Christ, whose royal court is filled with shepherds and magi, with the Holy Innocents of Bethlehem, with angels and saints and Isaiah's zoo full of peace-loving critters, including the ox and ass (Isaiah 1:3) and camels (60:6) that populate our nativity scenes.

*I*n these merry days, within the mystery of the liturgy we claim that Christ is born not only years ago but today, here among us. And make no mistake! This newborn child is our God and Lord, our Savior and our judge, who comes to us in mercy and gentleness and compassion.

To announce God's epiphany—the glorious appearance of heaven on earth—we sing out loud, "Joy to the world, the Lord is come!" We sing what might be called the first Christmas carol, Psalm 96:

> O sing to the LORD a new song!
>   sing to the LORD, all the earth!
>
> Then shall all the trees of the forest sing for joy
>   before the LORD; for he is coming.
> He will judge the world with righteousness,
>   and the peoples with his truth.
>
> —Psalm 96:1, 12b, 13a, 13c

(Anyone making the claim that the Christmas tree is a pagan symbol has forgotten Psalm 96.)

In the birth of Christ, so says Saint Leo, the church is born. No wonder we give one another gifts! No wonder we throw our doors wide open and extend hospitality to every guest.

As the year ends and a new year arrives, we imagine what heaven must be like. We leap out of the humdrum circle of time and try to live in God's own timelessness. That's why so many of the signs of Christmas are prepared as circles and spirals and braids—from round fruitcakes, to a holly wreath on the front door, to circular dances, to carols sung in giddy rounds. When in the company of guests you slice a fruitcake or divide a mince pie, you're breaking the circle of time, you're sharing a sweet first taste of the joys of eternity.

At Christmas we hear that the restored Jerusalem will be God's holy crown. "Rise up in splendor," the prophet Isaiah shouts, "the glory of the Lord shines upon you" (Isaiah 62:3). "Rejoice before the Lord as at the harvest" (9:2). Behold how "your sons come from afar, and your daughters in the arms of their nurses" (60:1–3). No wonder this season above all is a time of homecoming.

*A*lthough they are filled with heaven, the days of Christmas are the most earthy of the year, the most crammed with all manner of materials in nearly nonsensical profusion. The festival is kept with shiny bugles and drummer boys and toy soldiers, with wassail and glögg and champagne punch, with straw goats and teddy bears and red-nosed rein-

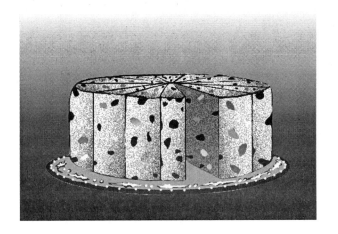

*D*ecember

25 **Solemnity of the Nativity of the Lord**

26 **Feast of Stephen, first martyr**

27 **Feast of John, apostle, evangelist**

28 **Feast of the Holy Innocents, martyrs**

29 Optional memorial of Thomas Becket, bishop, martyr

31 Optional memorial of Sylvester I, pope

*J*anuary

1 **Octave of Christmas: Solemnity of the Virgin Mary, Mother of God**

2 Memorial of Basil the Great and Gregory Nazianzen, bishops, doctors of the church

4 Memorial of Elizabeth Ann Seton, married woman, religious founder, educator

5 Memorial of John Neumann, bishop, religious, missionary, educator

6 Optional memorial of André Bessette, religious

7 Optional memorial of Raymond of Penyafort, presbyter, religious

12 Memorial of Marguerite Bourgeoys, missionary, religious founder

13 Optional memorial of Hilary, bishop, doctor of the church

Sunday between January 2 and January 8:
Solemnity of the Epiphany of the Lord

Sunday after Epiphany, unless Epiphany falls on January 7 or 8, in which case it is the Monday after Epiphany:
Feast of the Baptism of the Lord

deer. In Christ, God is made one with the world, and we seem determined at Christmas to shut nothing and no one out.

The Christmas season brings us into the presence of a wealth of holy signs that reflect the scriptures. We gather around a light-spangled tree as an image of paradise, of the garden where our story began and where, God willing, it will end. We hang a wreath of greens on the front door as an emblem of eternity, of our coronation as the heirs of the kingdom, of our confidence in Christ's promise of victory. We hang

In Short, during
Christmas

- Decorate for the Christmas season during the final week of Advent. That way everything's waiting for your return from the Christmas break.

- The usual Christmas decorations may seem too hackneyed after months of their being used by advertisers and shops. Broaden the scope and turn to ethnic folk expressions of the season for a traditional yet fresh approach in the classroom.

- On the first school days of the new year, be sure to host parties and pageants and other festivities. No one should dread the return to school.

- Keep the nativity scene in the classroom fresh with flowers and evergreens. Add the images of the magi at Epiphany. Keep adding figures of animals, and perhaps create figures of every member of the classroom. It's customary most everywhere to leave the nativity scene up until February 2, the feast of the Presentation of the Lord.

- If you're not accustomed to doing so, the first years you keep the Christmas season according to the liturgical calendar might feel odd. The feeling passes. In time you won't be able to imagine why anyone would end Christmas too soon.

Christmas Season

- Seasonal vesture color: *white, gold or silver*
- Other seasonal vesture colors from the tradition: *black*
- Some complementary colors: *red, forest green*

overhead a cluster of mistletoe as a token of peace and reconciliation—like the olive branch borne by Noah's dove—as if to echo these words of Psalm 85: "Justice and peace shall kiss."

But the keeping of Christmas is not easy. On the day after December 25, the after-Christmas sales begin, as if Christmas were over. But it's not over. It's just begun! Like any person who is bound to a religion, we Christians have to rely on our own resources when it comes to keeping our festivals according to our calendar.

And we have so many days to keep! There's the feast of Stephen, when "Good King Wenceslas looked out." There's Saint John's Day, when people toast each other's good health. There's the feast of the Holy Innocents, the sad day of the season.

Christmastime includes the New Year celebration, when we ring out troubles and ring in blessings. In fact, we might even say that Christmas—all the days of the season—is the New Year festival of the church, the manner and context in which we renew the year.

Epiphany is not the conclusion of Christmas but its merriest day, when we follow a star to our heart's desire, when we come fully into the presence of God. The Christmas season ends on the feast of the Baptism of the Lord. Usually that falls on the second Sunday in January. But the season echoes again on February 2, Candlemas, the fortieth day, when we praise Christ, the light of the world. Like old Simeon, we take Christ into our arms. Think how much we'd miss if we ended Christmas on December 25!

Advent and Christmastime—the preparation and the celebration—bring us from the old year to a new one. The Christian year is not a circle, leading nowhere. Rather, our years form an ascending spiral, like the ladder of angels in Jacob's dream, a spiral stairway into heaven. Step by step the year leads us ever upward into God's bright eternity.

The Nativity Scene

Christmas is not the anniversary of the birth of Jesus. Christmas, the liturgy says, is the festival of the birth of Christ, not his birthday. (Think about the subtle difference here!) *Hodie Christus natus est!* sings the Latin of the liturgy: "Today Christ is born!"

♕ ♕ ♕

That's something that we need to get deep into our bones before we can grasp what Christmas (or any festival) means to us as members of the church. The liturgy takes place within God's *hodie,* the eternal "today" where the past, present and future are rolled up into one, grand "now."

Traditional nativity scenes in Latin America, in Europe, among the Pennsylvania Dutch or French Canadians are not depictions of something that happened 2,000 years ago. Instead, the scenes situate the birth of Christ here and now, in one's own community. Old-fashioned nativity scenes may look quaint to us now, but to their creators the scenes depicted what could be seen in their neighborhoods, with real people going about their business: Today Christ is born.

Another tradition is to fashion the scene anew each year. Even in Europe's ancient churches, in many cases the statuary of the nativity scene is a contemporary creation. The birth of Christ is shown in the here and now. Perhaps the neighborhood is depicted as a backdrop, perhaps parishioners craft depictions of themselves and these are added to the scene, perhaps their photos are gathered near the scene.

In Italy, central Europe and many places in Latin America, the scenes sometimes sprawl outdoors in a town square. The intention again is to make the event appear to occur squarely in our midst. And the effect, which is amazing, is of a birth that has taken place in public, a birth that demands our attention to the needs of the child and the family.

*I*n the classroom you, too, might create a Bethlehem scene from scratch each year, creating figures of the Holy Family, the animals, the shepherds and magi, and also of all the members of the classroom. By locating the scene in some central spot, perhaps even an inconvenient and oddball spot, you are making the claim that the birth of Christ happens in our midst, today.

Around the scene add plenty of flowers, straw, branches and greens—and perhaps also a whole galaxy of stars overhead. All four seasons can be represented, all forms of weather, all the corners of the earth, even the entire cosmos. Like Christmas itself, a traditional nativity scene shuts out no one and nothing. Everyone is welcome.

*T*he scene has room for our hopes and dreams for a better world, a world where justice is stronger than injustice, where peace crowds out war. Are there factions in the school and among neighbors that need reconciling? Perhaps this can be addressed in your nativity scene. Perhaps the best and brightest and most unifying moments of the past year can be brought into the scene, for example, with pictures of those times set into stars and hung overhead.

*D*isplay idea

In one school each student fashions a paper cutout of one hand, and then writes her or his name on the cutout. The cutouts are glued one to the other to form a chain, and the chain is festooned onto a small tree that's set over the nativity scene. In another school a medley of photos of students' efforts at peacemaking are set inside cut foil snowflakes and raindrops. These are strung from "clouds" cut from fluffy white Dacron® batting and then placed behind the nativity scene. The words of Isaiah are called to mind: "Let the clouds rain down the Just One, and the earth bring forth a Savior."

*E*astern Christians imagine the Bethlehem scene to be like the tomb of Christ, a cave cut into rock. The manger appears like a sarcophagus, the newborn Christ is tightly wrapped in swaddling that is almost indistinguishable from graveclothes, and the star descends from the skies and enters the pitch-black cave. The scene tells us that Christ comes to free us from death. In becoming human, God embraces our death and transfigures it into the fullness of life.

Western Christians have generally depicted the birthplace of Christ as a rickety shack, like the *sukkah* of the Jewish festival of Sukkot (see pages 84–85). All sorts of creatures perch in the rafters or peer down through the decrepit roof. The rickety stable reminds us of the fragility of flesh and blood. In being born in Christ, the Creator takes on the fragility and vulnerability of the created world. The entire universe rejoices in this union, which, when complete, will raise creation into glory with Christ.

*I*n times past the day before Christmas was a day of abstinence. Meat was not eaten out of respect for animals. As a rhyme runs: "Who were the first to cry 'Noel'? Animals all, as it befell!" Not shepherds or magi or even angels, but animals were the first to see the newborn Lord, lying in their own manger. The Syrian poet Saint Ephrem wrote of Christ being the first lamb born in spring, the firstborn of all the many lambs born in the waters of baptism. A Silesian carol speaks of Bethlehem's stall as a new Noah's ark. All animals enter it eagerly, because they see in it a place of safety, a vessel that will transport them to the fullness of life.

Keep adding images of animals and birds—and even insects—to the classroom nativity scene and tree throughout the Christmas season and on through Candlemas. Search the scriptures for stories about animals. The prophet Isaiah told us that even an ox and an ass have the good sense to recognize the Lord, even if we humans do not. The Christmas season is a great time to visit a zoo, to set up a feeding station for birds, to offer pets and farm animals extra helpings of food. In these and other small ways at Christmas we hasten the day that death will be no more, that we will find homecoming in paradise.

Christmas Customs

During the days of Christmas we are welcomed back to paradise. The angel who barred our way to the garden puts aside the flaming sword and then throws open the gates of Eden and leads us to the tree of life. In Eden, creation joins with all the company of heaven to sing glory to God.

The custom of the Christmas tree—also called the "paradise tree" or "Christ-tree"—began in villages in Austria and Germany, but about 150 years ago it spread among Christians in many lands. Kept true to tradition, this custom is far more than a pretty thing to look at. A Christmas tree is meant to be a focus of prayer. In Scandinavian countries this prayer takes the form of singing and dancing around the tree.

The strongest tradition of the tree is that it is lit for the first time on Christmas Eve and not beforehand. We make a great burst of light to welcome the Lord. Then Advent is over, and our Christmas festival is here at last.

Simply by lighting the Christmas tree in the classroom at the beginning of prayer in the morning, you are using it as a vehicle of prayer. Perhaps when you light the tree you can say aloud these words: "Jesus Christ is the light of the world, a light that darkness cannot extinguish!" Or say this: "Rise up in splendor, Jerusalem! The glory of the Lord shines upon you."

You don't need a tree in the classroom, of course, and if you do have a tree, a small fresh one may be easy to find on December 26. Nor does the tree need to be inside: A tree can be set up outdoors for the birds, full of edible ornaments such as strips of suet, strings of berries and orange-peel cups filled with peanut butter. (Once a bird feeding station is begun it should be maintained, since the critters come to depend on it.)

*I*f students exchange cards or gifts, hold these exchanges during the days of Christmas and not during Advent. Writing those cards and preparing the gifts can be done over the break. Students and their parents can take advantage of the sales following Christmas Day. These gifts can be assembled around the tree or nativity scene, and the exchange held perhaps on January 6, the "twelfth day of Christmas," or on the day you add the figures of the magi to the nativity scene and tell the gospel story.

Traditionally, the nativity scene is placed beneath the tree. In this way all of creation (the tree ornaments) gives witness to the birth of the Lord. In the words of Psalm 96, all the trees of the forest clap their branches in joy at Christ's coming. In some places in Italy, the nativity scene, or *ceppo,* is a kind of trellis shaped like a candle-lit tree, hung with greenery, fruits and flowers, and filled with gifts. In Finland, paradise is represented by a canopy of straw and stars set over the dining table.

All the many evergreens and flowers and fruits of Christmas also are presentiments of paradise. (What a wonderful way to regard a poinsettia!) Perhaps loveliest of these signs are branches, such as forsythia, coaxed into early bloom. Southerners can make use of camellias, sweet osmanthus and witchhazel, which bloom at this season. Folks in the subtropics can decorate with orange blossoms, which magically come into bloom at the same time the fruit grows ripe.

*C*hristmas, New Year's Day and Epiphany are called, in some places, the "three feasts of guests." On these three occasions above all, it's essential to invite guests and to be a guest, as if the entire world should have an open house. That same spirit of hospitality extends throughout the days of Christmas and on through the winter. Just sing the jolly carol "Deck the halls" and you'll catch the spirit.

*A*ctivity Idea

During the first school days of January make sure to host guests for lunch, perhaps, or go all out and throw a schoolwide open house. Perhaps the magi can arrive to bless the school and classroom. This week is perfect for Christmas pageants and parties.

Although the year-end recess is a good time for janitorial staff to give the place a thorough cleaning, it's a bad idea to have teachers strip the place of Christmas decorations before the break. The first days of the new year are Christmas days, and these days need their decoration and celebrations. January is dreary enough in most places and doesn't need to be made drearier by ending Christmas too soon.

*I*n winter we are between the harvest that is past and the harvest that is to come. Christmas and Epiphany are harvest festivals. That's why we bake and serve so many good, rich foods. Perhaps keeping the twelve days of Christmas is like saying a long grace after the meals that have fed us in the past year, and like saying one before the meals that will feed us in the year to come.

*A*ctivity Idea

The cafeteria staff can catch the spirit and make the school days of the season a time for special breads and pastry, and your classroom rules about snacking can be adjusted to accommodate extra treats during breaks.

*U*se lots of straw and straw ornaments and wheat in your decoration of the classroom. Ornaments made of bread or cornstarch dough are popular and easy to craft. Straw makes a traditional groundcover underneath a Christmas tree. On these days in many households a loaf of bread is broken and dipped in honey and then shared with kisses and wishes for a sweet year. Sometimes this bread looks like the unleavened bread of communion. Sometimes it is rich and yeasty and filled with fruit. And sometimes it isn't bread at all but a porridge of grains and sweet berries—which in some homes is tossed around the home, making a merry mess. In central and eastern European households, it's customary to spread straw and hay throughout the home, even beneath the tablecloth.

We are reminded in these rituals that Bethlehem means "house of bread." The newborn Christ is placed in a manger, a feed trough, to be our bread of life. We too must offer our lives in Christ to sustain one another.

*I*n January make sure to continue food and clothing drives. Perhaps bless and send off the gifts for the needy just before the feast of the Baptism of the Lord, then again at Candlemas in early February, then again at Mardi Gras, before Lent begins. Create worthy containers in which to collect these items. Place them near the prayer corner.

Blessing of Baked Goods at Christmas

Christmas baked goods can be blessed with this prayer. The blessing can take place while treats are being prepared, while they are being put away to keep until Christmas, or when they are being enjoyed.

Some of the best baked goods need to ripen several weeks, including fruitcake, cranberry bread and spice cookies. We store them away to save for the happy season to come. The storage can offer a lesson in Advent patience and self-control, as well as teaching that some things reach their potential only after a good, long wait.

God of all who hunger,
we praise you for the fruits of the earth
and the work of human hands.

As the farmer longs for the harvest
so we are anxious for your coming.
Sow the seeds of peace in our land,
and let them spring up and bear fruit abundantly.

When we share these foods of Christmas,
in spirit may we enter Bethlehem,
the house of bread,
and find completed in us your harvest of justice.

All glory be yours, now and for ever. Amen.

The Epiphany of the Lord

Another name for Epiphany is "Twelfth Night." Everyone knows the carol "The Twelve Days of Christmas." The English begin the count of the twelve days on December 26, which makes New Year's midnight the centerpoint of the count and January 6 the twelfth day.

👑 👑 👑

Central Europeans begin the count on Christmas Day, making January 6 the thirteenth day. By either count we have a baker's dozen days of Christmas. The mystical number 13 reminds us of Christ and the apostles, or of God and the twelve tribes of Israel.

January 6 is the ancient day for celebrating Epiphany. Among Roman Catholics in the United States and Canada, Epiphany is now kept on the first Sunday after January 1. In Europe and Latin America and in many of the Christian churches of North America, Epiphany is celebrated on its ancient day.

It's hard to talk about Epiphany without sounding like we're exaggerating. Today is a day of superlatives. Epiphany is the grandest, merriest, brightest and best day of Christmastime. At Epiphany we celebrate three wonders: The magi offer the Lord gifts of gold, frankincense and myrrh; the Lord comes to the Jordan River to be baptized by John; the Lord turns water into wine at the wedding feast of Cana.

Epiphany means "appearance" and "revelation" and "manifestation." In the gospel stories of Epiphany, we hear that God appears in creation. God is revealed in a star, in the waters of a river, in the shining skies, on the wings of a dove, in stone jars of everyday water. Whenever heaven breaks forth on earth, we have an epiphany.

Gather in the prayer corner signs of Epiphany's "three miracles" of the magi, of the Jordan River and of Cana. Begin with the three gifts of the magi; it's not difficult finding real frankincense and myrrh in a religious goods store, although the "gold" might be a coffer of candy coins wrapped in gold foil. Add a handsome star, three crowns, a seashell and an icon of the baptism of the Lord, a figure of a dove, six stone or crockery jars, a wedding veil and rings.

Follow That Star

In our celebration of all the seasons in the classroom, we try to recognize physical things as images of the good news, as images of heaven. We take our cue from the magi who followed the star. They recognized the good news within a sign. But notice what the gospel tells us: Before the magi got to Bethlehem, they first came to Jerusalem, to God's holy city. There, from the pages of scripture, they learned how to interpret the star. Only after they encountered the scriptures did the star lead them to Christ.

And there was a catch: In searching for Christ, the magi also encountered wily and wicked King Herod, who attempted to "follow" the scriptures and the star in order to destroy Christ. Searching for Christ will lead us face-to-face with those who, like Herod, do not "hunger and thirst for holiness" or "show mercy"—those who do not live according to the beatitudes. God's signs can lead us where we'd rather not go.

A yearlong task in a Christian classroom is to follow authentic traditions—our holy signs—under the guidance of the scriptures. Like the star of Bethlehem, they can lead us to Christ.

*T*he custom of gift-giving at this season is meant to remind us of the gifts given to Jesus by the magi. Among Catholics in many places around the world, Epiphany is the day for exchanging gifts. In Puerto Rico on Epiphany Eve, children fill their shoes with hay for the camels and horses (and in some places, even the elephants) of the magi. The next day the hay is gone and the children find their shoes filled with candy and toys.

In Italy a woman named Befana leaves people gifts. A cranky fellow named Rodolfo joins her, threatening to punish people who need to mend their ways. (Before there was a reindeer named Rudolph, there was Rodolfo!) The story of Befana matches a Russian tale of a grandmother who had wanted to join the magi in their search for Christ. But, at the last minute, the woman decided she had more important things to do. She missed the opportunity to find the Lord. In contrition, she now wanders the streets, going door to door in search of Christ, her heart's desire. And in the mystery of love, she sees Christ in everyone she meets.

If students exchange cards and gifts, January 6 (or the closest school day) is the perfect day each year for this. It's good to save such an enjoyable activity for the first days of the new year.

A famous Epiphany tradition is to have a meal in honor of the visit of the magi. A cake in which a bean or coin or tiny figure of the Christ Child has been hidden is sliced and served. The lucky person who finds the bean or coin or figure in her or his slice is crowned queen or king.

It's easy to do this in a classroom or even at a schoolwide celebration. Everyone can wear gold paper crowns, and there can be a procession for bringing in the Twelfthtide Cake (or even a tray of brownies or some other easily dividable treat in which one piece has the hidden token). New Year horns and noisemakers (for a royal salute) and a royal robe and scepter, and perhaps a taped fanfare or live music will add much to the festivities. (In Italy Epiphany is just about synonymous with horn-blowing—which supposedly drives out the old year and welcomes the new, and is a royal welcome for Christ.) (See also An Epiphany Journey with the Magi in LTP's *Blessings and Prayers through the Year.*)

 *R*esource Idea

A Bulletin Board for Epiphany
The Three Wonders

Epiphany is a celebration of a triplet of gospel events: the adoration of the infant Jesus by the magi (Matthew 2:1–15), the baptism of Jesus in the Jordan River (Mark 1:9–11), and the wedding feast at Cana, where Jesus turned water into wine (John 2:1–11).

Begin by reading these gospel stories and paying attention to details. Divide a bulletin board by using three background colors: gold in the center, green above (or on one side), purple below (or on the other side). For visual interest perhaps the three colors are set on the bias rather than arranged horizontally or vertically. Gold, green and purple are traditional colors of Carnival time, which begins at Epiphany. The colors represent the gifts of the magi and also are said to represent the attributes of God's nobly born children—generosity, faith and justice.

On the gold panel depict the adoration of the magi. You might simply show a crock of gold, an urn of myrrh and a smoking censer of frankincense, with a star over the three. Or you might try to re-create the entire scene. Matthew tells us that "they saw the child with Mary his mother," and so, in traditional art, the infant Jesus is often shown sitting regally in his mother's lap, her lap forming his royal throne, with the magi kneeling around the pair.

On the green panel depict the baptism of the Lord. You might include flowing blue water and, over the water, a dove emerging from a bright cloud. Or you can show the whole scene, described on page 158.

On the purple panel depict the wedding feast at Cana. You might have six grey stone jars, half with blue water at the brim, half with purple wine. Or you might show the entire scene, with Jesus and Mary and other guests, with the bride and groom and steward.

The scene might stay up from Epiphany until Candlemas. After Candlemas you might leave up the three background colors— Carnival colors—and add some images discussed on page 204.

*B*less the classroom and school doors. (See Epiphany Blessing of a Gathering Space in *Blessings and Prayers through the Year.*) The Twelfthtide monarch has two responsibilities. One is to host a Candlemas or Carnival party in the coming weeks. The other is to lead the blessing of the home for the new year: The numerals of the year are written with chalk over the front door. The initials of the legendary names of the magi are added next to three crosses. The names are Caspar, Melchior and Balthasar, and the blessing looks like this:

$$20 \ +C+M+B \ 02$$

That's how the home—and the classroom—can be dedicated to hospitality in the new year. In a sense, at Epiphany all of us are noble-born. In baptism we were anointed to be God's royal people. Heaven's star shines over us, who are baptized, who bear the name of Christ.

The Baptism of the Lord

When Advent began we heard the words of Isaiah: "O that you would tear open the heavens and come down!" Today God answers this prayer. Jesus goes into the Jordan River to be baptized by John. Suddenly the skies open. God's Spirit comes down in the form of a dove. Then God speaks for everyone to hear: "This is my beloved."

In the fifth century, Bishop Maximus of Turin wrote that we have every reason to celebrate this event with the same joy as Christmas: "At Jesus' birth his mother Mary held her child close to her heart. So today God the Father holds his beloved Son for all people to adore. Jesus is baptized so Christians may follow him with confidence as the child of Mary and the child of God."

In Hebrew the name of Jesus is Joshua. This name means "savior." In the days of the Exodus, after Moses died and the people's forty years of wandering were over, Joshua became the leader of the Hebrew people. He led them through the Jordan River and into the Promised Land.

Jesus is a new Joshua. Jesus leads us through the Jordan of baptism. We pass through the water to enter a new life. Sweetened dairy foods such as cheesecake and eggnog are customary during Christmastime in honor of our Savior, who leads us into "a land flowing with milk and honey."

Byzantine Christians celebrate the baptism of Jesus at Epiphany and make a point of blessing water on that day—often the water is from a lake or river, even if a hole has to be cut through its frozen surface. In some places in Russia,

blocks of ice are made into an outdoor cross and the cross is dyed red with beet juice or another natural dye. One school creates snow and ice sculptures of the baptism of the Lord for the front lawn of the school campus.

You might keep an icon or another image of the baptism of the Lord in the prayer corner as Christmas ends. Make a mobile of fluttering origami doves, or else at least hang an image of the dove of the Holy Spirit near the Christmas star. Keep a bowl of holy water in the prayer corner, and use it to sign yourself with the cross each morning.

January and February

Entering into the Mystery of Winter
The Gateway of the Year
Candlemas
Bless Throats—and More!
Saint Valentine's Day
Carnival

Entering into the Mystery
of *Winter*

*T*his chapter deals with the winter days between the Christmas season and Lent. These weeks of Ordinary Time in January and February vary in number from year to year, depending on the date of Ash Wednesday. In some years Lent begins even before Saint Valentine's Day, and more rarely Lent doesn't begin

until early March. Check this year's calendar before using the ideas in this chapter!

*T*he Catholic calendar came into existence after generations of handed-down wisdom and theological reflection—which was then tempered by old-fashioned common sense. Especially during winter, the Catholic calendar runs contrary to the commercial calendar. With almost no sense at all, common or otherwise, the commercial calendar has us feasting before December 25 and then dieting afterward. On the commercial calendar January is a bleak and characterless month.

According to the Catholic calendar, the days from Christmas to Ash Wednesday are some of the merriest of the year. They're a time to drive away the winter blues through human creativity and playfulness. They're a time for singing and dancing, for reminiscing around a cozy fire, for telling the old tales and for dreaming new dreams, for inviting the neighbors to share a hearty pot of soup or a sumptuous dessert.

*I*n making merry at the time of year that days begin to lengthen, we mirror who we want to be—the "children of light." At Christmas we came into the presence of the light. After Christmas we hear once again the Lord Jesus' assuring and yet challenging words, "You are the light of the world." We are called to reflect the light of Christ, like mirrors, light-bearers ourselves—God's lamps—in order to illuminate the dark corners of the world.

A key liturgical image in winter is of old Simeon taking the infant Christ into his arms—old age embracing youth, the lamp bearing the light, the human race taking God into its waiting arms. What a glorious image of winter itself, a season that seems to hold everything in potential, a season customarily given over to the hard and necessary groundwork that eventually bears fruit!

January

13 Optional memorial of Hilary, bishop, doctor of the church

17 Memorial of Anthony, abbot

20 Optional memorial of Fabian, pope, martyr

Optional memorial of Sebastian, martyr

21 Memorial of Agnes, virgin, martyr

22 Optional memorial of Vincent, deacon, martyr

24 Memorial of Francis de Sales, bishop, religious founder, doctor of the church

25 **Feast of the Conversion of Paul, apostle**

26 Memorial of Timothy and Titus, bishops

27 Optional memorial of Angela Merici, virgin, religious founder, educator

28 Memorial of Thomas Aquinas, presbyter, religious, doctor of the church

31 Memorial of John Bosco, presbyter, religious founder, educator

February

2 **Feast of the Presentation of the Lord (Candlemas)**

3 Optional memorial of Blase, bishop, martyr

Optional memorial of Ansgar, bishop, religious, missionary

5 Memorial of Agatha, virgin, martyr

6 Memorial of Paul Miki, religious, missionary, martyr, and his companions, martyrs

8 Optional memorial of Jerome Emiliani, presbyter, religious founder

10 Memorial of Scholastica, virgin, religious founder

11 Optional memorial of Our Lady of Lourdes

14 Memorial of the brothers Cyril, religious, missionary, and Methodius, bishop, missionary

17 Optional memorial of the Seven Founders of the Order of Servites

21 Memorial of Peter Damian, bishop, religious, doctor of the church

22 **Feast of the Chair of Peter, apostle**

23 Memorial of Polycarp, bishop, martyr

In Short, in *Winter*

- The winter images you put up during Advent can remain in place until Ash Wednesday.

- Don't be too quick about stripping Christmas decorations. Winter needs extra signs of light and life, if only some potted flowers. If at Christmas you added evergreens and flowers, these might be kept good looking until Candlemas.

- Leave up the nativity scene until Candlemas—this is a longstanding tradition among Catholics.

- The prayer corner might feature a few changing images that focus on saint's days and other observances of the season. The observances of Saints Blase and Valentine deserve no more and no less attention than other popular saints' days.

- Carnival (lasting from Epiphany until Ash Wednesday) has pride of place on the calendar in winter. The final days of the season are a time for Mardi Gras parties and an overload of gaudy and brilliant decoration. Yet all the days of Carnival are a customary time for the best inventions of the human imagination—for putting on plays, for music-making, for inviting guests and sharing special treats, and for storytelling, especially the scriptural stories that tell of roles being reversed, tables turned and God's justice breaking forth in surprising places and ways.

Winter Ordinary Time

- Seasonal vesture color: *green*
- Some complementary colors: *silver, gold, white, blue, violet*

---

*O*ur calendar uses the term "Ordinary Time" for the days that fall between liturgical seasons. A term for these days may be necessary, but "Ordinary Time" is probably an unfortunate choice. It troubled Dorothy Day, who was steeped in the spirit of the liturgy and who knew that, in Christ, no time can be called "ordinary." It would have troubled the liturgical founders who chose the word *feria,* "feast," to describe the days on which no saint is commemorated and no festival observed. Within God's reign, even the least of our days are feasts.

The word "ordinary" here means "counted"—not "plain" or "usual"—and perhaps a better name would be "ordinal time." We keep count of the weeks in order to organize our liturgical books to know which readings to read and which prayers to pray.

*T*he span of Ordinary Time that falls between Christmas and Lent takes its character from these two seasons. In the gospels of the Christmas season we heard about beginnings—the birth and baptism of the Lord. Stories about beginnings continue in the Sunday gospel passages during winter, as we hear about the call of the first disciples and about the first sermons of the Lord. In winter we often hear the word "light" in the readings. So, too, the readings at Sunday Mass seem to prepare us for the great paschal seasons to come. We hear sobering, lenten words from the books of Isaiah, Job and Jonah.

The classroom might reflect this transition from the glories of Epiphany to the simplicity and new life of Lent. Until Candlemas, February 2, you might keep some of the merry decorations of Christmas in place—especially the nativity scene, which traditionally is left up until this day. After February 2 the classroom can be decorated for Carnival.

The notion here is that winter puts us in need of extra light, color and camaraderie. In true Catholic tradition, in some places around the world the gaudy decorations of Christmas are left up in winter and then covered in the even gaudier decorations of Carnival. Then all of it is removed on Ash Wednesday, and the place is given its spring cleaning. In this manner Lent appears as the true "new year" of the church, the strongest turning point in the church's year of grace.

*W*inter Ordinary Time is peppered with occasions that need decoration. There's the national holiday commemorating the life and work of Martin Luther King, Jr. (observed on the third Monday of January). (LTP has published a handout for the occasion that can be purchased in quantity.) There's Anthony (January 17), Agnes (January 21) and Agatha (February 5). Beginning on January 18 and concluding on January 25 with the feast of the Conversion of Paul is the Octave of Prayer for Christian Unity. (Again, LTP has a handout for the occasion and there are pages for all these days either in *Take Me Home* or *Take Me Home Too*.)

The brightest festival during this period is February 2, Candlemas, the fortieth day of Christmas and the close of "Yuletide." More about the day is found beginning on page 194. February also includes the national holiday commemorating the lives and work of Abraham Lincoln and George Washington, as well as the birthday of Susan B. Anthony, the champion of women's rights, and the anniversary of the death of the abolitionist and writer Frederick Douglass.

The most well-known and well-kept festival that usually falls during this period is Saint Valentine's Day. The shops, as well as many people at home, treat this day as if it were February's theme. Some practical advice for keeping this folk festival in the classroom is found beginning on page 202.

*C*arnival, traditionally speaking, begins at Epiphany. In some places Carnival is observed with three customary colors—gold, green and purple—which echo the gold, frankincense and myrrh of the magi and look forward to Easter's gold, spring's green and Lent's purple. Carnival reaches its crescendo and conclusion on the Tuesday before Ash Wednesday—in French called Mardi Gras, "Fat Tuesday."

Carnival is one of the richest times on the calendar and is discussed beginning on page 206. The more we take Lent seriously, the more we need Carnival to get soul and body into gear.

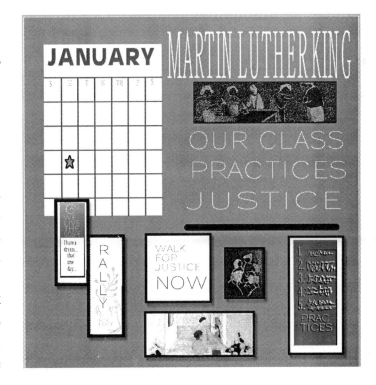

The Gateway of the Year

In a lovely sense winter Ordinary Time complements November. In the northern hemisphere days dwindle down in November. Then, in December, the winter solstice brings transition. In January and February—even as the winter cold settles in most intensely—there is a slow and subtle increase in the light.

Ordinary Time in winter has a certain character—the way it has a certain character in November—owing to the gospel passages we hear on Sundays. In November we hear Jesus' predictions about the end of the world and the dawning of God's reign, and these gospels give the month its eschatological flavor. In January we hear about beginnings—about Jesus coming on the scene, beginning his ministry, summoning his disciples, and causing a stir.

January begins with the great and splashy festival of Epiphany, and the month continues to echo Epiphany's richness. The month is named for the Latin word for doorway, *janua,* which also gave the name to the Roman personification of endings and beginnings, the two-headed god Janus. January, like Janus, looks backward and forward at the same time. The Epiphany blessing of doorways has this venerable heritage.

 **D**isplay Idea

Images of the magi and their gifts might stay in a prominent place until Candlemas (February 2). So, too, the star and dove and water jars, and other emblems of Epiphany's gospel stories, might be kept somewhere prominent.

Another "king" who makes a royal entrance into the month of January is Martin Luther King, Jr. The national holiday in his memory, the third Monday of the month, often occurs just as the Octave of Prayer for Christian Unity commences. In the middle of this octave comes Saint Agnes's Day (January 21), which, like Saint Lucy's Day five weeks earlier, is a children's holiday and is filled with folk traditions. Agnes's Day generally falls during the coldest days of the year. The end of the eight days of prayer for Christian unity is the feast of the Conversion of Paul, a great story found not once but three times in the Acts of the Apostles. Then, as the month ends, comes Catholic Schools Week, coincident with the memorials of several teacher-saints. February begins with Candlemas, Saint Blase's Day and Saint Agatha's Day (the last of the wintertime "wise bridesmaids" that accompany the Christmas arrival of the Bridegroom). The middle of the month brings the popular observances of Presidents Lincoln and Washington, of Frederick Douglass and of Saint Valentine. Depending on the year, Mardi Gras and Ash Wednesday interrupt the flow of winter days and propel us into a new time altogether, the church's spring.

$\mathcal{P}$erhaps the best approach during the winter days of Ordinary Time would be to give the classroom an overall decorative approach that reflects the winter. Then add to the prayer corner some changing piece of art as the special days or weeks come and go.

$\mathcal{P}$rayer Corner Idea

As an example, for Saint Agnes's Day, on the Internet you might find a picture of the martyr, print it and frame it. (Photo-quality paper, about 50 cents a sheet, gives better results than ordinary stock.) Or you might make use of a student's portrait of the saint or of a picture in a book or of a holy card. The name Agnes means "pure" in Greek but sounds like the Latin word *agnus,* "lamb." On this day lambs are shorn in Rome, and the wool is used to make palliums, the cloth "yoke" given to bishops. On a red cloth, with a palm or evergreen branch (images of martyrdom), place the framed print on a bed of real lamb's wool (available in some pharmacies), and perhaps add an image of a lamb, even one borrowed from the nativity scene. Or, especially if your school is named after the saint, you might go all out and have students craft paper lambs to hang from the light fixtures or from the bare branches or vine you set up to hold small ornaments through the year.

In a few days, on the feast of the Conversion of Paul, you might change the framed print to one of Paul's experience on the road to Damascus (usually showing Paul being knocked off his horse) and then add signs and symbols that remind us of Paul—a quill pen (for his writings), a ship (for his travels), a sword (for his martyrdom). Be sure to open the book of Acts to one of the accounts and leave it open on a handsome book stand.

A Bulletin Board for Winter Ordinary Time
Christian Unity

January 18 to 25 is observed as the Octave of Prayer for Christian Unity. The dates were chosen to conclude on the feast of the Conversion of Saint Paul, who first spread the gospel throughout the Mediterranean region.

As a border around a wintry colored paper, such as deep blue or forest green, add as many different styles of cross as you can find. Do some research into traditional shapes of the cross, for instance, the Roman, Greek, Maltese, Celtic and Byzantine. The crosses can be made in an array of metallic shades.

Students can prepare drawings (or even take photographs) of the exteriors of neighboring churches, or else prepare an array of church signs with the actual full names of churches in the neighborhood or town. These drawings or names can be overlayed one against the other on the bulletin board. The center image might show the story of Saint Paul's conversion.

This is a week of prayer for Christian unity. Perhaps someday we'll have a day of prayer for the unity-in-diversity of all the world's peoples. You may need to explain to students what distinguishes Christians from people of other religions.

If you use actual names of churches, be careful to get the names right. Check the phone book and perhaps make a call to find out the full and correct names. Often the names are interesting and speak volumes about the church's history and how a congregation understands itself. You may need to take some class time to define such words as Catholic, Orthodox, Methodist, Baptist, and so on—as well as words such as apostolic, congregational, evangelical, missionary, pentecostal and others that are featured in a church's name.

In early Ordinary Time we will hear again about Jesus' baptism (and the dove) and the summoning of the disciples. In this context we will hear about fishing and about boats. Our ancestors in the lands where winter meant heavy rains thought it was marvelous that wintertime signs of the Zodiac were the fish-tailed goat Capricorn, Aquarius the water-bearer, and Pisces, two fishes snared on a line. (These constellations have dim stars that were imagined to be underwater!) The stories of Jesus' baptism and the call of the fishermen are perfectly suited to such a watery season.

*O*rnament bulletin boards and other classroom sites with images of nets, boats, shells, fishes and other sea life. Or use images of clouds, rain, snow, sleet and the colors of water such as aquamarine and teal, and all the many shades of green and blue. Ordinary Time's green might be featured somewhere in the prayer corner and reflect the kinds of green you see around you—perhaps a deep and wintry pine green, or, in the south, the first-flush-of-spring green, or else, in maritime locations, the strange and indescribable colors of the sea. Ordinary Time's green can be complemented in January and February by wintry colors such as silver.

"Let There Be Light"

The imagery of light keeps appearing in the prayers and readings of the first weeks of Ordinary Time. In a time of year when we are starved for light, the liturgy offers us a hearty helping. After Christmas you might find sale-priced lights shaped like icicles and snowflakes to put to good use in the classroom. You also might clean the overhead lights and make sure everything's in working order. Do the windows need cleaning? Make a special effort to remove bits of tape and other leftover junk.

*W*inter weather requires extra housekeeping. What's the state of coat closets and the piles of winter gear that need to be stored? Mud and salt and other snow-melting chemicals can make a mess of interiors. All this affects the appearance of the classroom and the slipperiness of the floors.

Candlemas

When preparing the school calendar, be sure to set aside this day for festivities. Celebrate the blessing of candles and the procession, at the very least. The procession can lead into a eucharist in church or else lead into morning prayer, followed by some warm refreshment. Pull out the stops and get everyone on board today, especially the cafeteria staff, to prepare a full day of fun. The following ideas can guide your decisions.

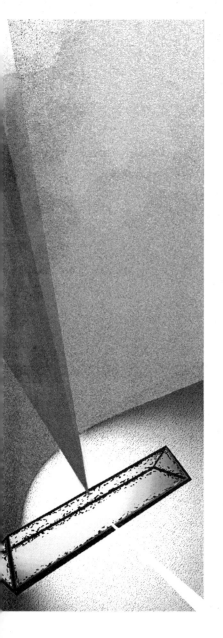

*B*y Candlemas, February 2, the feast of the Presentation of the Lord in the Temple, the worst of winter is past. The days are lengthening rapidly. The "lengthen season"—the original meaning of Lent—comes soon. The world aches for springtime. Forty days ago, on Christmas Day, a light was kindled. On Epiphany this light rose to twinkle from the stars. And today this starlight is placed in our arms. Like Simeon, who this day takes Christ into his arms, today we are hand-in-hand with God.

*M*any people, especially in Latin America and Europe, leave the Bethlehem scene up until February 2. A few flowers are tucked into its straw as promises of spring, even if these have to be brought inside and coaxed into early bloom. Then, at the end of the day, the stable is packed away. Like old Simeon himself, Christmas departs in peace. A Hispanic custom is to bring the image of the Christ Child into church today—to "present the Child in the Temple."

Even if you put away the Bethlehem scene weeks ago, you can put out the statues of the Holy Family for Candlemas and surround the figures with some lights and spring flowers.

*T*he feast of the Presentation comes midway between the winter solstice and the spring equinox. No wonder today we take a final look back at Christmas and a first look forward to Lent. Candles and oil lamps seem the right symbols for the day because they are sources of light that consume themselves in order to shine. The marvelous images of light shining in darkness and of loving self-sacrifice are strong common denominators throughout winter.

This imagery suggests that we shouldn't be too quick to say farewell to the lights of Christmas. We need this light throughout the winter, if only as an antidote to depression. In the classroom, as long as this can be done safely, you might celebrate this day by filling the room with lights of every kind, brought from homes, perhaps, and collected in a wild display. While a cloudy day might make this more effective, on a sunny day make use of the sunlight and some prisms and mirrors to multiply the light.

*A*nother of the important signs of the church's winter is the imagery of courtship, weddings and married life. According to the imagery of the liturgy, during Advent the church was courted by Christ, betrothed to Christ. Christmas was the wedding and Epiphany the reception when, so claims a wonderful antiphon, the magi bring wedding gifts! Candlemas is the wedding night, and another splendid antiphon urges Jerusalem to adorn the marriage bed with flowers.

In the earthy and yet heavenly image-world of liturgical poetry, the snows of winter are imagined to be the garments of the bride and groom. The bright winter stars are imagined to be the bride's veil. The first snowdrops and crocuses of spring are said to greet the wedding and to hasten its fulfillment.

*L*iturgical poets recognize in the sign of the dove a reference to the lovers in the Bible's Song of Songs. We hear about doves today in the pair of birds offered in sacrifice. The dove, which has become a wedding symbol, also reminds us of the story of Noah's flood—and, oddest of all, a dove reminds us of the story of Jonah, whose name in Hebrew means "dove." In this story God is the persistent suitor, repeatedly spurned by Jonah. Take delight in this symbol and fill the room with images of doves—at least two!

While wedding imagery is mostly lost to us and is complicated by such matters as our attitudes about the roles of the sexes and the difficulty of talking about these subjects among children, it remains woven through our liturgical poetry. During the year it returns in folk customs and the liturgical texts of Lent and Easter. In the classroom you might choose an occasion each year to have students share stories of a wedding they have attended. Talk about the students' hopes for friendship and marriage, and for the virtues of fidelity,

compassion and tenderness. Winter offers a few natural opportunities for doing this, in Epiphany's telling of the story of the wedding feast at Cana, and especially surrounded by the hearts and flowers of Saint Valentine's Day.

*C*andlemas is a day for processions. Processions are emblems of our journey through life, of our march toward the kingdom. In the liturgy, processions have a special association with the conclusions to 40-day periods: on this day, on Palm Sunday, on the days leading to the Ascension, and, at least in the Middle East, on the fortieth day after someone dies. These occasions mark the crossing of a threshold, a homecoming.

Two favorite "traveling songs" for processions are Psalm 24 ("Lift up your heads, O gates") and Psalm 118 (with its lines "Open to me the gates of justice," and "Blessed is the one who comes in the name of the Lord"). Your own choice of "traveling music" can be settings of these psalms or can at least match the spirit of the psalms, and can also be enhanced by brass, handbells and percussion—music that carries and will be heard from front to back in the procession.

Activity Idea

Once again we have an occasion in the school year for decorating doorways and entrances, and for inviting guests. In keeping with the gospel today, which tells about the 84-year-old widow and prophet Anna, some schools make a point to invite the elderly to share in the Candlemas festival. In this manner youth and old age embrace, as Simeon and Christ did.

Prepare the physical accoutrements of the processions—censers, candles, the processional cross (made merry this day with an evergreen wreath and bright ribbons), banners and other pole-mounted signs of festivity—perhaps images of the turtledoves as well as portraits of Anna and Simeon, Mary and Joseph. Think of these as "walking sticks" that show those in the middle or rear of the procession where everyone is heading.

*L*ousy weather and ice-slicked sidewalks work against outdoor events. However, there's something splendid about a wintertime procession as an act of defiance against the elements, as a hastening of spring. Foretastes of spring surely have a place in our communal prayer throughout this time of year. Even in the north, an open eye can usually locate some stirring of nature—the flash of a cardinal's wing, the first snowdrop, even icicles formed from the melting and refreezing of snow on a roof. They are the signs that the sun is gaining power. For us they can be sacred signs that the love of God is stronger than death.

A Bulletin Board for Winter Ordinary Time
Candlemas

February 2, the Presentation of the Lord, is the best and brightest feast at this time of year! A festival in early February is an old idea. The Celtic calendar, which was profoundly oriented to day length, began the springtime quarter of the year on February 1. The quarter was called *lencten*—Lent! *Lencten* reaches its conclusion on May Day, when spring everywhere will be in full bloom.

Winter's bleakness can make it hard to believe that spring is around the corner, but that's what Candlemas proclaims. Even groundhogs seem eager to "rise and shine." An old custom is to surround the nativity scene—left up until today—with the first of spring's flowers, even if in your climate these need to be coaxed into bloom. Then the scene is dismantled and the last Christmas carols are sung. "Hark, the herald angels sing" and "Joy to the world" are fine choices.

Cover a bulletin board in wintry colors, such as an array of purple, blue and silver snowflakes or icicles overlaid one on the other.

Perhaps you already have such a background in place from Advent.

Students can create simple paper cutouts of spring flowers. A flower bulb catalog would have plenty of pictures of tulips, daffodils, irises, crocuses and other spring blooms, and the pictures can serve as models for student artists. Simple and strong cutouts, silhouette-style, will look handsome. Use just a few colors that complement the wintry ones, perhaps lavendar, mint green and pink.

Stud the wintry background with your paper flowers so it appears the blossoms are emerging from the frost. As a sign of Christ, add a gold or silver cross over the scene. Or a student artist might create figures of Mary holding the 40-day-old Jesus. Nearby stand the prophets Anna and Simeon. Mary is placing her child in Simeon's open arms.

Like winter passing from the scene so that spring might appear, old Simeon departs in peace. He embraces Jesus, who renews his youth, and calls Jesus "a light of revelation to the Gentiles and the glory of God's people, Israel."

For inspiration, read this story in Luke 2:22–38.

You may know February 2 as "Groundhog Day." According legend, on Candlemas even animals hope for spring. That's why the groundhog supposedly peeks out of its burrow to check the weather. A sunny day means it sees its shadow and returns to its burrow. A cloudy day means no shadow and so the groundhog emerges. There's a kernel of good sense to this folklore: Bright sunlight and harsh shadows—associated in winter with frigid air—ordinarily signify that winter still holds sway. But clouds and even storms are signs that the earth is stirring into life.

Lent is coming! The light in our arms must be sacrificed. We must be ready to lose our lives. We must ache for Easter.

Bless Throats— and More!

The blessing of throats on February 3, the memorial of Saint Blase, comes from a time not long ago when a sore throat was the first sign of a dreadful illness.

*I*n winter the indoor air gets dry, hampering immunity—and most folks are indoors much of the time. Viral infections can lead to far more serious bacterial infections—strep throat and scarlet fever, pneumonia, blood poisoning. Before the use of antibiotics, bacterial infections were the leading cause of death. Life-threatening bacterial illnesses came to mind when you said the word "winter." For many people, they still do. A story runs that prayer to the Armenian martyr-bishop Blase saved a child from choking on a fishbone. Blase is one of the "14 holy helpers" that medieval Catholic folklore identified as protectors against maladies and mishaps that people feared most—depression, backache, eye disease, cancer, lightning, fire, hail and even travel-related accidents.

*D*evotion to such saints formed a kind of confederacy and support group for the people affected by the troubles. In linking arms against a common problem, the church sees an image of itself, joined together for the common good, together offering itself to God as the body of Christ, united in suffering, in compassion and in hope.

While nowadays we might have medicines or other therapies for many of the life-threatening ailments that plagued our ancestors, not everyone on the planet has access to such medicines. Even the beneficiaries of modern healthcare are not immune from many of the fears of our medieval ancestors.

*T*he blessing of throats is one of many hundreds of saint's day blessings that once graced the Catholic calendar. This blessing survives as a relic from a time that, as the year progressed, most everything on earth—including the parts of our bodies—were held up before God in praise and thanksgiving, and with intercessory prayer, too. The ritual of blessing comes from a fundamental Catholic "attitude of gratitude" that brings words of praise to our lips whenever we see a shooting star, whenever we greet a friend, when we wake up each morning and go to sleep at night.

Without a year full of other blessings, the Saint Blase Day blessing is missing its proper context. Without the context this blessing can seem like superstition or a leftover from a way of life no longer lived, an exercise in nostalgia for nostalgia's sake. The trick isn't to dispense with this blessing but to reinvigorate the calendar with many other seasonal blessings.

The matter for a proper blessing is something important to our welfare, something crucial within the human community, something that's a matter of life or death—such as good health. That's what the liturgy of blessing accomplishes: We give thanks to God who created the thing we are blessing and who preserves and sustains us within the created world. We ask for God's continued care no matter what befalls us.

Resource Idea

*S*ome summer, sit down with the calendar, and craft for the classroom and for the school an annual series of occasions for liturgies of blessing. In creating the calendar of blessings, take your cue from such resources as *Catholic Household Blessings and Prayers* and LTP's *Blessings and Prayers through the Year*—and also, if possible, from the *Book of Blessings* and from the old Roman ritual. (The order of the blessing of throats, for instance, is found in chapter 51 of the *Book of Blessings.*) Read through the lives of the saints for natural associations between their lives and blessings.

In winter Ordinary Time, for instance, you might have a blessing in mid-January of efforts toward better race relations and cultural awareness on a day close to Martin Luther King Day, prayer for Christian unity during the week before the feast of the Conversion of Paul, and a blessing of pets on Saint Anthony's Day (January 17). At the end of January, to prepare for Catholic Schools Week, you might host a blessing of teachers on the memorial of one of the teacher-saints, such as Thomas Aquinas (January 28), Angela Merici (January 27) or John Bosco (January 31). In February you can have a blessing of candles (and even of the classroom lights) on February 2, a blessing of throats on February 3, a blessing of brothers and sisters on Saint Scholastica's Day (February 10; Scholastica was Saint Benedict's sister), and a blessing of valentines on February 14.

The calendar needs to maintain perspective, of course. In this period the blessing of and procession with candles on February 2 has pride of place and deserves your fullest attention. Something's seriously out of balance when a school celebrates the blessing of throats on February 3 and yet does not keep Candlemas with full vigor.

*B*lessings are liturgies, requiring trained ministers such as presider, cantor, reader. Blessings benefit from material signs, from decoration. The blessing of throats makes use of two candles blessed the day before; the candles are tied crosswise with ribbon. Attach some flowers or a small image of a fish to the ribbon, or evergreens. Keep the crossed candles somewhere dignified and prominent this week.

*P*rayer Corner Idea

Prepare something special, such as thank-you cards as a treat for the school nurse and other health care volunteers. In one school cafeteria, in honor of Blase, there are cookies for dessert shaped like fishes and crosiers (a bishop's staff) and miters (a bishop's hat). On a bulletin board you might feature a display of the many ways the school tries to keep students healthy and what students do to minister to the sick.

*A*ctivity Idea

After school, if possible, students might go to nursing homes and hospitals to help the people there celebrate the blessing. Students might prepare images of Saint Blase to distribute at these places. A useful handout that can be colored and decorated is found in LTP's *Take Me Home Too.*

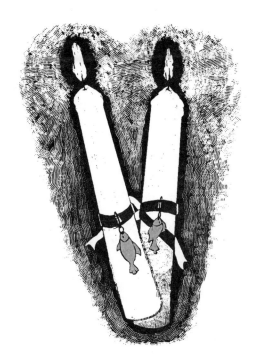

Saint Valentine's Day

On the church's calendar February 14 is the memorial of Saints Cyril and Methodius, evangelizers of much of central and eastern Europe. But the folk festival of Saint Valentine has grabbed the affections of many people, even the nonreligious.

The Roman martyrology—the list of martyrs and the anniversaries of their deaths—tells about two Saint Valentines, both martyred around the year 269. One of them may have been the bishop of Terni in Italy and the other a priest in Rome. A legend says that the priest sent letters of encouragement to people who lived in fear of persecution. The legend is meant to explain why people send valentines in his name.

Another explanation for the custom of sending valentines is that people noticed that in mid-February birds begin returning from their winter nesting sites and then choose mates for the springtime. All that raucous singing of birds is a method for claiming nesting territory. So the day was regarded as the perfect day to choose a sweetheart.

 *A*ctivity Idea

Encourage students to bring in flowers this day, or, earlier in the month, coax branches into growth and bloom by setting them in water. Take a walk this day and search for signs of spring. Clean and renew the bird-feeding station or else set one up.

*Y*ou might create or find an image of Saint Valentine—at least one of them—to place in your prayer corner. (For wonderful images of the saints, check out the art of Michael O'Neill McGrath at www.beestill.com.) The hearts and flowers associated with the day seem perfectly suited to the celebration, as is the color red, the color associated with the memorials of the martyrs.

The method in the classroom for keeping Valentine's Day is basic training in the art of being a decent person. The practice of exchanging valentines works only when everyone is challenged to exchange signs of respect and affection with everyone else, and not to show favorites or to leave anyone out. Decide this for yourself: Is this day primarily for showering our romantic sweethearts with signs of affection? (If this is the case, the exchange of valentines among small children makes little sense.) Or is this day also about the joy of caring for one another with kindness and respect and compassion?

Prepare something for folks who would be most surprised by it. Perhaps, instead of a classroom-wide exchange of valentines, small favors are prepared for the residents of a hospital or care center or for neighbors. (It is always a good idea to stay on good relations with the neighbors who surround the school.)

Advertisers try to convince us that homemade valentines on this day can't compare to store-bought cards and gifts. Instead of flooding the room with store-bought materials, make your own. It's hard to create something more wonderful this day than a multiplicity of hearts.

LTP's book *Blessings and Prayers through the Year* gives a useful blessing for a Valentine's Day celebration. Use it when exchanging valentines or when sending them off to others.

The commercial calendar has turned Valentine's Day into February's theme. Some stores actually displace Christmas materials with those for Valentine's Day as early as December 25! That, of course, is way out of proportion to the significance of this day.

In the Catholic classroom you might want to grab control of Valentine's Day and treat it as one of many saint's day observances in the year—and certainly not as a month-long theme. It's probably best if decorations for Saint Valentine's Day are put up a day or two before the holiday and removed soon after.

A Bulletin Board for Carnival
Esther the Queen

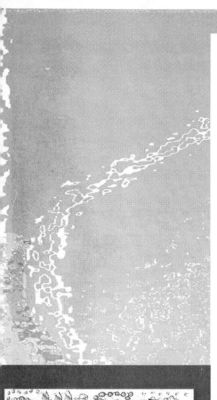

The story of Esther is the Bible's bawdiest. Most everything that happens involved roles being reversed, tables turned. The book of Esther can be read in a single sitting and makes the perfect biblical tale for Carnival time, the days before Lent begins.

The Jewish holiday of Purim, a month before Passover, is a celebration of this story, and the ways of celebrating involve masquerading, sharing gifts of sweet foods, and a riotous reading of the book; whenever the bad guy Haman is named, everyone joins in drowning out the name by shouting, stamping feet and sounding noisemakers.

For a Carnival-time bulletin board you might depict the characters of the story of Esther. Everything takes place in a fairy-tale-like setting in Persia. The people drip in beads, jewels and silks, with great amounts of cosmetics and perfumes—all of it sounds like Mardi Gras, doesn't it? Cover the board in the rich Carnival colors of gold, green and purple. Edge it with depictions of crowns, jewelry, fancy goblets and other signs of wealth. Party noisemakers such as horns and rachets (actual ones or depictions of them) might be used to ornament the board.

Add mask-like faces (or actual handmade masks) depicting the characters in the story. The characters seem to be in contrasting pairs, except for the king, who, in the words of the nursery rhyme, "stands alone." First we hear about haughty Queen Vashti, who dared to disobey the king. The menfolk are terrified that the queen's attitude will catch on among all women, so they turn against her. In contrast we hear of the Jewish girl Esther, who becomes the new queen. Esther, too, disobeys King Ahasuerus, but manages to pull it off to her advantage.

Esther's uncle Mordecai is the embodiment of loyalty, patience and wisdom. Wicked Haman, the bad guy in the story, embodies selfishness, rashness and the corruption of power. Haman plots to kill the Jewish people, Queen Esther included, and Esther is forced to act.

Notice in the story the importance of fasting and even of the use of ashes. A law forbids anyone, even the Queen, from speaking to the king. Esther stirs up her courage to speak to the king by first spending three days hiding her beauty behind ashes and by fasting. Notice too the importance of feasting. Esther's mask might show her two sides, beautiful and bejewelled, and covered in soot. The king, too, has two sides, the pompous husband of Vashti, and the tender and just husband of Esther.

Masquerading is a Jewish tradition for Purim and a Christian tradition during Carnival. Any of the bulletin boards in the school at Carnival time can feature all sorts of masks, but best of all would be to use these masks to act out the stories of the characters being depicted. But be warned, the story of Esther is violent and even raunchy. Still, the Jewish people do not hide this tale from their children. It ends, according to the book, in "feasting and gladness," with "gifts of food" and "presents to the poor," a fitting festival for all generations.

*W*hen Saint Valentine's Day falls during Lent, tone down the celebration of the saint's day a bit to give Lent its due. In Lent, explain the situation this year and request that edible valentines be kept to a minimum. (Conversely, at Mardi Gras you might encourage overindulgence!)

On a lenten Saint Valentine's Day, there's no rule that hearts can't be cut out of purple paper and placed alongside the red ones. Recognize in the hearts a reference to Psalm 51, "Create in me a clean heart, O Lord," and to the words of the prophet Joel, "Rend your hearts and not your garments, and return to the Lord your God."

*T*he classroom's approach to Saint Valentine's Day and to the balance between this day and other mid-February events is an important issue. In a Catholic school, something other than the priorities of a card shop or florist can be reflected in the school windows. If Mardi Gras and Ash Wednesday fall during the same week as Saint Valentine's Day, will the decorations in your school windows put the priority on Lent, where it belongs, or on the saint's day?

Decorate Windows!

School windows are indicators of the classroom's affections. They can reveal what you love most. Also, in a sense, the windows, reach out to passersby to help form the affections of your neighbors. A splash of life and color in those windows is a captivating sight. That splash can either work against or work toward the Catholic way of life.

Carnival

The name Carnival comes from the Latin words for "farewell to the flesh," or perhaps it can be translated "putting meat aside." Carnival is the feast before the fast. This oddball season lasts, according to tradition, from Epiphany to the day before Ash Wednesday—called Mardi Gras or Shrove Tuesday or "Ash Eve."

Thanks to the English Puritans, who banned liturgical festivals, most people in the United States do not keep Carnival. But it's a Catholic thing to do! The French Acadian people ("Cajuns") along North America's Gulf Coast keep it. In Italy the dusty Christmas decorations are left up and then get smothered with *Carnevale* serpentines and festoons. In the Brazilian city of Rio de Janeiro, street dancers move to the rhythm of the samba. The German cities of Mainz, Munich, Cologne and Dusseldorf hold *Fasching* parades with elaborate floats. The people in the French city of Nice use heaps of flowers as weapons in a fragrant but enormously messy street battle between the forces of winter and spring.

Carnival marks the time in between two liturgical seasons, Christmastime and Lent. In a sense, that makes Carnival Halloween's alter ego. According to folklore, at Halloween life and death meet, shake hands, do battle, and then declare death the victor. Now it's time for a rematch!

Most everywhere during Carnival it's customary to run winter out of town, or at least to give winter a tongue-lashing. Winter is burned in effigy, tossed into a lake or set into a boat and left to drift away. In the classroom a great way to mimic these customs is to bash a snowman piñata. Or bash a real snowman outdoors. Or melt one in a bonfire, if this can be done safely.

A city teacher worked with the cafeteria staff to adapt this custom for lunchtime on Mardi Gras, borrowing the old English Christmas game called "snapdragons." In the original game, a large, heat-proof platter covered with raisins is prepared. Rum is warmed carefully, poured over the raisins and set alight. (The alcohol content burns off.) The object is to pluck as many raisins as possible from the dancing, blue flames. Of course, the room has to be darkened. The safer variation on this custom has the students plucking bits of melting "snowmen" made out of marshmallows stuck together with toothpicks. Over a hotplate set on "warm" or in a Chinese wok they melt slowly into a gooey but delicious mess. Outdoors, marshmallow snowmen might be roasted around a barbecue, which is all the more fun if the weather is wintry.

*A*ctivity Idea

*I*n many places the foods of Carnival are anything and everything not eaten during Lent. When Lent meant not eating animals products—meat, lard, dairy dishes, eggs and even marshmallows (which are made from gelatin, an animal protein)—Carnival came to mean a festival of cholesterol-rich foods, such as fritters, pancakes and doughnuts. Also, with the weather beginning to grow warmer, foods that would spoil had to be eaten or would be lost.

If you're searching for something traditional to serve during these days, round foods especially—such as the many different kinds of pancakes and doughnuts—are prepared as edible wishes for the return of the springtime sun. A wonderful Russian tradition during Carnival is the making and eating of buckwheat *blini* that are drizzled in butter and served with plenty of sour cream. The festivities include a mock-battle between

a gruff old man representing winter and a flower-clad girl representing springtime. The man grouses and groans, but the young woman wins the day.

*S*hrove Tuesday is the English name for Mardi Gras—from the word "shrive," meaning "to be forgiven." The English (and others) have a tradition of making pancakes this day—and of holding outdoor races while flipping pancakes in their skillets. A nearly universal Carnival tradition is the seeking of forgiveness, regarded as the only way to enter properly into Lent. Before we can seek God's forgiveness we first turn toward one another.

*I*n the spirit of reconciliation, Carnival is a high-steppin', high-calorie antidote to winter. It's a time to dance, attend plays, sing around the piano and make merry! In winter the weather can be miserable for long stretches of time. Bad weather and the extra time spent indoors can encourage people to cultivate their "inner world," the world of fantasy and imagination. Carnival is a season for music, plays and art, and also for wild and crazy behavior, including the wearing of disguises and masks. It's a time to master an ethnic tradition of the season, from puppetry to pantomime, from the polka to the samba.

Carnival Is a Time for Stories, Too

The tales of Pinocchio ("little pine nut"), Cinderella ("ash girl"), Rapunzel ("beet root"), and many, many others were first fashioned to be told late into a winter night. A particularly lovely tale by Hans Christian Andersen is about the emperor of China and a tiny nightingale that sings each evening in the forest. A splendid 1987 telling of this tale (and of many other folktales) is available on video from Rabbit Ears Productions.

The stories, like the biblical tales of Esther and Jonah, tell of roles being reversed, about the nature of reality and of what gives something value, and about heaven's amazing and compassionate and life-giving justice winning the day—to everyone's surprise. Art, drama, music, literature and religion students might join forces to act out these stories at this season. Find an authentic source for the tales, which often are far richer than the popular animated versions.

*H*old a classroom or schoolwide Mardi Gras masquerade on the "Fat Tuesday" before Ash Wednesday. Gather friends and enemies, strangers and the all-too-familiar for a final fling before lenten fasting. Turn your Carnival celebration into a feast of open-door hospitality.

The costumes can represent what we want to be, or what we are but don't want to be. At the end of the party, remove the masks, wipe off the greasepaint, and prepare to welcome Lent, the season when we see each other as we truly are. Such a moment needs a ceremony, and tradition provides the perfect one,

the "burial of the alleluia." (See the description and song on page 211.) Gertrud
Mueller Nelson describes the burial in her wonderful book, *To Dance with God.*
LTP's *Blessings and Prayers through the Year* includes a version for the classroom.

*I*nscribe the word "Alleluia" on a banner, scroll, or even, as in one classroom, with gold-leaf on an ostrich egg. Find a suitable place to put the
alleluia throughout Lent until its exhumation at Easter. The container can be a
chest, handsome box, sealable cupboard, even the earth itself, if the container
for the alleluia is watertight. One class shuts the container with a wax stamp
and wraps it in a velvet satchel. Everything about the alleluia—its container
and its place of rest—should be beautiful and noble.

With the help of percussion instruments, especially bells, everyone sings
alleluia and carries it to its resting place. The church provides an ancient song
of farewell, "Alleluia, song of gladness, voice of joy that cannot die." Then the
instruments are gathered up and the procession returns in silence.

*I*n addition to removing masks and burying the alleluia, the conclusion of
the Mardi Gras party is a good time to burn palms to make ashes for Lent.
(See page 210.) Again, the rite is also found in *Blessings and Prayers through
the Year.* During the weeks before Mardi Gras a large basket or hamper can be
set up in the school or in each classroom for collecting last year's dried palms.
The reverent burning of blessed objects is a traditional way to dispose of them.
Usually the parish does this, and the parish school can help.

Making Ashes

Ash Wednesday's ashes are the burned remains of last Lent's palms. What a wonderful sign of the change of seasons!

In many parishes and parish schools during the weeks before Lent, people gather dry palms to burn them. For safety's sake, the burning must be done outdoors. To make the ashes useful for the blessing and imposition, they are sifted through a wire colander and collected in an earthenware jar or other handsome container. The burning of palms can follow a Carnival party.

Although it is not traditional to bless this fire, and the ashes themselves are blessed as part of the rites of Ash Wednesday, the burning of ashes may be preceded by an invitation to prayer and a blessing and song. The blessing suggested here includes the *Shehecheyanu*, the Jewish prayer proclaimed at turning points of life.

My friends, nearly a year ago, at the end of Lent,
we carried these branches to welcome the Messiah.

In preparation for a new Lent, the church's holy springtime,
we have gathered these holy branches to be burned.
On Ash Wednesday, as Lent begins,
the ashes will be placed on our foreheads.

Ashes are the leftovers of life. They are reminders of death.
At one time ashes were scattered on fields to make them fertile.
They were used with other ingredients to make soap.
For us the ashes signal an ending and a beginning,
a season of repentance,
a time of purification and cleansing,
a time of fresh growth.

My friends, let us bless the Lord,
the maker of all our endings and beginnings.

Blessed are you, Lord our God, the sovereign of creation.
You preserve us in life, you sustain us,
and you have brought us to this season.

And to this let us all say: Amen.

Burning Ashes

During the burning of palms a psalm or other song may be sung, such as the following text by Alan J. Hommerding, sung to the tune for "These forty days of Lent," called ST. FLAVIAN:

"From ashes to the living font"

> *From ashes to the living font*
> *Your Church must*
> *journey, Lord,*
> *Baptized in grace,*
> *in grace renewed*
> *By your most holy word.*
>
> *Through fasting, prayer,*
> *and charity*
> *Your voice speaks*
> *deep within,*
> *Returning us to ways of truth*
> *And turning us from sin.*
>
> *From ashes to the living font*
> *Your Church must*
> *journey still,*
> *Through cross and tomb to*
> *Easter joy,*
> *In Spirit-fire fulfilled.*

Burial of the Alleluia

Alleluia means "praise the Lord." We imagine that alleluia is the never-ending song of the saints. During Lent we do not sing or say "alleluia." Instead, we call to mind that we have been exiled from heaven, our true home. Like the exiles in Babylon, in contrition we refuse to sing the Lord's song. We hang up our alleluias like harps on the willow trees.

Because we sin, we bring this exile on ourselves. We are like the prodigal son, a runaway. The good news is that, at Easter, when Lent is completed, we come to our senses. Like the prodigal son, we return home to our Father who loves us. We feast on the fatted calf. We sing our Easter "alleluias" with all our might.

Before Ash Wednesday, many school communities bid farewell to the alleluia. Saint Augustine said that "we say goodbye fondly, like parting friends." This may be done by singing a favorite alleluia or a song filled with alleluias, such as "All creatures of our God and king" or the eleventh-century hymn "Alleluia, song of gladness," which was translated in the nineteenth century by John Mason Neale. The hymn fits the tune for "Let all mortal flesh keep silence," "Praise, my soul, the King of heaven," "Tantum ergo" or "Pange, lingua":

Alleluia, song of gladness,
Voice of joy that cannot die:
Alleluia is the anthem
Ever dear to choirs on high;
In the house of God abiding
Thus they sing eternally.

Alleluia now resounding
Through Jerusalem the free!
Alleluia, joyful mother,
All your children sing
*   with glee,*
But by Babylon's sad waters
Mourning exiles soon to be.

Alleluia we deserve not
Here to chant for evermore.
Alleluia our transgressions
Make us for a while give o'er,
For the holy time is coming
Bidding us our sins deplore.

Trinity of endless glory,
Hear your people as they cry!
Grant us soon to keep
*   your Easter*
In our home beyond the sky;
There to you for ever singing
Alleluia endlessly.

The Season of Lent

Entering into the Mystery
of Lent

*F*or North Americans, Lent begins in winter, a season that almost always overstays its welcome. By the time Lent rolls around we're probably wishing that cabin fever would give way to spring fever. We're likely to have spent too many nights like Noah in the ark, like Daniel in the lion's den, like Jonah in the fish's belly, like Lazarus in the tomb. Lazarus, too, the gospel tells us, began to stink.

But the hibernation is over. It's time to get off our duffs and roll up our sleeves! Outside of Eden the children of Adam and Eve have work to do "by the sweat of their brows."

*L*ent is spring-cleaning time, a task made necessary as the land thaws and mud gets tracked into cars and on carpeting. In the beginning God made Adam from clay, which is what Adam's name means. The Bible's (and Lent's) other "dirty stories" include one about Jeremiah being tossed into a cistern and one about Esther concealing her beauty under ashes. That's how Lent begins, a muddy mess. Dust we are and to dust we return. Lent will end, thank God, by a pool of clean water, in the Easter bath of baptism.

By a pool of water Jesus rubbed mud on a blind man's eyes, and the fellow's eyes were opened. An old name for Lent is "enlightenment." Some of the catechumens—the people who year-round are being formed as Christians and readied for baptism—are chosen ("elected") to celebrate the sacrament at Easter. These chosen people are then called "the elect." Lent is their time of enlightenment.

*T*he word "Lent" comes from the same root that gave the English language the words "long" and "lengthen." The word originally referred to the quarter of the year between Candlemas and May

Day, when days lengthen rapidly. During Lent the light of the world gains strength, unquenchable, irresistible. Lent, the Paschal Triduum and the Fifty Days of the Easter season—a quarter of the year—are the church's springtime.

This is plowing and planting season, when, in the language of parables, the sower goes out to sow seed, the grain of wheat is buried in the earth, the farmer spreads manure in hopes of a fruitful yield. The span of days from late winter to early spring is a birthing season. Farm animals are born. Birds nest and lay eggs. Creation is at its most vulnerable.

Lent's abstinence from meat shows empathy with this fledgling generation. We will not add to its struggles by butchering it. Keeping the abstinence makes us like the travelers aboard Noah's ark. What if one of them had a sudden urge for a hamburger? It would have meant the end of cattle, forever. During Lent's 40 days and 40 nights we refuse to take bites out of one another. Instead, aboard this ark called "earth" we grow hungry together for a fresh harvest. Lent's fast is like a table grace at the beginning of the agricultural year, a thanksgiving not for what we have in hand but for what is promised in the future.

The saints and mystics of the church, in tandem with the scriptures, speak of prayer, fasting and almsgiving as the three pillars of discipleship. The pillars form the foundation of the year-round regimen of Christian living. They are disciplines that, many would say, form us as disciples. During Lent we try as best as we can to get back to these basics.

If Lent is understood in this way, as a time to get back to basics, the conclusion of Lent doesn't mean backstepping to undisciplined ways. Instead, Lent is rehearsal for living the Christian way of life year-round. Lent leads to Easter, to the time of living the fullness of life.

For the elect, those adults and children roughly age six and older who have been chosen by the bishop for the sacraments of baptism, confirmation and eucharist at Easter, Lent means final preparations for initiation into the church. Lent also is a time for those who have broken their baptismal vows to seek reconciliation. Through communal prayer, fasting and almsgiving, all for one and one for all, the already baptized link arms with the soon to be baptized, and together they march toward homecoming at Easter.

Lent is often called a journey. We march not through space but through time, and the march is rarely merry. Like the prodigal son, we are a long way off from where we want to be. In many of the lenten scriptures, like the tale of Noah's flood, people are on the move. God told Sarah and Abraham, "Go from your country and your kindred." And so they set out in search of the Promised Land. Their children and their children's children continue the adventure.

As in the tale of Noah, the number 40 often gets connected to the tales of travel. One such story is

In Short, during Lent

- Absorb this principle deep into your bones and make it shine in all you do: In small ways and in large, difficult ones, the seasons of Lent, the Paschal Triduum and Easter affect everything and take precedence over almost everything. The only thing that would take precedence at school is a death within the community, which is itself a "passover." Anything less than that takes a backseat to Lent.

- Convince yourself of this: Lent can be popular. Like Advent, the season overflows with images and practices and special events that grab the heart and stir the soul, although it seems the church as a whole needs to rediscover the time, especially to rediscover what it means to fast.

- Lent, the Triduum and Eastertime are storytelling seasons. The great paschal scriptures provide the seasons' biblical foundation—and also provide you with your principal source for images to use in the classroom.

- Saint Leo the Great reminded the church, "What Christians should be doing at all times should be done during Lent with greater care." Lent is the church's retreat. The prayer, fasting (simple living) and almsgiving (sharing charity) that is part of a Christian's year-round way of life is reinvigorated and renewed during Lent. Devote a corner of the classroom or one of the common spaces in the school to share the ways students are praying, fasting and giving alms this Lent.

- Lent is kept in special sympathy with two groups: the folks making final preparation for baptism at Easter, and the folks preparing to be reunited with the church at Easter. Much of Lent's power and the season's traditional rites, practices and symbols arise from the church's empathy with these two groups of people. Get to know these folks in your parish. Pray for them daily. Invite them for lunch.

- Anyone celebrating the sacraments of initiation—baptism, confirmation and eucharist—are VIPs at this time of year. No matter when we were baptized, Easter is the "anniversary." All Christians (especially by witnessing the rites) are called to renew their baptism during Lent, the Paschal Triduum and the Easter season. Where in school can you list the names and perhaps photos of students preparing for the sacraments?

- Lent is spring-cleaning time, indoors and out. Start with windows. They are your classroom's eyes. The days between Ash Wednesday and the First Sunday of Lent are a customary time for changing the classroom from Carnival exuberance to Lent's simplicity. The final days of Lent are a time to give everything a thorough cleaning.

- With the sense that absence makes the heart grow fonder, customarily during Lent we place emphasis on certain things by their absence. We do not sing alleluia. We keep flowers and decorations to a minimum. We don't leave treats out for nibbling. An ancient custom during Lent was the veiling or putting away of iconography. Since we are preparing for baptism at Easter, during Lent we don't jump the gun on the signs of baptism; instead we leave the bowl of holy water dry. The things emphasized by their absence during Lent are emphasized by their abundance during the 50 days of Easter.

- The poet Emily Dickinson wrote about the purple coloring of hills in March, caused by the flowering of the native red maples with their oddball fuzzy bloom. How will violet, Lent's liturgical color, have pride of place in the classroom and throughout the school campus? What other colors can be used alongside Lent's violet? The white and greys of late-season snow? The browns and beiges of the thawing earth? The pale and yellowish greens of early spring?

Lent

- Seasonal vesture color: *violet (rose on the fourth Sunday, red on the final Sunday)*
- Other seasonal vesture colors from the tradition: *unbleached linen (ecru), gray, black, brownish red, carmine red (especially during the final days)*
- Some complementary colors: *brown, green*

harsh and difficult, but a key to entering into the mystery of Lent: In the days that the Hebrew people journeyed from slavery in Egypt to freedom in the Promised Land, the slave-born generation was condemned to perish in the desert, so that only their freeborn children would enter their homeland in Canaan. This passing of one generation to another took 40 years.

The number 40 has come to represent an unsettled life spent hungering and thirsting for justice, a life spent embracing our baptismal heritage as freeborn children of God. Lent is a rehearsal for living this kind of life.

*C*ent is about a tenth of the year. Church poets called the time a "tithe" of our days given back to God. During the other nine-tenths of the year the work of the church is supposed to be directed out to the world, but during Lent we pull back to examine ourselves and to face our unhealthy ways. "Physician, heal thyself," we say. The word "quarantine" is an old word for Lent—literally meaning 40 days of imposed recuperation.

Jonah shouted to the inhabitants of Nineveh: You have 40 days to repent! And they did. Even their cattle fasted. Like the story of Noah's flood, creation conspired to save itself. And in case we miss the connection, a pun makes clear the link between the stories of Jonah and of Noah: "Jonah" is the Hebrew word for "dove."

*T*he Hebrew word for repentance is *teshuvah,* "return." The dove returned to Noah to announce the reconciliation of heaven and earth. Jonah, however, was far less willing to announce forgiveness to the inhabitants of Nineveh. He thought they were worthless—after all, they were foreigners. God had to force Jonah to go to that city, with the help of the big fish.

*F*ebruary

8 Optional memorial of Jerome Emiliani, presbyter, religious founder

10 Memorial of Scholastica, virgin, religious founder

11 Optional memorial of Our Lady of Lourdes

14 Memorial of the brothers Cyril, religious, missionary, and Methodius, bishop, missionary

17 Optional memorial of the Seven Founders of the Order of Servites

21 Optional memorial of Peter Damian, bishop, religious, doctor of the church

22 **Feast of the Chair of Peter, apostle**

23 Memorial of Polycarp, bishop, martyr

*M*arch

3 Optional memorial of Katharine Drexel, virgin, religious founder, missionary, educator

4 Optional memorial of Casimir, prince

7 Memorial of Perpetua and Felicity, martyrs

8 Optional memorial John of God, religious

9 Optional memorial of Frances of Rome, married woman, religious founder

17 Optional memorial of Patrick, bishop, missionary

18 Optional memorial Cyril of Jerusalem, bishop, doctor of the church

19 **Solemnity of Joseph, Husband of the Virgin Mary**

23 Optional memorial of Toribio de Mogrovejo, bishop

25 **Solemnity of the Annunciation of the Lord**

*A*pril

2 Optional memorial of Francis of Paola, hermit

4 Optional memorial of Isidore of Seville, bishop, doctor of the church

5 Optional memorial of Vincent Ferrer, presbyter, religious founder

7 Memorial of John Baptist de la Salle, presbyter, religious founder

11 Memorial of Stanislaus, bishop, martyr

13 Optional memorial of Martin I, pope, martyr

At the end of the story we read that the vine that shaded Jonah withered, so he whined like a brat. Elijah did the same thing while sitting under a broom tree. Happily, an angel brought Elijah a little refreshment, and soon the prophet was off and running 40 days to Horeb, God's holy mountain. The gospels tell us that Jesus himself, in his 40 days in the wilderness, was refreshed by angels after his temptations by Satan.

Lent, too, has its oases, its moments of refreshment, its ministering angels. These are the Sundays and the few—the very few—feast days during Lent.

Amazingly, when Lent is complete we will find ourselves right in the middle of the stories we have been telling all along. During the Paschal Triduum—those three days from Holy Thursday evening until Easter Sunday afternoon—we will gather around the cross—a tree of life, an ark, a burning bush where we learn God's name. In joy we will fill the font of baptism—a pool, a flood, a Red Sea, a great fish that swallows us and that spits us out alive, safe on a new shore.

A Lenten Blessing of Grain

What follows is text for a flyer to describe the custom mentioned on page 222, as well as to send home a blessing to pray over specially prepared small bags of grain. For each student, prepare a small, sealable plastic bag filled with about a cup of perlite and 3 tablespoonfuls of annual rye seed.

The Flyer

Christians have long kept the paschal custom of nestling dyed eggs into sprouting seedlings to make "resurrection gardens." Start some "Easter grass" today. Place the blessed grain and perlite in a bowl. Keep it moist but not waterlogged. When Easter arrives tuck in a few dyed eggs.

We who are baptized must become as buried grain, rising to a fruitful harvest. We must become as Easter eggs, opening into the white and gold of risen life. We ourselves must become the burial garden in which our wonderful gardener lives.

The Blessing of Grain

My friends,
the Passover of the Lord comes soon.
The world grows green; the birds return.
The moon waxes brighter each day
until at last it will be full
and our feast will come.
Our eyes turn toward Jerusalem
and we run with joy to the holy city
    to keep the Passover.

It is again time to plant our Easter grain.
We remember the words of Jesus:
"Unless the grain is buried in the earth,
    it cannot grow.
But if it is buried, it rises to bear fruit
    a hundredfold."

When we sprout this grain,
we foretell the day of resurrection
when we will rise from our graves
in the harvest of God's reign.

My friends, let us bless the Lord:
    Raise arms over the grain.
Blessed are you, Lord our God,
for you create the seeds of the earth,
and you raise the world to life.
All glory to you, almighty God,
in the death, burial and resurrection
    of your Son,
our Lord Jesus Christ,
now and unto endless ages, and for ever. Amen.

The Shape of Lent

Lent is long. To young people it may seem interminable. Happily, the season, as well as the Easter season to come, shows many faces, like a journey through a changing landscape. In some ways this change mirrors the volatile weather at this time of year. One day is frigid, the next mild, the next stormy, the next calm—and as the weeks progress there is a dramatic movement from winter to spring, from darkness to light, from lifelessness to an abundance of life.

Let's take a look at the "shape" of Lent, from beginning to end, and how images build in intensity as Easter approaches.

The first few days of Lent following Ash Wednesday are days of transition from Carnival. They're a time to simplify, to clean, to set agendas, to adjust schedules as the classroom and the school community and the entire church settle into Lent. A satisfying exercise that nevertheless takes time and fore-thought to accomplish is to give the classroom a real cleaning, scraping tape off windows, putting things away and finding places to store things. Work with the janitors on this. Don't clean anything unless you know the proper method for doing so.

Activity Idea

Clean outside too. One school sets aside a day at the start of Lent to eradicate graffiti from school property, something that has to be done with great care and some specialized skills and equipment. Most schools have one or more clean-up days in spring. Why not combine this with an hour of kite-flying? That's a traditional activity on Annunciation Day (March 25), perhaps because the March winds are a sign of the Holy Spirit. In the South and on the West Coast, Lent is planting season. Planting a tree or even a whole garden is an event that has its rite of blessing, which calls for songs and prayers.

Finally, early in Lent choose a way to keep a count of the days or weeks. Ways for doing so are given beginning on page 243.

*T*he first two Sundays of Lent, liturgically speaking, are entrances into the season. We hear about Jesus' 40-day fast in the wilderness and then about his transfiguration on the mountain, an event that tradition says took place 40 days before his death. Not everything of Lent, not even the classroom's approach to the season, needs to be in gear immediately but can be worked on and developed during the season's first weeks.

The entire season of Lent is an invitation to enter into its spirit, whether, in the words of a parable, at the third, sixth, ninth or even the eleventh hour. That's why, in the liturgy, Lent seems to deepen, grow stronger, mature. If you missed a week or two or three and didn't do something you intended to do during Lent, then begin with gusto as soon as you are able.

Our School Keeps Lent

Figure out a way to make it visually apparent outdoors to folks driving by that the school community is keeping Lent, that Lent is all-important in the life of this school, and that the church invites all to share in the blessings of this holy time. Ways of doing this might include an array of purple and grey and brown hangings in weatherproof fabrics outside the main doors. A large vine and pussy willow wreath could be hung near the sign that bears the school's name. A collection of fish-shaped nylon windsocks can flutter from bamboo poles on the lawn. Purple, rose and green nylon kites can be hung from lights in the parking lot. A series of well-crafted letters can stretch from window to window to form the slogan "Our school keeps Lent." Or, with some ambition, an outdoor display can be prepared to keep count of the 40 days, perhaps as a countdown to Easter.

The Fourth Sunday of Lent, Laetare Sunday, is a crest on the hill from which we catch our first sight of Jerusalem, the motherland where we shall keep the Passover. The Sunday gets its name from the Latin entrance antiphon: *Laetare Jerusalem, et conventum facite omnes qui diligitis eam* ("Rejoice, Jerusalem, and come together all you who love her"). Not to trivialize the liturgical image, but it's amazingly similar to the wonderful scene in the Wizard of Oz where the travelers along the yellow brick road catch their first sight of the Emerald City shining in the distance. (On Palm Sunday we will reach the gates of God's holy city, which will swing wide for us to enter.)

Halfway through the Forty Days, on this Sunday of rejoicing, flowers are permitted in celebration of spring, and in some parishes flowers are handed out to everyone. The art students in one school prepare paper roses for distribution in church on the Fourth Sunday of Lent. Rose-colored vesture is customary (although not required). The color is not pink but a dusky rose, a softening of Lent's violet. In England this fourth Sunday became "Mothering Sunday," a day for honoring Mother Jerusalem and Mother Church and one's own mother. The day is meant, in the words of the opening prayer at Mass, to make us "hasten toward Easter with the eagerness of faith and love."

Activity Idea

In schools on a weekday before or after Laetare Sunday you will want to do something that revs up energies and has us "hastening toward Easter." Perhaps your "Laetare Schoolday" is the occasion in Lent for observing birthdays and other reasons for indulgence that fall during the season. Gertrud Mueller Nelson suggests making "Laetare sundaes" that day! Like those of Carnival, the traditions of Laetare Sunday were formed by people for whom Lent was important. If Lent is kept with vigor and care, we need this mid-Lent celebration to strengthen us to finish the journey.

*A*nother custom for mid-Lent is to plant wheat or rye or other grain. (See the text for the blessing of grain on page 218.) In a pretty bowl or foil-lined basket the grain is covered lightly with

earth, sand or a growing medium such as perlite and kept moist but not water-logged. At Easter these now-green "resurrection gardens" are studded with a palm-cross and a few Easter eggs. Real "Easter grass" certainly is more beautiful than shredded cellophane—and a lot safer around pets. The custom of sprouting grain in springtime is truly ancient, observed by Persians to celebrate their new year at the vernal equinox, and kept also among Christians in Mediterranean countries in celebration of Easter.

Activity Idea

*M*ark a calendar in the classroom with the dates of the new moon and then the full moon before Easter. During those weeks make a point to remind students to try to catch a glimpse of the moon as it grows more and more full. Easter Sunday is set each year as the first Lord's Day after the first full moon after the vernal equinox. As Christians we are a people in love with holy signs. Once each year, at Easter, we rejoice that all the signs of nature seem to point in the same direction, straight into the kingdom of heaven, straight toward the life that is stronger than death.

Following the vernal equinox, daytime is longer than nighttime. Light is victorious over darkness. This is the first sign of Easter. When the moon grows full, it rises just as the sun sets so that no moment of the day and night is dark. That is the second sign of Easter. The Lord's Day is the first day of the week, the day God said, "let there be light," the day that Jesus Christ was raised from the dead, the day the Holy Spirit was given to the church. The Lord's Day is the third sign of Easter.

Your work as a religious educator means that you are a teacher of such signs. You open eyes and ears to their mystery. The paschal language of the church is at heart the church's sacramental language, its "sign language." This language involves every form of human communication and every sense.

Prayer Corner Idea

*I*f you enshrine the Bible in the classroom, then open it to John's gospel during the final weeks of Lent and on into the Easter season. Overlay the book stand with violet cloth. Just before Palm Sunday, ornament the classroom cross with red and violet fabrics, with pussy willows, with a crown of thorns and other handsome emblems of the passion.

*P*lacing palms in the classroom is an important event. You can go a few steps further than simply tucking palms behind the classroom cross. Instead of just bringing palms from church, do as the children did when they welcomed the Messiah into the holy city. A day or two before Palm Sunday, gather your own palms from yards and fields. Palms don't grow in your neighborhood? Then do as generations of Christians have done and substitute another branch. Pussy willow, yew and olive (or its northern relative, forsythia) are traditional.

John's gospel is the only one that mentions palm fronds. Matthew's and Mark's gospels simply say "branches of trees," and Luke doesn't tell of branches at all, only that people threw their cloaks on the road. The branches call to mind the processions at the Jewish harvest festival of Sukkot (which is discussed beginning on page 84). Willows, myrtle (a fragrant evergreen shrub available from florists) and date palm fronds are woven together for the festival.

*D*ate palm fronds and olive branches have strong biblical significance for Jews, Christians and Muslims as emblems of lasting and abundant life. That's why martyrs are shown carrying the branches. That's also why throughout the Middle East palm fronds and olive branches customarily are attached to gravestones. Perhaps the reason for the "lively" association is that date palms live in oases in the desert. To ripen properly, the fruit of the date palm requires months of 100-degree heat, deadly to other plants. Olive trees are famous for their longevity, living for centuries. Of course, the olive has been a symbol of peace and forgiveness ever since the dove carried a branch in its beak as a sign that the great flood was past.

In North America we generally substitute Gulf Coast palmettos for date palm. It's strange in America that on a commercial basis we seem to have no problem substituting one species of plant for another but haven't developed the same tradition as in other countries of gathering branches from our backyards. Early in Lent talk this over with the folks responsible for liturgy in the parish so that students and perhaps all parish households are encouraged to bring backyard branches on Palm Sunday to mix with the commercial palms for the blessing in church. That way the gathering of the branches becomes one of the active, hands-on rituals of Easter.

*F*rom Guatemala to Germany, there are splendid customs for weaving clusters of branches with ribbons and bells and other ornamentation for Palm Sunday. The clusters are often ten feet tall and just as wide, lovingly fashioned at home, carried to the great ingathering in Jerusalem (the parish church), and then, after Mass, brought to cemeteries to announce to the dead that Easter is coming.

 **A**ctivity Idea

Students also might prepare other decorations for the Palm Sunday procession, including bright banners and a donkey piñata hoisted high on a pole. Using a donkey in the Palm Sunday procession is as old as the day itself. A donkey is a scriptural sign of humility and service. It calls to mind Zechariah's enigmatic words about a humble king who will arrive to end war and "command peace to the nations."

*A*nother animal associated with the paschal festival is a mother hen and her chicks. Jesus looked down on the holy city of Jerusalem and mourned its coming destruction. He said he wanted to protect the citizens of the city like a hen gathering its chicks under its wings. In some places hens and chicks are fashioned from paper, bread dough or chocolate and hoisted on dowels to carry in the Palm Sunday procession.

*F*or Holy Week and the Paschal Triduum, figure out a handsome way to decorate classroom doors and the main doors of school, as well as the windows. If the school breaks for Easter week, use decorations that will look right throughout these days. One parish school ornaments windows with traditional designs of *pysanky* (batik Easter eggs) executed in paper and featuring such biblical images as the cross, deer, rooster, sun and moon, fish, willow,

A Bulletin Board for Lent
A Journey through the Desert

The idea on page 240 about a "burning bush" that gathers representations of Lent's scripture stories might be adapted for a bulletin board. So too might the ideas for keeping count of the 40 days of Lent and then the 50 days of the Easter season. The way these days are counted is explained beginning on page 243.

For a "lenten desert," cover the board in sand-colored paper (or why not use bits of actual sandpaper, if this can be found in sand colors?), or cut rough half-circles of several shades of browns, purples and sand colors, and overlap these on the board like shingles to create a hilly effect. You might edge the board with depictions of desert plants, such as cactuses and other succulents. Or edge the border in a single, rippling, purple-and-green snake that winds around the circumference.

Depending on the shape of the board, work a meandering path in purple from one corner to another. Divide the path into seven areas, perhaps by using several shades of purple, to represent the seven weeks of Lent. (If you use shades of color for the path, use rose for the fourth area and red for the final one.) On either side of the path, add images of desert animals, such as lizards, tarantulas, scorpions, ravens, tortoises and owls.

The beginning of the path, representing Ash Wednesday, might have an animal skull as a sign of mortality. At the end of the path you can place a domed city with twelve gates, representing the Paschal Triduum kept in Jerusalem. The entrance into each new color (each new week of Lent) can be represented by a symbol, perhaps something simple, such as a water well or thorny rose bush, to indicate that Sundays are the oases in Lent's desert. Or the symbols can be chosen from the Sunday readings, for instance, on the first Sunday, the devil or a tree of life or a rainbow. The entrance into the red area, Holy Week, can be marked by a triumphal arch or a donkey or both, representing Palm Sunday.

The simplest image, especially on a long, horizontal board, could be the meandering path in seven colors along which a traveler is moved. Or, more elaborately, each day from Ash Wednesday until Holy Thursday could be distinguished by adjoining colors. Two travelers representing Sarah and Abraham, or even a small caravan including Isaac, Hagar and Ishmael might represent your lenten pilgrims.

A version of this notion might be a sequence of 40 fishes in various shades of purple in a wandering line, head to tail, over an aqua-colored board. As each day passes the fish can be marked with a number or else the board could begin with no fish, just the aqua "water" and perhaps some bubbles and seaweed for interest. Each day another fish is added.

snake, tree and rose. There are other beautiful scriptural images for this week: the phoenix rising from its own ashes within the fronds of the date palm tree; the mother hen gathering her brood; the olive tree and Noah's dove; the lamb seated on the throne within the holy city. LTP's *A Lent Sourcebook* (in two volumes) and *A Triduum Sourcebook* (in three volumes) can help us recognize the wondrous imagery of this holiest of times.

*D*isplay Idea

Read the passion accounts and try to find suitable images to portray: You might gather in the prayer corner or near the cross a wood-handled hammer, three large nails, a ceramic rooster, dice, thirty silver coins in a satchel, a sea-sponge on a reed, a lance, a purple robe and a seamless white tunic. Find beautiful depictions of the passion in books of art reproductions and leave the books open on book stands. Splendid art can be found on the Internet.

Enter God's Gates in Joy!

A "triumphal arch" is a traditional outdoor seasonal decoration worth returning year after year. The arch—a sturdy wooden trellis that is in scale and complementary to the doors—is set up from Ash Wednesday to Pentecost. It receives changing ornamentation as the weeks pass, perhaps purple fabrics and bare vines during Lent, red fabrics and palms and pussy willows added for Palm Sunday and the Triduum, a switch to pastel fabrics and flowers for Eastertime, and green branches and bundles of fresh grasses at Pentecost.

One school's arch becomes the nesting spots for birds every year, which is an annual source of delight as well as a place for watchful care. Something of an arch can be created more simply from a large swag of fabric used as bunting over the main doors. This is a customary emblem of triumph or mourning.

The biggest and most worthwhile lenten challenge in a Catholic classroom is to get ready to celebrate with the parish the mysteries of the Paschal Triduum. Take time during Lent or even earlier to talk about the importance of freeing schedules and putting everything else aside in order to participate in the parish liturgy of the Triduum. Cooperate with parish liturgical ministers to maximize student participation.

In several schools students volunteer to help in church during the latter part of Lent for the many tasks that need doing to make the place ready for the Christian Passover. There are participation booklets to staple, bulletins to stuff, hymnals and other liturgical books to get in good order. The grounds and just about everything else need a careful cleaning.

It's possible in an active parish to put just about all hands to work preparing the physical requirements and embellishments of the liturgical rites of the Triduum. For instance, in some schools students are responsible early in Holy Week for getting the physical requirements of the Triduum out of storage and into place. The foot-washing vessels are cleaned and polished, the holy cross is sanded and oiled, the towels are folded, the wood for the Easter fire is cut and put in a dry place. Student artists prepare handheld flags for use during the Palm Sunday procession and the procession with the eucharist on Holy Thursday night. Attractive bobeches are fashioned around the candles used on Easter Eve; containers of water are filled for distribution at Easter.

In one school early in Lent an art teacher runs off copies on card stock of a marvelous Ethiopian design of the holy cross. The crosses are given to all students in school and in the religious education program. Students are instructed to cut the crosses out and color and ornament them on both sides, and then to sign their family's name on one side. The crosses are gathered up before Palm Sunday, then on Good Friday the crosses are blessed and distributed for parish families to hang on their front doors.

Just before the Triduum, students might take a "liturgy tour" if someone can act as tour guide to talk about the upcoming rites, for instance, the bringing in of the chrism and holy oils, the washing of feet, the gathering of gifts for those in need, the procession with the eucharist, the veneration of the cross, the kindling of the paschal bonfire, the rites of baptism and confirmation. LTP's video series for Holy Thursday, Good Friday and the Easter Vigil might be watched and discussed.

*B*ack to Basics: Prayer, Fasting and Almsgiving

Early in Lent decide with the students some real, accomplishable and practical ways to embrace the lenten disciplines of prayer, fasting and almsgiving, and then stick to them. Let tradition guide you.

*T*he notion here isn't to determine this year's gimmick. The notion is to take on disciplines that are sustainable from year to year, practices that students can grow into and not grow out of. That's why traditional practices are best—they've been tested by time.

In getting back to basics during Lent, focus on what needs work. Some things might be just fine as they are. For instance, your classroom prayer may be healthy and good and in need of only minor refinement. So this year focus instead on almsgiving and fasting.

*W*ays of fasting require their being geared toward age and abilities, and also require parental cooperation. Don't let those very real hurdles prevent you from tackling the subject of fasting and abstinence.

The fasting regulations of the church don't offer us much guidance. Over the past several generations most regulations were abolished not to put an end to the practice but to enable Christians to make fasting a free gift we do for one another, a gift we offer the church. But legalism and minimalism remain a plague on Catholic practices. For instance, the rule about fasting on Ash Wednesday and about not eating meat on lenten Fridays is bare minimum observance without which a person can hardly be called "Catholic." The laws are not some sort of ideal or even foundational way to keep Lent's fast.

Uncovering traditional ways to fast and then deciding how to accomplish it will take hard work.

$\mathcal{O}$n a bulletin board display student's research into customs of religious fasting. Get to know what people do the world over. Determine how such practices are different from dieting. Robert Farrar Capon distinguished the two by observing that a dieter says that food is bad and a faster says that food is good. Fasting leads to a feast. In your classroom corner devoted to the lenten disciplines, share ways in which students can embrace the spirit of such fasting, a spirit that places high value on the goodness of food.

Fasting usually means eating less food and skipping meals. A once-common Christian tradition of fasting, still observed by Muslims during their holy month of Ramadan, is not eating from sunup to sundown, from Morning Prayer to Evening Prayer. Growing children and the very old, those who are sick and those who are pregnant are not asked to fast. Fasting is regarded as a privilege. If you can fast safely without compromising your health, that's a reason to give thanks to God.

Abstinence means not eating certain foods, such as eggs, dairy products and meat, and replacing these with vegetables, grains and legumes. The traditional lenten abstinence from eating anything derived from animals was once nearly universal throughout the church, east and west. This abstinence makes sense of the traditional foods of Carnival and

Easter. Such a low-cholesterol diet sounds amazingly contemporary, doesn't it? This kind of healthy eating is suited to almost everyone of any age.

$\mathcal{I}$n paradise our first parents ate the forbidden fruit and brought death upon themselves and upon their children. In marvelous contrast, the Lord Jesus refused to eat when tempted in the desert. His gift to us is eternal life. Mark's gospel tells us that during Jesus' 40-day fast he lived in peace with the wild beasts. He made the desert a new Eden. The lenten fast is a way of showing

God that we've learned our lesson. We want to return to Eden. The ban on butchering animals during Lent was intended to be a further sign that we are ready to live in the peaceable kingdom.

Connect the stories of Eden and of Jesus' 40-day fast with your classroom presentation on the ways people fast. Connect fasting and abstinence also with the new life coming to birth as winter passes over into spring. You might ornament this presentation with pictures of newborn farm animals and newly hatched chicks, as well as art depicting Eden.

Bulletin Board Idea

Activity Idea

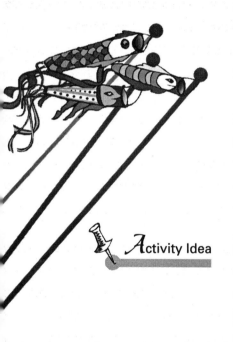

Even among small children the spirit of the fast can be kept by not sharing between-meal treats in the classroom and by skipping many forms of entertainment. Birthdays in Lent might be celebrated in some unique way, not with shared cake and candy but perhaps instead with flowers. Work with the cafeteria staff on appropriate lenten meals. Some ingenious efforts arise when even the foods served in the cafeteria get "back to basics." Work with the full school staff, including the athletic department, so dances and other entertainment are not scheduled for Lent. Saint Valentine's Day and Saint Patrick's Day are not enough of a reason for an exception. Lent means that it's not business as usual in a Catholic school.

John Chrysostom called fasting a "medicine." It's meant to make us healthy in body and mind. Hunger, so Jesus tells us in a parable, brought the prodigal son to his senses. For this medicine to be effective, religious tradition insists that fasting be accompanied by prayer and almsgiving. "Alms" comes from a Greek word meaning "compassion." The book of Tobit reminds us that "prayer with fasting is good, but better than both is almsgiving with justice."

Activity Idea

Do you invite guests to take part in your prayer? If the prayer life in the classroom is good, it might be made even better if on occasion you invited outsiders to participate, especially during Lent. Parents and grandparents might join in daily or weekly prayer. If it's still your practice to have prayer led over the public address system, stop doing that and instead have students lead prayer in the classroom.

An excellent lenten improvement in prayer is to replace recitation with singing. Make sure the books and other accoutrements of prayer are handsome, noble and beautiful.

How and where will you gather gifts of charity—alms—during Lent? Who will receive your gifts? The money gathered in "rice bowls" benefits

Catholic Relief Services, an agency that helps people of any or no religion. Another form of alms box or mite box can have a secure and prominent place during Lent and throughout the year. Piggy banks originated as alms boxes, a visual reminder that Lent's fast prepares for a feast. The pig (or other alms box) gets opened on Holy Thursday and the money is brought to church to purchase an Easter feast for others. The word "pyg" is an old word for clay—that's what the banks were made of. It's a great lenten image.

*P*rayer Corner Idea

*Y*ou'll need substantial baskets and hampers to gather gifts of food and clothing. In one of the common areas of school, instead of in separate classrooms, the baskets and hampers make the perfect sign of Lent as long as they're put to use. This public spot is a good place for a display about the recipients of the gifts, if this can be done in a way that respects the privacy of the recipients.

*A*ctivity Idea

No matter how it's done, Lent's alms should be made part of the special procession of gifts for the needy on Holy Thursday evening. Even if you can't bring up everything you've collected throughout Lent, work out with the pastor and worship coordinator a way for the school's almsgiving to be represented in this procession.

On Holy Thursday evening, as the Triduum begins, the gifts themselves become a key sacramental sign that this community is ready to keep Easter. The school art department and student artists might take some time to see that the gifts and the containers for the gifts are beautiful.

Welcome the Lenten Spring!

In her book *To Dance with God,* Gertrud Mueller Nelson tells of a ritual following the Mardi Gras bonfire during which the old palms are burned to make Ash Wednesday's ashes. After the ashes are made, paper flowers are handed out with a motto attached to each flower: "Lent means spring."

*T*hose words are short and sweet, and they convey something important. Spring isn't incidental to the season but cuts to the core of what we are about as a church during these days. A fuller expression of this sentiment is found in an antiphon from the Byzantine liturgy: "Welcome the lenten spring! Welcome the time that brings light to the soul."

During Lent the northern hemisphere of the planet turns toward the sun, the source of life. In the lengthening brightness from Ash Wednesday to Holy Thursday—our lenten spring—we are called to turn away from sin and death. We are called to turn to God as our source of life.

A great addition to the prayer corner during Lent, and even to the school entryways, is a small, flowery foretaste of Easter, such as a potted primrose, a few daffodils, a cyclamen or a branch of forsythia. Perhaps remove any bows or other festive wrappings and instead repot the plant in a simple clay or wicker container.

What other signs of the season are true to what's happening in your neighborhood and can be reflected in the decorations in the classroom? A clay vessel to hold ashes? Bare branches? An earthenware jar of seeds? Sprouting bulbs?

*P*rayer Corner Idea

*T*ake a lenten walk in the wild. You'll likely return with clods of dirt stuck to shoes, hair messed by the wind, perhaps eyes a bit blinded by the strengthening

sun. Our ancestors named the lenten months "February," from the word for purification, and "March," from the name of the god of war. Lent can be a stormy season.

Lent is not so much a settled time of flowers and butterflies but a season of struggle—of transfiguration, of conversion, of "passing over." In some places the lenten spring looks like a flowering orchard, but in some places Lent brings flooding rivers engorged with mud and drowned animals. Death and life are never far apart.

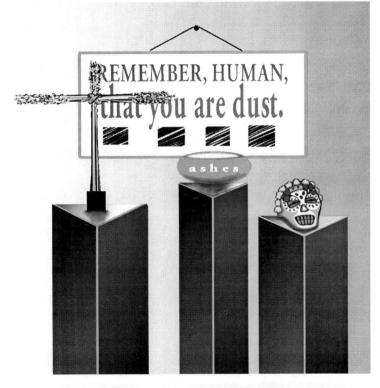

*W*hat signs of spring can you bring into the classroom that show something of the messy, muddy struggle that early spring entails? Be sure to keep an earthenware bowl of ashes in evidence. Perhaps nearby you might keep a small skull of some kind, a *memento mori,* a reminder of death. (Because "Calvary" is derived from the Latin word for skull, old-fashioned crosses often included a small skull at the base, a reminder that the cross of Christ is victorious over death.) Perhaps this is an animal skull found on a hike through the woods, or a Mexican sugar skull, or a carved ivory skull—the effect is not meeting to be silly or hokey.

*A*ctivity Idea

A class trip to see newborn farm animals might be an inspiration toward keeping the lenten abstinence as well as a time to gather a few signs of the season from the wild, with the landowner's permission, of course.

*D*isplay Idea

Bare branches can evoke the lenten scriptures of the wilderness, the burning bush, the fig tree given another chance to bear fruit. A large, bare branch or vine may look good hung against a wall or hung overhead, even between light fixtures. Small branches can look good arranged in a pot of sand or gravel or some other material, such as perlite. This is a two-person task: Put the branches in the pot, hold them roughly where you want them to stand, then add the sand. This is easier than trying to stick the butt-ends of branches into the sand.

Now arrange the branches attractively by pushing them apart a bit without lifting them out of the sand.

Brightly colored red- and yellow-twigged dogwood branches are often abundant in yards and fields and are not harmed by heavy pruning. Thorny locust and hawthorn branches are handsome—but keep them somewhere away from eyes. Pussy willows are customary on Palm Sunday and during Holy Week. (Don't put them in water or the catkins will fall off.)

*B*ranches that flower in early spring are a welcome sight—alders, elm, willows, hazels, birches, aspens, forsythia, witch hazels, maples, peach and plum trees! Some of these species have flowers that are hardly recognizable to most people as flowers. But they do have a strange and welcome beauty that fits the season. They can be signs of the brevity of life and perhaps even heralds of the life to come. A few branches might go in a crock of water put in a place where they can be appreciated up close. A drop or two of bleach will keep the water fresh.

*P*rayer Corner Idea

Many tree flowers produce abundant pollen. Aside from the matter of allergies, pollen makes a mess. Because most trees are wind-pollinated, the pollen is light and more likely to get up one's nose than the sticky, heavy pollen of insect-pollinated flowers.

*W*illows are among the first trees to green up in springtime. In Christian poetry, the willow tree's thirst for water is compared to the catechumen's longing

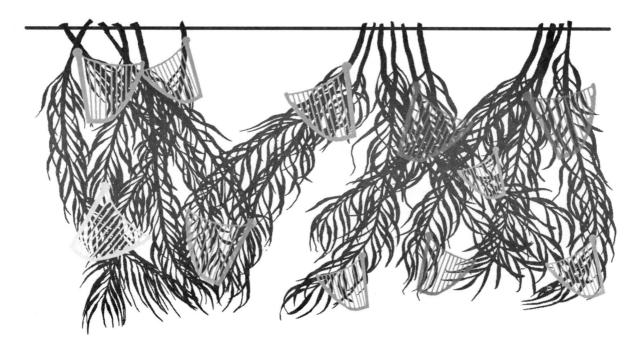

for baptism. Weeping willows are mentioned in Psalm 137, the song of the Babylonian exile, and the species name shows the link—*Salix babylonica. Salix,* the Latin name for willow, means "leaping," from the tree's ability to root at its branch tips, which enables a grove of trees on one side of a stream to "leap" over the stream and to establish a grove on the other side.

Weeping willows look great suspended from a wall with wire, with stump ends anchored against the wall. To echo Psalm 137, hang a few "harps" cut from tagboard or other material on your willows. Somewhere near your lenten willows is the perfect place to bury the alleluia (or to hang the word on the harps) as Lent begins—because that word is the song we yearn to sing once our lenten exile is past. Alleluia will be our song of homecoming at Easter.

The supple branches of weeping willow, no doubt abundant under a tree after being broken off by winter storms, are great to weave into wreaths or chains or other classroom ornaments.

In one class at the beginning of Lent every student gets a four-foot length of fresh willow. One of the branches is woven into a circle simply by weaving the branch around itself into a ring. The next branch goes through the first and is woven into a ring round and round, in and out of itself. This continues as each student adds her or his branch to the growing chain. The chain is hung across a wall during the season and represents the classroom keeping Lent together, united as one. At Easter the chain is hung with all sorts of seasonal ornaments including paper flowers, butterflies, lambs and other signs of the season.

Transfiguration

Metamorphosis is the Greek word for transfiguration and transformation. On Lent's second Sunday we hear about the metamorphosis of Jesus, a transfiguration mirrored by the earth during springtime.

Bulletin Board Idea

*Y*ou might include among the lenten decorations in the classroom a gradually transfigured "work in progress." For instance, you might gather on a bulletin board or even an entire wall images of the wilderness. More and more features are added each week—of desert creatures, of a path through the desert, of oases springing up along the path, of a sudden storm, of cactuses and other appropriate plants that bloom after rain, of the holy city coming into view at the end of the path.

You might gear the images, as the church does, to certain biblical stories. When we hear about Jesus' conversation with the Samaritan woman at the well, add a well to the desert oasis. When we hear about the pool of Siloam, add a pool.

As an image of metamorphosis, some people set branches or small trees in water to leaf out over a several-week period. That's hard to do successfully. Even with a suitable species, such as poplar, what's likely to happen is that within a couple of weeks or even days after the new leaves emerge, the entire branch will suddenly die. This is certainly not a good sign of transfiguration and, in any case, it's one that won't last the season.

*I*n every classroom it seems that the metamorphosis from caterpillar to chrysalis to butterfly has become a favorite, if overused, image. Frogs also undergo a metamorphosis from eggs to tadpoles to adult frogs. They also hibernate and then in early spring emerge noisily from their sleep. Their emergence and vocalization is itself a sign of resurrection. An ancient Christian tomb is decorated with a carving of a frog and the words "in the twinkling of an eye," words that refer to Paul's first letter to the Corinthians, which speaks of the metamorphosis of the dead "at the last trumpet."

In traditional iconography, the primary images (of Jesus or the saints) are expressions of the church's communal faith, so the iconographer is taught to uphold accepted and traditional ways of depicting the images. But the artist has more leeway in using secondary images—such as butterflies or frogs—which may be added in secondary positions, say, tucked into a corner. Secondary images offer a kind of commentary on the primary images and can delight the viewer who happens to notice them.

The same principle can apply to our work with images in the classroom. A lenten caterpillar that is transformed during the Paschal Triduum into a chrysalis and then, for the Easter season, into a butterfly might go in an oddball corner of the room that is not a focus of prayer—certainly not directly alongside the classroom cross or in the prayer corner.

*O*f course, the most striking "transfiguration" in the classroom will be the metamorphosis from Lent into Easter. That's why it's best to plan to use the same sites in the classroom and throughout the school complex for decoration from Ash Wednesday through Pentecost. Establish through this visual tactic something of the unity of these days.

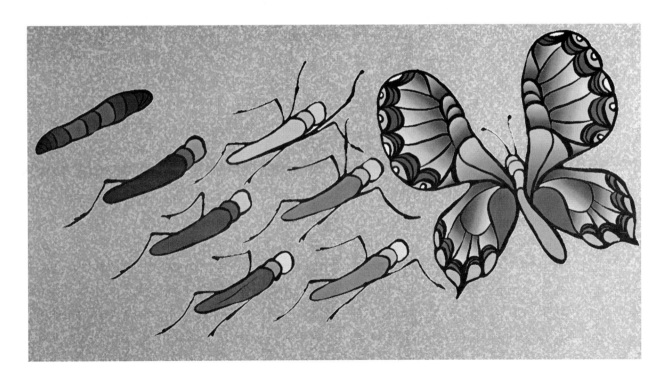

Paschal Literacy

When Christmas rolls around, the mind is flooded with images in near nonsensical profusion. Magi, shepherds and angels get jumbled in our brains with the little drummer boy and Santa Claus. The same giddy overabundance of images should fill the mind at Easter, the richest of times on the church's calendar, the "festival of festivals" that gives life and meaning to all others.

The scriptures form the richest treasury of paschal images. One of our tasks in the classroom is to lead students to learn and appreciate, and then fall in love with, such images. In part, that's what this book is all about.

Begin with the scriptures of the season: The animals aboard the ark, the Hebrew slaves marching through the Red Sea, Jonah in the belly of the fish, Daniel in the lions' den, Esther in the court of the king of Persia, the three children in the fiery furnace, Susanna on trial for her life, the prodigal son—these tales can be depicted in some way and the depictions displayed. The characters are our companions on the paschal journey, and parts of their stories are heard at daily Mass during Lent.

Activity Idea

In one classroom each student has to choose and sign up to read and then depict a different lenten story. The stories are read directly from the Bible, not from paraphrases. Each student, with the help of her or his family, fashions a depiction of the characters in the story from foam core and beautiful papers. When finished, all the students' efforts are gathered in one place. Students are responsible for researching likely modes of dress or other details to attempt an accurate portrayal. (This is another of umpteen examples of the benefits of art, history and religion teachers working together.)

Finding Art

Many of us have trouble depicting the human form and so may need to borrow a bit. The Internet offers some sources for artwork to borrow (or at least from which to derive inspiration), and you might begin simply, for instance, by typing "Daniel the prophet" (along with variations on this name) into a search engine. Clip art collections are also sources of images, and LTP's books of clip art by Steve Erspamer and Suzanne Novak are gems. To create a template, one teacher uses an overhead projector to shine an enlarged image of figures from clip art onto paper.

Bulletin Board Idea

Prayer Corner Idea

Where would you display the gradually accumulating depictions of Lent's scripture stories? A traditional way to display depictions of the lenten scriptures, a nice one for parish schools, is called a "burning bush," a cousin of Advent's "Jesse tree." Branches are set into a pot of sand or gravel (red-twigged dogwood is beautiful). Day by day, onto the twigs are hung representations of characters from the lenten scriptures. If you made a lenten willow chain, that might be a good spot to suspend depictions. If you hung a willow branch or a vine, that's a good spot, too.

The "burning bush" might be located in the classroom or in a common area of the school. The spot needs to be reasonably suited to such a construction. (In church, a beautiful spot might be in the church vestibule, a reverent location that doesn't vie for attention with the pulpit and altar.)

The burning bush on Mount Sinai is the place where God spoke to Moses, where Moses learned God's name. As Easter nears, the "burning bush" will grow bright. In the study of the scriptures and in learning these stories, we too hear God's voice and learn God's name.

Anything like this that you do for Lent might stay in place and be embellished during the Easter season. It's not so much that the church has particular lenten stories and then Easter stories. Instead, it's almost as if the same story unfolds over the 90-plus days of Lent and Eastertime. Here's an example: The paschal season is often compared to a journey. The lenten leg of the trip takes us from slavery in Egypt to the shore of the Red Sea. During Eastertime we travel onward to Sinai, where at Pentecost we meet God face to face.

As the weeks pass between Ash Wednesday and Pentecost, your depictions can change gradually to tell a particular story. As an example, on a bulletin board in the parish school or on a window during Carnival, the animals might be shown marching aboard Noah's ark. As Lent begins God shuts the hatch of the ark and the rain begins. During Lent the people and animals huddle inside the boat and eye one another hungrily. At the Triduum, the ark sets to rest on the mountain, and Noah releases the raven and the dove. During Eastertime the earth grows green and flowery, the animals come out of the ark, and the rainbow appears.

Rather than displaying the characters during Lent, perhaps you read about and discuss the stories during Lent and craft the depictions, but then wait until Easter to display them on a kind of "Easter tree." In one school, on 8" x 11" white card stock an art teacher runs off a variety of Ukrainian Easter egg

A Bulletin Board for Lent
Noah's Ark

Subdivide a bulletin board with sea-blues on the bottom third and sky-blues on the top two-thirds. (A border of fishes on the bottom third and clouds on the top two-thirds would be appropriate.) Out of 40 pieces of paper, heavy on the purples, create a great, fat half-circle shape floating on the sea, rounded side on the bottom, flat side on the top. (It should bear a strange resemblance to a map.) Add on top of this half-circle "boat" a house shape, and within the house add figures of Noah and his family.

On the first few days of Lent glue a pair of animals to each of the 40 sections. Then, just before or after the First Sunday of Lent, which is the first of the 40 days, cover all the sections (overlaying the animals) with a single sheet of paper or with strips of paper (to look like planks) so the animals are hidden beneath the paper. A corkboard that can be stapled will make this easier, but a less-sticky tape (removable tape is available from office supply stores) can be used, too. Portholes might be added to the covering so a few of the critters peek through.

During the first week of Lent cover the blue sky with storm clouds. These can be created from cotton or Dacron® batting. As the season moves along, add lightning, hail and plenty of raindrops descending from the clouds. (Strings of blue beads would be magical as rain. Mylar® film or foil works for lightning.)

Fishes and other sea creatures can be added to the water, perhaps one a week or even one each day. Each day you might place the appropriate number across the hull of your ark to count up the days of Lent.

When you return from Easter break, the covering over the animals is removed, the darkest clouds are taken away to reveal the blue sky, and the sun, a rainbow, a raven and a dove should be added to the sky. The same board can be used to count up the 50 days of the Easter season with a new number added to the sky each morning.

designs. (These are taken from a book about decorating Ukrainian eggs and enlarged to about ten inches.) Each student receives an egg, blank on one side and printed with the design on the other. Instructions tell students to cut the egg out, decorate the design as brightly and imaginatively as possible, and then, on the blank side, to portray one of the Bible stories given in a list of possibilities. These include the readings from the Paschal Triduum. Ribbons are attached to the eggs, which are used to ornament the ceiling of the "gathering space" inside the church building throughout the Easter season.

Lenten Sunday gospels from John—about the Samaritan woman, the man born blind and the raising of Lazarus—express powerful, archetypal images of water, light and life. These stories lend themselves to being acted out, complete with costumes and props.

In some places, symbols of light or water are used as decorations because the gospel that week mentions light or water as a central image. This is not a good idea. Keep in mind that these (and other) baptismal images are woven throughout John's gospel and are hardly unique to any one story. We will surround ourselves with these sacramental signs in abundance at Easter—not as secondary decoration but as the blessed material of the sacraments.

The lenten way of emphasizing baptismal materials is through their absence, an absence that more than makes the heart grow fonder.

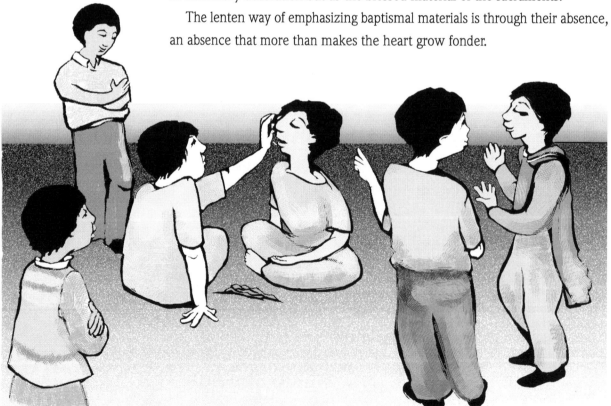

Counting the Days

The springtime of the church, the days from Ash Wednesday to Pentecost, are so important that each day counts—and is counted! The numbers 40, 3 and 50 resonate with biblical significance. Together the days add up to a quarter of the year, a full season, the church's spring.

The biblical practice was to count the days of the barley and wheat harvests, the all-important harvests that brought the community its daily bread. The count of seven weeks, 50 days, was begun after Passover. (See Leviticus 23:15–16 and Deuteronomy 16:9.) Jewish tradition includes elaborate calendars for counting the 50 days between the festivals of Passover and Shavuot.

Christians might take a cue from this custom. A paschal calendar running from Ash Wednesday to Pentecost can grace the vestibule or classroom. The calendar can be a construction of cut paper, cloth or wood, perhaps made more elaborate with small doors, as in an Advent calendar. It could designate both the day of the week—say, Monday of the second week in Lent—as well as the day of the count—in this case, the ninth of the Forty Days of Lent.

Activity Idea

The Jewish calendars for keeping the count usually involve a vertical scroll attached top and bottom to two dowels. On the scroll is written the series of numbers from 1 to 50, each number often embellished with illumination. The scroll and its dowels are mounted in a box with a window that shows each day's portion of the scroll. This kind of construction is fairly easy to make. The trick is to find a roll of paper and then make the scroll. Or use separate cards and slip each day's card into an ornamental, windowed box or frame.

Another good form for a calendar for counting the days is a ladder with numbered rungs. The ladder might take the form of a "Jacob's ladder," a *ziggurat,* which is a staircase that spirals around a tower. Each step can be numbered in an ascent to Pentecost.

A Bulletin Board for Holy Week

Daniel in the Lion's Den

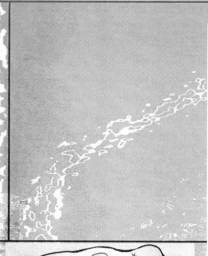

Easter is more than the celebration of the death, burial and resurrection of the Lord Jesus. To this story we attach other scripture stories of "passing over." We add our own stories, too, as a church, as a parish, as a school, as a family—especially the stories about the time we were baptized, confirmed and celebrated our first communion.

Some key paschal stories that can be depicted on bulletin boards are the ones we will hear on Easter Eve: the story of creation, the story of Abraham's near-sacrifice of his beloved son, Isaac, the story of the exodus from Egypt. Add to these stories the tale of Noah and the great flood, the story of Esther and the king, of Jonah in the fish's belly, of Susannah on trial, of Daniel in the lions' den, of the three youths in the fiery furnace.

Throughout Lent you might depict as many of these stories as possible, cumulatively, a new one each week, in a place where you have the space to keep adding to the depictions, such as a hallway or the cafeteria. Student artists can prepare these, and their efforts can be put on display.

Perhaps during Lent you show a scene from a story that leaves the story unresolved. Then during the weeks of the Easter season, you finish the telling. As an example, during Lent when you depict Abraham's near-slaying of his son Issac, perhaps you show Abraham raising the knife over his son. Then during the Easter season you add the angel that stops Abraham from harming the boy, and you show the ram caught in the thicket.

A great story to depict in stages is the one about Daniel in the lions' den. (There are two versions of this tale in the book of the prophet Daniel, although different translations of the Bible locate the second version in different places. The first version is found in chapter six of the book of Daniel.) Just before the Paschal Triduum you can leave the story at the point that Daniel spends the night in the den. Daniel's friend, the king (who threw him into the den!), stays awake all night, fasting and praying—and hoping beyond hope that the lions are fasting, too. Then, once Easter has arrived, you can show Daniel coming out of the pit of lions—and the king and the lions and Daniel having their breakfast.

Rather than making each figure out of a single sheet of white paper that you color, you might instead use various richly colored papers, foils and acrylic sheets or other substrates that are pieced together to form a figure. For instance, Daniel's body might be brown paper, his hair black felt, his robe bright blue paper with real buttons glued on, his belt gold Mylar® film, and his sandles thin cork.

It's customary in much iconography to add the person's name to the figure, sometimes within the folds of the person's clothing or else in a halo.

Another possibility is to fold an origami paper crane or fish each day of the season and to add it to a chain or to suspend it from the ceiling. In one classroom at the start of Lent, students fashion 40 paper fish and set them swimming (from fishing line, of course) from the light fixtures. The fish are made from papers in various shades of purple, rose and green, just to underscore the association with Lent. Numbering the fish enables students to keep track of the count. Each day of the "40 days of Lent" a fish is cut down and added to a paper net tacked to a bulletin board.

Fish became lenten symbols because, among Western Christians, the only meat permitted during Lent was fish and other sea creatures. A fish marked on the calendar meant a day of abstinence. (Eastern Christians include fish among the foods not eaten during Lent.) Also, the zodiacal sign of Pisces, the fishes, always falls during Lent. And, of course, the fish is a symbol of Christ. The Greek word for "fish," *ichthus,* is an anagram for the Greek words for "Jesus Christ, God's Son, Savior." Ancient church poets described those who are baptized as "little fishes protected by Christ, the big fish."

*B*esides customs for counting the days, there are customs for counting weeks. Some of these are venerable but bizarre, for instance, as the Sundays of Lent pass an orange is stripped of six feathers that have been poked into it at Lent's onset. A more interesting custom, from Spain, is the crafting of an eight-legged (or 46-legged) paper scorpion. The scorpion is a symbol of the "sting of death" that Christ's victory abolishes. On Ash Wednesday a leg is removed. Each lenten Sunday (or each day) another leg is removed, and then on Easter Eve the final leg is removed and the scorpion is tossed into the Easter bonfire.

A variation on this custom would be the gradual construction of a butterfly. At the beginning of Lent the legless, wingless body would be caterpillar-like. The six legs are added on the six Sundays of Lent and the wings added at Easter. Another construction could be six feathers added to a peacock or six flames added to a phoenix, both birds being symbols of resurrection. (Or, with eight feathers or flames the birds could be used to count the weeks of the Easter season, completed at Pentecost.)

*V*ariations on the form of an Advent wreath designed for Lent are new-fangled gimmicks. One such variation has six candles arranged on a cross that lies flat. Four candles are purple, one candle is rose (for the fourth Sunday) and one is red (for Palm Sunday). If that's done, then the logical thing would be to have the centermost candle be a large paschal candle for the Easter season.

A seven-branched candelabra might be put to this service (the final light is kindled at Easter). For the Easter season the cross might be surrounded by a crown of eight candles; one more candle is lit each week until the crown is fully illuminated at Pentecost. If you do anything like this, make sure that you do it well, that the materials are beautiful, noble and in scale with their surroundings. Also, figure out a way to show the continuity between Lent and the Easter season. It would be unbalanced to make it seem that Lent is more important than the Easter season.

Candles can be dangerous and are not especially effective during the day. Perhaps the counting of the weeks can be shown through the addition of depictions of the characters of the Sunday readings (see page 244 for more about this), or through the addition of lenten and then Easter symbols to ornament the wall behind the classroom cross.

*H*ow does the church count the 40 days of Lent and the 50 days of the Easter season? The count of the 50 days is straightforward, day by day from Easter Sunday to Pentecost. The count of Lent's 40 days is more complicated. Most people are surprised to learn that the "Forty Days of Lent" begin on the first Sunday of the season, not on Ash Wednesday. The fortieth day is Holy Thursday, the day during which Lent ends and the Paschal Triduum begins.

But there is another 40-day period to consider at this season: 40 days of fasting. Because Sundays are never days of fasting, the 40 days of Lent (from the first Sunday to Holy Thursday) include only 34 fasting days. In the sixth century in Rome, the day we now call Ash Wednesday and the three days afterward were "added" to the lenten fast so that there would be 38 fasting days before the Paschal Triduum. The two fasting days of the Triduum—Good Friday and Holy Saturday—are counted with Lent's 38 to total 40 days of fasting before Easter Sunday.

LTP's *Forty Days and Forty Nights* calendar and *A Lent Sourcebook* reflect this ancient method for counting the 40 days, beginning on the First Sunday of Lent. The books of LTP's sourcebook series are anthologies of seasonal prose and poetry arranged day by day through the seasons. Perhaps a place can be found to leave *A Lent Sourcebook* (and then the *Sourcebooks* for Triduum and Easter) open to each day's entries as an invitation to prayer and meditation. For younger children LTP publishes Melissa Musick Nussbaum's *Bible Stories for the Forty Days.*

Saints' Days in Lent

Saints' days take a backseat in Lent. Any memorials of the saints are optional in Lent, and even if they are celebrated the vestments remain lenten violet, with readings and prayers from the lenten texts. That means—and this is news to some people—that the proper liturgical color for Saint Patrick's Day is violet!

*H*ere we have the spirit of Lent, which permits no distraction. Another way to look at the matter is to say that we have our hands full during Lent. Anything that interrupts Lent had better be worthwhile. With a very few exceptions, saints' days take a definitive back seat to the observance of Lent.

*S*aint Joseph's Day (usually kept on March 19) and the Annunciation of the Lord (usually kept on March 25) take precedence over weekdays of Lent. These two solemnities are celebrated with white vesture and great festivity. The observances are transferred to another day if March 19 or 25 falls on a Sunday or during the two-week-period from Palm Sunday to the Octave Day of Easter.

These two solemnities wrap around the vernal equinox and so occur nine months before Christmas. A saint's day is usually the day of the saint's death, and that's what Saint Joseph's Day is. As winter comes to an end we gather around Joseph, imagined in legend to have been surrounded by his family when he died, the most blessed and peaceful death celebrated by the church.

In a week, after the equinox has passed and spring begins, the church gives witness to the moment that the angel appeared to Mary with the good news that she is to become the Mother of God. Life leaps up where no life had been.

And in that life all members of the church, along with Mary and Joseph, find their life.

*T*he angel's annunciation to the sleeping Joseph or to Mary is a favorite subject for artists. So is the death of Joseph. Find such a depiction and high-light it for the day with flowers, candles and other ornamentation. (Carnations, meaning "flesh colored," are the "flowers of the incarnation" and are customary in some places on March 19 and 25.) Statues of Mary and Joseph should be ornamented and crowned with flowers on these days.

Another event commemorated in some places on March 19 is the marriage of Mary and Joseph. This is curious, but almost every church in Europe has a portrait of this event and almost none in America do. In some places in Europe the days between March 19 and 25 are kept as Mary and Joseph's wedding.

In our orderly way of thinking it may be hard to celebrate what seem like Christmas events in a lenten context. Another way of thinking—one that cannot imagine Christmas separated from Easter—is reflected in a diptych (a double-paneled painting) that couples the annunciation to Mary with Jesus' agony in the garden. In the panel that shows Gabriel appearing to Mary in her garden, the sun illuminates the scene, which overflows with insects, nesting birds and reptiles basking in the light. In the other panel an angel offers Jesus the cup of suffering. The paschal full moon rises, and its pale light glows in the eyes of bats and other creatures of the night. Overarching the two scenes are the words "Thy will be done."

The classic collect for the Annunciation, still used as the final prayer of the Angelus, links this event with Easter:

> *Pour forth, we beseech you, O Lord,*
> *your grace into our hearts:*
> *that we, to whom the Incarnation of Christ your Son*
> *was made known by the message of an Angel,*
> *may by his Passion and Cross*
> *be brought to the glory of the Resurrection.*
> *Through the same Christ our Lord. Amen.*

*W*hat about Saint Patrick's Day? The occasion has been turned into March's "theme" by the greeting card industry. Some of us follow suit and cover walls with shamrocks weeks before the occasion. Something's seriously off-kilter in a Catholic school when Saint Patrick's Day receives visual prominence over Lent.

 *D*isplay Idea

That being said, many (but not all) of the traditional images of Saint Patrick's Day fit well throughout Lent. The abundance of the color green seems to welcome and even hasten the springtime. Shamrocks supposedly were one of Patrick's teaching devices as he prepared the catechumens for baptism at Easter. The snakes Patrick is said to have driven out of Ireland are emblems of evil and chaos, hearkening back to Eden. The snake is a perfect lenten image.

Another of Patrick's images, the bonfire, never gets the same attention on this day as leprechauns and their pots of gold, but is a strong reminder of Ireland's Druid heritage. Supposedly Patrick "christened" the Druid spring bonfire by kindling it on Easter Eve. The sense here isn't a rejection of non-Christian practices but a new interpretation of them in light of the gospel.

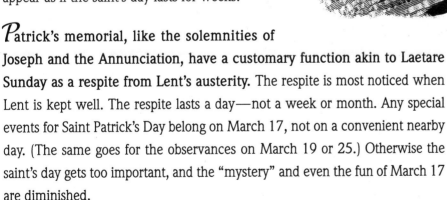

The trick in a Catholic school is to make use of appropriate images during Lent that may borrow a bit from the card-store decorations for Saint Patrick's Day but that do not make it appear as if the saint's day lasts for weeks.

*P*atrick's memorial, like the solemnities of Joseph and the Annunciation, have a customary function akin to Laetare Sunday as a respite from Lent's austerity. The respite is most noticed when Lent is kept well. The respite lasts a day—not a week or month. Any special events for Saint Patrick's Day belong on March 17, not on a convenient nearby day. (The same goes for the observances on March 19 or 25.) Otherwise the saint's day gets too important, and the "mystery" and even the fun of March 17 are diminished.

The Season of Easter

Entering into the Mystery of Easter
First Things First: Easter Water, Easter Candle, Easter Cross
Frolicking in the Pasture of the Good Shepherd
Mother Mary in May
The Ascension of the Lord
The Solemnity of Pentecost

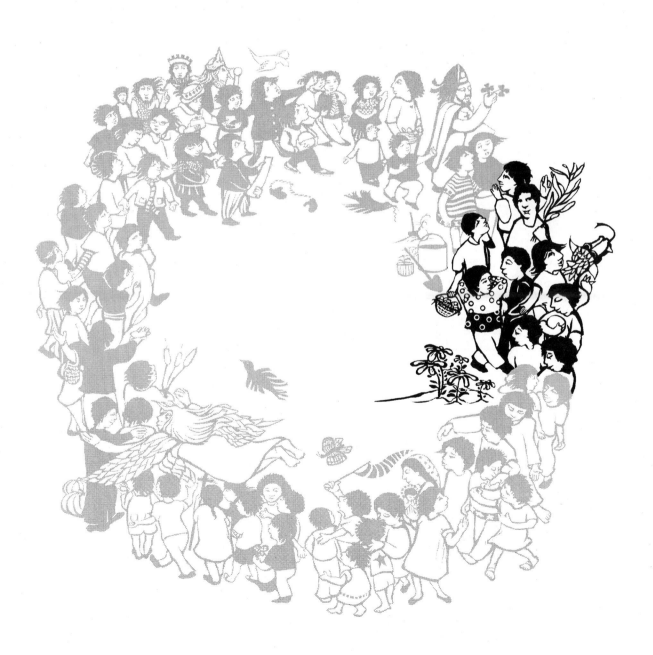

Entering into the Mystery
of *Easter*

*T*he word "neophyte" means "newly planted." That's the name we give to those newly baptized. Anything freshly planted requires tireless care to keep it from drying up or from going into transplant shock. A time of settling in and sending down roots is necessary. "Mystagogy" is the name for the church's care for the "newly planted."

*F*or the people baptized at Easter, the seven weeks after the Paschal Triduum are a season of **mystagogy, which means "the learning of mystery."** But here mystery doesn't mean a puzzle to figure out, it means a new way of life to embrace. We "learn mystery," a life-long task, by entering into it and by living it—by sending down roots deep into its fertile soil.

The mystery encompassing all mysteries is Christ—Christ crucified, buried and risen in glory. When the newly baptized rise from the water, the church sings the words of Saint Paul: "You have put on Christ." To "learn mystery" is nothing less than to "put on Christ," to become the mystery into which we are baptized.

The Triduum

The three most holy days of the year are the Paschal Triduum. From sunset Holy Thursday to sunset Good Friday is day one. From sunset Good Friday to sunset Holy Saturday is day two. From sunset Holy Saturday to sunset Easter Sunday is day three.

Mysterion is the Greek word for "sacrament." A sacrament is not so much a rite that the church does as a mystery that the church becomes. In the sacraments we become Christ. We enter into God's own life. More than any other time, the Easter season overflows with sacramental imagery, and the newly baptized and confirmed and those who have celebrated their first communion are the loveliest signs of the season.

If you're one of the folks who care for visuals in the classroom, Easter will keep you busy. During the Easter season it's as if the church, following the amazing rites of the Triduum, is so overwhelmed with joy that it babbles like a child in awe. No wonder Easter's favorite word is "alleluia," sung again and again in untiring profusion.

The season lasts 50 days, from Easter Sunday until Pentecost. Why 50? Seven is a sign of fullness—there are seven days in a week. Seven weeks signify "fully full." And when one more day is added—to make 50—we have a sign of the fullest fullness. That's where we have been rocketed by the Paschal Triduum, into the fullest fullness. And so we keep Eastertime by "playing heaven," by learning how to live with one foot on earth and one foot in heaven—both feet planted firmly in the reign of God.

"Playing heaven"—what a great expression! Take some time to ponder what it means to live as if we were already in heaven. What might this look like, sound like, feel like? What are the challenges and consequences? Notice that Lent is shorter than the

April

2 Optional memorial of Francis of Paola, hermit

4 Optional memorial of Isidore of Seville, bishop, doctor of the church

5 Optional memorial of Vincent Ferrer, presbyter, religious founder

7 Optional memorial of John Baptist de la Salle, presbyter, religious founder

11 Memorial of Stanislaus, bishop, martyr

13 Optional memorial of Martin I, pope, martyr

21 Optional memorial of Anselm, bishop, religious, doctor of the church

23 Optional memorial of George, martyr

24 Optional memorial of Fidelis of Sigmaringen, presbyter, religious, martyr

25 **Feast of Mark, evangelist**

28 Optional memorial of Peter Chanel, presbyter, religious, missionary, martyr

29 Memorial of Catherine of Siena, virgin, doctor of the church

30 Optional memorial of Pius V, religious, pope

May

1 Optional memorial of Joseph the Worker

2 Memorial of Athanasius, bishop, doctor of the church

3 **Feast of Philip and James, apostles**

12 Optional memorial of Nereus and Achilleus, martyrs

Optional memorial of Pancras, martyr

14 **Feast of Matthias, apostle**

15 Optional memorial of Isidore and Maria, farmers, married couple

18 Optional memorial of John I, pope, martyr

20 Optional memorial of Bernardine of Siena, priest

25 Optional memorial of Bede the Venerable, presbyter, religious, doctor of the church

Optional memorial of Gregory VII, pope, religious

Optional memorial of Mary Magdalene de Pazzi, virgin, religious

26 Memorial of Philip Neri, presbyter, religious founder

27 Optional memorial of Augustine of Canterbury, bishop, religious, missionary

31 **Feast of the Visitation of the Blessed Virgin Mary to Elizabeth**

In Short, during
Easter

- Teach the school community about the Fifty Days. Many folks remain unfamiliar with the season, a tremendous loss, since the season is the church's most ancient and most joyful of times.

- The Fifty Days require some visuals that stay mostly the same from week to week to help us sense the presence of the season. This books suggests you focus first in the classroom on Easter water, the Easter candle and on ornamenting the cross. Of course there are special days and events within Eastertime, such as May-crowning and Ascension Day, but any additional decorations shouldn't replace the seasonal materials.

- Not everyone will agree, but in this season it's probably better to err on the side of excess than of paucity. Eastertime is splendidly rich in sensory images. There's a lot to work with. Lent is a kind of fasting from these, a time when we veil and otherwise put away the things of earth. Easter is a season where the things of earth are recognized as signs of the Holy Spirit.

- Easter, like Christmas, is a time for wreaths and garlands, classic decorations that signify joy, triumph and eternity. Customary materials for these at Easter are boxwood (which stays a good green even after it dries), pussy willow and laurel. Cloth and paper garlands and chains are wonderful folk decorations. A way to make garlands appear richer is to suspend two or three in parallel swags.

- As a source for images in decorating the classroom at Easter, immerse yourself in the readings proclaimed during the Paschal Triduum. Turn also to the Song of Songs and to John's gospel, the Acts of the Apostles, the first letter of John, the first letter of Peter and the book of Revelation. These scriptures are foundational to the season.

Easter season. That's deliberate. It means that in the course of the liturgical year the balance is tipped from fasting to feasting, from contrition to celebration, from remorse to joy and contentment.

These 50 days are one-seventh of the year. Bishop Athanasius called them the "Great Sunday." As the Lord's Day is to the week, the Easter season is to the year. The Lord's Day every week and the Easter season every year are meant to be times of rest, renewal and recreation that leave us created anew.

Amazingly, this is our most ancient season, older even than Lent. The scriptures, psalms and sacramental rites of the Easter season are wonderfully rich and foundational to faith. But many people still are unaware of the season. Catechesis is in order here.

Even if the Easter season is unfamiliar, it brings with it familiar and well-loved observances: Most every Eastertime we play baseball, celebrate Mother's Day, have a picnic, clean windows, plant tomatoes and geraniums, and chat with neighbors whom we may have barely seen all winter. It's light enough to play outside after supper, lily-of-the-valley blooms, and the social calendar gets into high gear with confirmations, first communions, awards ceremonies, graduations, and perhaps a wedding or two. One of our tasks is to help others recognize these familiar activities for what they can be—encounters with the risen Christ and bestowals of the Holy Spirit.

Easter

- Seasonal vesture color: *white, gold or silver (red on Pentecost)*
- Other seasonal vesture colors from the tradition: *rose, yellow*
- Some complementary colors: *pastels of all kinds*

Be patient. This year is rehearsal for the next, and it will take years to get into our hearts and souls that these days have their own sounds, sights and aromas. These Fifty Days are no ordinary time. They are our *laetissimum spatium*, our "most joyful season." The liturgical mood is "alleluia." And what does that mean? Consider this: Alleluia is the praise we offer at the sight of an apple tree in bloom, the praise we offer when witnessing a wedding, and the praise we offer over the graves of the dead.

*O*n Easter Eve we sang that heaven is wedded to earth. If the Paschal Triduum is like a wedding, the Easter season is like a honeymoon, a time of romance, fresh discovery, and sometimes a bit of brooding and even storminess.

In the synagogue the Song of Songs is read on the Sabbath during the seven days of Passover. That book, a love poem, has been regarded by Jews and Christians alike as the most sacred in the Bible (even though God is never mentioned!). The book is a singular wellspring of images of the Easter season. Get to know this book and relish it. Christian poets have imagined that, on the final day, when the Lord Jesus raises the dead, he will take each of us by the hand and say in the words of the Song of Songs, "Arise, my beloved, my beautiful one, and come away! For behold! The winter is past, the rains are over and gone. The flowers appear on the earth . . . and the song of the dove is again heard in our land."

In this romantic, revealing and sometimes stormy season, the lover and the beloved welcome the spring. A stranger is recognized as a beloved friend. The good shepherd leads us into a verdant pasture. The gardener plants us in paradise.

June

1 Memorial of Justin, martyr

2 Optional memorial of Marcellinus, presbyter, martyr, and Peter, exorcist, martyr

3 Memorial of Charles Lwanga, catechist, martyr, and his companions, martyrs

5 Memorial of Boniface, bishop, religious, missionary, martyr

6 Optional memorial of Norbert, bishop, religious, missionary, martyr

9 Optional memorial of Ephrem of Syria, deacon, doctor of the church

11 Memorial of Barnabas, apostle

First Things First: Easter Water, Easter Candle, Easter Cross

Three things deserve special attention in the classroom throughout these weeks: baptismal water, the paschal candle, and the cross. These holy things might be "noted by their absence" during Lent and would receive prominence during Eastertime.

*P*erhaps you keep holy water in the classroom year-round. (The one exception would be during Lent.) If not, keep holy water there at least during the Easter season. The vessel holding the water should be beautiful and in good repair. It can be any handsome bowl and really doesn't need any special markings. Some people think clear glass is best for a water bowl.

Keep the vessel brimming and spotless. The use of a de-scaler such as Lime-Away® (an acid) is necessary every so often, and the cleaning and filling of the vessel might be a task each Monday morning. If the vessel isn't too crusted, a weaker (and safer) acid, such as vinegar, does the trick.

Activity Idea

If possible the water should be drawn directly from the baptismal font, and any leftover water should be reverently returned there. On your first class day after Easter break make a holy procession of getting the water from the font and bringing it into the classroom, perhaps when you "resurrect the alleluia."

*O*rdinarily the water is kept by the door or else in the prayer corner. The location needs to be accessible. Having a holy water "stoop" (as it's called) in a classroom or home is an extension of the practice of having a stoop by each entrance to a church. (In churches that have the baptismal font near the entry-way, people draw water directly from the font and stoops aren't needed.) The signing with water calls baptism to mind, which makes perfect sense when entering a church but less sense when entering a classroom. In school it's probably better to use holy water when beginning prayer rather than when simply entering the room.

Especially if you keep holy water in the classroom year-round, during these 50 days keep something special near the vessel, such as a few fresh flowers. Floating a flower or burning candle in the water can be beautiful, but it also can seem as if the water is secondary to the ornamentation. Figure out what's best in the classroom. An image of a dove might be hung over the water. In one classroom a lovely hand-carved figure of Jonah emerging from the fish is kept near the bowl of water throughout the Easter season.

*N*o matter where it goes, be sure to use the holy water each morning of the Easter season. Students might learn the ritual of signing themselves with it during Morning Prayer. When you begin this ritual it may feel peculiar and garner some laughter or even irreverence, but if you keep to it, it will develop into true ritual, and the action will become second nature.

A paschal candle is a large candle lit every day of the Easter season, at least during times of prayer. The wax—beeswax is customary—is an ancient symbol of the body of the Lord. Wax is an amazing material, appearing to be almost magically produced in a beehive, clearly packed with enormous energy that is released with a spark of fire. The work of the bees to create wax is an image of the church working together to give arms and legs to the mystical body of Christ.

By tradition a paschal candle has five grains of incense fixed into it cross-wise. Beautiful amber chunks of incense can be lit (they catch fire easily) and

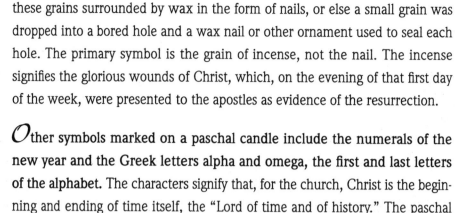

then quickly pressed into the wax. The paschal candle in church might have these grains surrounded by wax in the form of nails, or else a small grain was dropped into a bored hole and a wax nail or other ornament used to seal each hole. The primary symbol is the grain of incense, not the nail. The incense signifies the glorious wounds of Christ, which, on the evening of that first day of the week, were presented to the apostles as evidence of the resurrection.

*O*ther symbols marked on a paschal candle include the numerals of the new year and the Greek letters alpha and omega, the first and last letters of the alphabet. The characters signify that, for the church, Christ is the beginning and ending of time itself, the "Lord of time and of history." The paschal festival is, in many ways, the new year of the church.

Some people leave the candle plain, some add the symbols, and in some classrooms you may want to add all sorts of ornaments to the candle. A good way to do this is to cut out thin sheets of brightly colored beeswax (available in craft stores and from craft catalogs) and to fix these onto the candle by pressing with a warm finger or tiny pins. Wax ornaments can be cut into geometric shapes or perhaps into more classical designs: the dove returning to Noah with a branch of olive in its beak, the paschal lamb sitting upon the book of life, the phoenix rising in splendor from the ashes, the pelican feeding its young on its own blood.

Activity Idea

Beeswax makes a wonderful art medium especially at this season. In one school during Lent, students use beeswax to decorate Easter candles for their classroom and for their homes. In another, beeswax is used to decorate wax or real eggs.

A paschal candle is lit from the new fire on Easter Eve. At the Easter Vigil, someone might preserve the flame from this fire by kindling a glass-enclosed votive candle and then taking it home. This flame might be used when you first light your paschal candle in the classroom. Or perhaps the flame is carefully taken from the sanctuary lamp in church (which should have been lit from the new fire), and this flame is carried to the classroom to light the candle. The use of such "holy fire" connected to the Easter Vigil is worth the effort. You might bring over the flame at the time you bring over the baptismal water.

Activity Idea

*I*t's best if the paschal candle is big enough to last from Easter Sunday to Pentecost. Wax is expensive, and a large candle will cost a bit of money. A candle needs to be well-crafted in order to be safe, with a properly made

wick. Many of the pillar candles sold in card stores, such as the ones sold for weddings, can burn erratically and dangerously, and often do not tolerate being lit repeatedly. A beeswax candle requires a "follower" (ordinarily made of brass or glass) to burn safely. The candle holder needs to be secure.

Some students save all year for a good candle at Easter. (If you can't use a real candle, don't use a substitute.) Having it stand within the bowl of holy water can be beautiful and add a certain measure of safety.

A really fine, old tradition is to melt down the stub of last year's candle and to remold the wax (or to stamp it) into the shape of lambs. The wax lamb is called, appropriately, *Agnus Dei.* These are distributed to everyone and make a splendid Easter decoration. The tradition tells us how the substance of beeswax is highly regarded as a sign of the body of the Lord.

*A*ctivity Idea

*T*he classroom cross should receive special attention during this season. The holy cross is our tree of life. Keep some flowers nearby it. Flowering branches seem especially suited to honoring the cross. Another sign of affection for the cross is a victory wreath hung behind it, such as a ring of aromatic laurel (bay) or myrtle leaves.

Some people hang a white shroud on the cross. Recognize that this cloth is not just a decoration but represents the burial shroud of the Lord. If used, it should be handsome, full, pressed, of some appropriate material, perhaps rough cotton or wool or linen or some other natural fabric. It may have a place alongside other symbols of Jesus' passion kept nearby throughout this season.

*A*n Easter tree, like a Christmas tree and the maypole, is a European custom that makes use of the biblical imagery of wood and of trees, especially the wood of the cross. You might set up an Easter tree in the classroom in a way that beautifies the area around the cross. In one classroom an Easter tree is set up in a corner and hung with decorated eggs, handcrafted flowers

*D*isplay Idea

and birds, and other adornments. The classroom cross is set on an embroidered pillow beneath the tree.

You can decorate an Easter tree with an enormous number of symbolic ornaments, most all borrowed from the scriptures and from Christian art. The key to deciding on appropriate images is to be fluent in the language of the scriptures. A small sampling of such images includes sun, moon, stars, serpent, gardening implements, lock and keys, ladder or stairway, hammer and nails, fish and nets, dove, clouds and flames, sheep and shepherds, deer, pelican, phoenix, peacock, water well and bucket, throne and crown. If you illustrated scripture stories and hung the illustrations on a "burning bush" during Lent, it can be transfigured into your Easter tree.

Display Idea

*O*ther Eastertime decorations also can be related to the scriptures and rituals of the season. In one school a series of areas in hallways and other public spots, such as the cafeteria, are geared to readings proclaimed during the Easter Vigil. For instance, near illustrations of the story of creation have been gathered a display about students' work to preserve the environment. Near illustrations of the story of the exodus are the results of students' research into ongoing struggles for freedom around the world.

The exodus, of course, is a key paschal story. Eastertime may be likened to the journey from Egypt to Mount Sinai, from liberation to the receiving of the law. (And Easter candy and other treats have been compared to the sweet manna that strengthened the people on their journey.) Eastertime has also been likened to the crossing of the Jordan and the entrance into the Promised Land.

Other biblical stories of travels are associated with Easter and Pentecost, in particular the story of Ruth and Naomi, a story that takes place during the springtime barley harvest and that is proclaimed in the synagogue at Shavuot. The events of the book of Tobit begin at Pentecost. Both of these tales are love stories and can be read in one sitting. These scriptures deserve pride of place throughout Eastertime and especially at Pentecost.

*F*our New Testament books in particular are associated with these 50 days. The cryptic book of Revelation is filled with marvelous and weird images that inspire artists and lyricists. The first letter of John and the first letter of Peter are rich in baptismal lessons, and some people think the letter of Peter was intended to be a homily given to the newly baptized. (Many writings of the earliest poet-saints are just such "mystagogical catecheses" presented to those baptized at Easter.)

Truly Risen

An eastern European legend claims that Mary Magdalene came to the tomb with a breakfast of hard-boiled eggs in a basket. The soldiers guarding the tomb harrassed her. Suddenly the eggs turned all the colors of the rainbow. They leapt from the basket and began rolling in every direction from the tomb—like apostles! As they jostled and cracked, they sang out the good news: "Christ is risen." The earth's tombs cracked and groaned in reply, "Truly risen."

Day by day at Mass throughout the Easter season the church reads the book of the Acts of the Apostles. It's the sequel to Luke's gospel, and, like the gospel, is filled with interesting characters, exciting stories, even a number of tales that can only be described as comedies. Members of the church can have their hands full during the Easter season simply by reading and discussing this book day by day. Students can illustrate the stories or even act them out.

On a bulletin board in a hallway, be sure to offer evidence of what transpired during the Triduum, especially when students were responsible for certain moments. For example, photos and a bit of biography about the newly baptized and confirmed can be gathered in a display. Perhaps someone took pictures of the procession on Holy Thursday evening in which the previous year's and coming year's first communicants carried flowers. Perhaps someone took pictures of the "living stations of the cross" produced by the religious education program youth group or of the Easter fire built by the Scouts. These pictures and some explanation can be displayed on a bulletin board.

$\mathcal{F}$rolicking in the Pasture of the Good Shepherd

The Easter season has an extraordinary number of images drawn from the outdoors. That's a good thing, especially after a winter of being cooped up inside.

An Easter Pastime

A lovely way to keep a count of the Fifty Days is to add one sheep for each day to a bulletin board. At the beginning of the season students can prepare depictions of 50 sheep. (In one classroom these are crafted from lambswool, often available in drugstores to pad sore feet, although cotton also serves the purpose.) Sheep can be numbered from 1 to 50 and kept in a basket, one sheep added each day to your "Easter pasture." In one classroom each sheep is named for a student, with as many sheep as there are students. To add up to 50, other creatures are crafted and numbered, including the Good Shepherd's sheepdog, ducks on the sea, and bees in a beehive (an ancient symbol of the church).

$\mathcal{K}$ey scriptural stories at this season also bring us outdoors. We hear that locked doors cannot keep the risen Christ away from the disciples. We hear that Jesus served his disciples a barbecue breakfast by the seashore. We hear that Jesus led his disciples to a hilltop and ascended into the sky; angels descended to tell the disciples to quit cloud-gazing.

Just these few accounts of encounters with the risen Christ offer us a tremendous amount of inspiration for celebrating the season with students. Have a lavish breakfast. Visit a lakeshore. Climb a mountain. Study clouds. Decorate the classroom with images of fish and other watery creatures on the bottom half of the room and with clouds and birds and other creatures of the air overhead.

$\mathcal{T}$wo stories especially have led to traditions still kept in many places, of taking time during the Easter season to get outside for picnics and parades. One is the story in Luke's gospel of the two disciples on the road to the village of Emmaus. The risen Christ becomes their companion. The other story, at the beginning of the sequel to Luke's gospel, the Acts of the Apostles, tells of the Jewish festival of Shavuot. The Holy Spirit drives the disciples of Jesus outside, out of hiding and into the crowd who is celebrating the festival.

Figure out some way—and many ways—to worship and rejoice with students outside. Outdoor egg hunts, egg-rolling contests and other springtime games such as tug-o'-war are customary especially during the first days following

 $\mathcal{A}$ctivity Idea

A Bulletin Board for the Easter Season
An Easter Garden

John's gospel tells us that Jesus was buried in a tomb within a garden. When Mary Magdalene first encountered the risen Christ, she mistook him for the gardener. In a sense, Jesus really is a gardener. Around his tomb Jesus planted a new Eden! The cross has become the tree of life in the garden. The fruit of this tree, so say Christian poets, is the eucharistic body and blood of Christ, the food that grants the fullness of life.

Cover a bulletin board with spring-green paper. For a background you might use a fun print already covered in flowers. One teacher used Easter cellophane printed with violets. You can add blue sky to the top third. To one side, add a lakeshore or some other body of water.

In as dignified a manner as possible, add figures of the Lord Jesus and of Mary Magdalene. In traditional scenes of their meeting, Jesus is dressed as a gardener, in white and other bright colors, with a wide-brimmed hat. Mary usually wears brilliant red robes, the color of life. She carries an urn of myrrh because she intended to anoint the Lord's dead body. She's also shown carrying a basket of Easter eggs or simply one red-dyed egg. The eggs signify that she was the first to be commissioned to spread the good news of the resurrection of the Lord.

To this scene, throughout the Fifty Days of Easter, you can gradually add flowers, clouds, birds, newborn animals—anything to remind you of Eden.

(If you number these things from 1 to 50 and add a figure each day, you can keep count of the 50 days. Perhaps once a week some time is devoted to creating appropriate images to add to the scene: one week, benevolent insects such as bees, butterflies, ladybugs, dragonflies; the next week, weather signs such as the sun, clouds, raindrops and a rainbow.

A marvelous scriptural foundation for the imagery of the garden is found in the Bible's own love song, the Song of Songs. This book is read in the synagogue at Passover time. If you're stuck for traditional images to add to your Easter garden, begin by reading the Song of Songs. You'll be overwhelmed and delighted.

To your Easter garden you also can add your own depictions of the appearances of the risen Lord. These stories are told at Mass during the Easter octave (the first eight days of the season) as well as on the Third Sunday of Easter. For instance, we hear John 21:1–19, about the risen Lord preparing a seaside barbecue for the disciples. The account mentions a small fire, over which is a grill. On the grill is a fish. Nearby you can add a basket of bread.

If you're especially ambitious, you can use the same background landscape but change the characters to tell a different story each week or perhaps every two weeks. Early in the season you might show the appearance to Mary Magdalene (John 20:11–18). Later you can depict the story of the disciples on the road to Emmaus (Luke 24:13–35). At the solemnity of the Ascension you can depict this event (Acts 1:1–11). A traditional way to show the Ascension is described on page 271.

the Paschal Triduum. Easter games such as these become a living parable of the Easter sequence hymn, with its line *Mors et Vita duello conflixere mirando* ("Death and Life fought a wondrous conflict"). An egg hunt seems to bring to life the words of the angels to the women: "Why do you search for the Living One among the dead?"

An "Emmaus walk" is a jaunt around the neighborhood during which anyone you meet is to be treated as Christ. In Europe such walks are an Easter Monday tradition that have evolved in recent years into political rallies, especially by environmental groups. That seems to suggest an "Emmaus Clean-up Walk" is in order. At least clean windows and open them when the weather permits. Clean and decorate the outside doorways and school sign in a handsome way that stays in place throughout the 50 days.

The Good Shepherd

At some point in the Easter season be sure to depict Jesus as the Good Shepherd. Each year on the fourth Sunday of the season, we hear about the Good Shepherd or about another pastoral image, such as Jesus the gate of the sheepfold. Such images echo in the liturgy throughout Eastertime.

*D*uring Eastertime at daily Mass the church reads from the gospel of John. This gospel overflows with paschal images that you may want to include in classroom decorations—the Good Shepherd; the door to the sheepfold; the way, the truth and the life; the vine and its branches. Traditional depictions of the risen Christ are often allegorical—a lamb, a phoenix, a pelican, a shepherd, a gardener, the Sacred Heart. Of course, the shining paschal candle is a sign of the Risen One.

It's untraditional to show Christ rising from the tomb. Yes, artists try, but those who try forget an old discipline: The gospels do not speak of the moment of Jesus' resurrection. This has been interpreted as a sign of reverence.

The Byzantine icon called *Anastasis,* "Resurrection," sticks to this discipline. Here the departure from the tomb is not that of Jesus but of all humanity. The scene shows Jesus among the dead, in the depths of the underworld. The Lord pulls Adam and Eve from their graves. Behind them stand all the dead. Fetters and chains and broken locks fall from their bodies. The demons are trapped beneath the cross. They howl in anger that their captives are being released.

*I*n the northern hemisphere Eastertime falls in April and in flowery May, when spring is often at its best. But even in spring not everything is sweetness and delight. In North America, May is the month of the greatest number of tornadoes and hailstorms.

The story of Noah's flood is a favorite with children and brings together the beneficent and the destructive sides of springtime weather. In some Greek villages the festival of Pentecost has another name: *Kataklysmos.* Pentecost is regarded as the anniversary of the great flood and the renewal of creation.

Popular Easter images are clouds, rain, rainbows and the dove bearing an olive branch. Apart from the neophytes themselves, it's difficult to imagine stronger signs of the new creation, of covenant and of christening. The images from the story of Noah's flood keep recurring throughout the scriptures.

Rainbows are formed from the interplay of light and water. They are mythological signs of the union of heaven and earth. Genesis tells us that their purpose is to remind us of God's covenant with the whole of creation. The dove calls to mind the lovers in the Song of Songs as well as the Spirit who descended on Jesus at his baptism. The story of Jonah, whose name means "dove" in Hebrew, adds a rich layer to this image. The olive branch also has become a sign of anointing with oil, of christening, of the peace and forgiveness of the risen Christ: "Christ" and "Messiah" mean "anointed."

Sheer fabrics in a spectrum of colors can rise from several spots in the room to a common point overhead. A rainbow array of flags can hang from the light fixtures. If all the classes go in this together, perhaps a florist can supply a spectrum's worth of colored ribbons for all the rooms to share. The colors need not complete a spectrum but merely suggest it, and instead of hot colors perhaps the colors can be pastel, always a welcome sight in springtime.

Clouds, rain and lightning might be incorporated into the rainbow. Dacron® pillow filling can be cut into the shape of clouds and each can be hung high. A cascade of beads or prisms or pendants or strips of blue or silver Mylar® film can suggest rain. Gold foil can be cut into jagged bolts to suggest lightning, and into a great, smiling disk to suggest the sun. The image of a dove—beautifully designed and in scale with the space—can be set among the clouds.

*A*n ancient image of the season is the sowing, sprouting, growth and eventual harvesting of grain. In Mediterranean lands, barley and wheat grow ripe during these days, and a sudden squall can devastate a field. Farmers must be vigilant. On the Jewish calendar, the 50 days from Passover (Pesach) to Pentecost (Shavuot) are a time of anxiety over the success of the grain harvest, a symbol for any such periods in a human lifetime when vigilance and prudence are necessary.

Paul uses the image of ripening grain to speak of the resurrection: Christ is the firstfruits of the dead. Christ is the first, but then will come the resurrection of all who have died, like a harvest. Bishop Maximus of Turin, one of the poetic writers of the early church, spoke of the resurrection as a flowering, and of the ascension as a ripening, with the full harvest gathered at Pentecost.

In most places around the country grasses flower and form seedheads in springtime, and especially at Pentecost the fluffy heads of green grasses make a splendid decoration. If you sprouted grain during Lent, tuck in some Easter eggs during the Easter octave. A lamb or two might be placed near this grain, an image of the pasture of the Good Shepherd. If it isn't overwatered and the location isn't too warm, the "Easter grass" will stay green for weeks. If it dies, start some more. Although the sprouted grain will not flower, in the final weeks of the Easter season in a field or roadside you might find flowering grain, such as green rye or wheat, and bundle it to decorate the room.

Of course, the Easter season is a time to plant and tend gardens. Be sure to bless school yard plantings. A blessing of flower seeds for distribution is a tradition in many schools. Some of the easier varieties of annual flowers to grow include cosmos, cleome, morning glory, nasturtium, lavatera, four o'clocks and zinnia. (These do better if sprouted directly from seed in the garden than if sprouted in a greenhouse and transplanted to the garden.) Some schools sell annual flower and vegetable seedlings as a fundraiser.

*T*hroughout these 50 days we can take a cue from the first reading at the Easter Vigil and renew our efforts to restore this good earth to the freshness of creation. April 22 is Earth Day. Its observance is strengthening, especially in schools. April 23 is Saint George's Day, which we might call an earlier version of Earth Day because George's name is Greek for "earth worker." George is a patron of gardeners, farmers, ranchers and all who live close to the land, and his legendary battle against the dragon is an earthy sign of the paschal victory. Perhaps that is why the martyr George is considered the patron of spring.

May 15 is Saint Isidore's Day. He and his wife Maria Torribia are also patrons of farmers, and the U.S. Catholic Rural Life Conference sponsors celebrations and blessings of farmers and farmlands on this day.

Mother Mary in May

The Roman Catholic practice of dedicating the month of May to Mary is beloved by many. A problem arises when the practice takes precedence over the Easter season.

*S*omething's askew, for instance, when the parish school puts more energy into the ceremony of May crowning than into the solemnities of Ascension and Pentecost. Something's also askew when devotion to Mary during May is stronger than devotion during more ancient and richer Marian times, such as the Advent season and the late summer days between the festivals of the Assumption and the Nativity of Mary.

As schoolchildren we were taught (and now are teaching children) about devotion to Mary during May. Are we teaching the practices of Eastertime? Reorienting priorities takes time. We're involved here with human affections, and those take generations to form.

*D*evotion to the Blessed Mother during May has an interesting pedigree. Naturally, the cultures of northern Europe observed springtime rites later than their southern neighbors. In the north the weather at Easter could be cold and wintry, and so springtime festivities were held a month or more later. (For example, some Scandinavian villagers customarily decorate eggs at Pentecost simply because birds are not laying eggs at Easter.)

One of the springtime rites reflected an understanding of the season's burgeoning life as a "mystical marriage," with husband and wife imagined as the source of the new life of spring. In some places the husband was called the May Lord and the wife the May Lady. A maypole (a pole topped by a wreath) symbolized their union. Is this a pagan image? The "mystical marriage" is an image found throughout the scriptures: God is called Israel's spouse; Lady Wisdom is called God's bride; Jesus is called the groom and the church called the bride; the city of Jerusalem is bejewelled for its marriage to the Lamb.

In Christian lore, the Virgin Mary also is compared to a bride, to a dove, to the church, to holy Wisdom, to the Spirit. (Much of this nuptial imagery comes into play at Pentecost.) Naturally, springtime became a season of devotion to Mary and to the Holy Spirit.

In this imagery the contrast between women and men is not the focus. The images are of desire, courtship, loving union, cooperation, fidelity, and the birth and raising of children.

Mary is called "the mother of the church." The title has two echoes in scripture: When he was dying on the cross (John 19:26–27), Jesus told his mother and the beloved disciple that they were now mother and child to each other. The last mention of Mary in the scriptures, Acts 1:14, tells us that she was present with the other disciples praying together in the upper room. This mention is the reason artists have shown Mary at events that flank this passage: the ascension of Jesus, the election of the apostle Matthias and the descent of the Holy Spirit.

The spirit of the liturgy suggests that we shape May devotions to the Blessed Mother to coincide if possible with the Pentecost novena (the days between Ascension Day and Pentecost) or with the feast of the Visitation of the Blessed Virgin Mary to Elizabeth, May 31. Or May Day every year (which always falls within the Easter season) might be the annual occasion for the ceremony of crowning an image of the Blessed Virgin.

Mary's shrine in the classroom can be decorated for the whole of Eastertime (which always includes at least two or even all the weeks of May). Place a beautiful fabric behind Mary's statue. Especially fitting here are spring flowers gathered from backyards and brought to the shrine—tulips, violets, lily-of-the-valley, spirea, peonies. Encourage this practice. Crowning the statue with fresh flowers might take place every morning as a simple act at the conclusion of Morning Prayer.

Certainly the students will be expected to learn the Marian antiphon of the Easter season, Regina caeli, "O Queen of heaven." The hymn can be foundational to the rites around Mary's shrine at this season and certainly would be sung during the May-crowning ceremony.

For Mary's shrine, student artists might create a handsome scroll with the words and the music of the Regina caeli. The lines of chant can be illuminated with floral designs, insects and animals in the medieval style.

Other seasonal art, including the Byzantine icons of the ascension and Pentecost, can be included in Mary's shrine. The ascension icon shows Mary with arms uplifted in the posture of supplication. Here she is an image of a Christian's lifelong expectation of Christ, our unending Advent. The Pentecost icon sometimes shows Mary at the head of the gathering of the apostles. Beneath this gathering is a small figure called "Kosmos," a personification of creation, which is being renewed by the Creator Spirit.

Mary's shrine is a fine place to gather many of the small-scale folk arts of Easter: a carved balsa bird of paradise, finely woven ringlets of palm fronds, an inlaid enamel icon of Saint George slaying the dragon, and batik-dyed Easter eggs, or eggs overlaid with geometric designs cut from wheat straw. A basket of freshly sprouted wheat can form a living carpet for the eggs.

*I*t would be great to make a connection between Mary's shrine in the church and the shrines in classrooms. In one school students gather near Mary's shrine in church to bless and to receive the crowns of flowers they will use to honor the statues of Mary in their classrooms.

Crowns made from flowers and herbs are not only traditional for Mary's statue but for all sacred images during the Easter season. These crowns are a festive counterpart to the lenten veiling of images. When the veil comes off, the crown goes on. The practice is suggested by the special chants and prayers used for the saints during the Easter season that speak of the martyrs as "lilies in God's garden," that tell of the saints "wreathed in virtues," and that acclaim the company of heaven as "crowned in everlasting glory."

Regina Caeli

O Queen of heaven, be joyful,
    alleluia.
For he whom you have humbly
    borne for us, alleluia,
Has arisen, as he promised,
    alleluia.
Offer now our prayer to God,
    alleluia.

Regina caeli, laetare, alleluia.
Quia quem meruisti portare,
    alleluia,
Resurrexit sicut dixit, alleluia.
Ora pro nobis Deum, alleluia.

The Ascension of the Lord

The fortieth day of the Easter season falls on a Thursday. This fortieth day is observed as the solemnity of the Ascension of the Lord, although in more and more places the celebration is transferred to the following Sunday. The Pentecost novena (from the Latin word for "nine") lasts from the fortieth day until Pentecost, the fiftieth day.

Of course, because Pentecost (and often Ascension) is a Sunday celebration, rather than have these days slip from the school calendar, the traditions of Pentecost might be kept during the novena and the celebration of the Ascension in school might take place every year on the fortieth day.

We miss the point of the Ascension of the Lord if we think the day is about a departure. The festival, and every Christian festival, is about the everlasting presence of the risen Christ.

Any festival needs its special signs. Today's signs are added to those of Eastertime, joy upon joy. The second reading at Mass, Ephesians 1:17–23, tells us that Christ fills the universe. Celestial signs seem right this day—the earth, the sun, the moon, the planets, stars, sparkling comets, or the wheeling spiral of an entire galaxy.

Images of blaring trumpets and clapping hands are from Psalm 47, the psalm for the day. (So be sure to add brass instruments and plenty of hand-clapping to your prayer today.) From the account of the ascension in the Acts of the Apostles we have the holy sign of the cloud, perhaps the strongest image for this day.

One of our "clouds" today might be a cloud of incense. Can you use it in the classroom without setting off smoke detectors? Otherwise use it outdoors.

A Bulletin Board for Ascension
Why Do You Stand Staring at the Skies?

An idea for a bulletin board comes from a traditional manner of depicting the ascension of the Lord. It shows the disciples gathered on a hilltop and looking up at the sky. They are watching Jesus ascend into heaven. All that is visible of Jesus is his feet and the bottom hem of his robe. From the side the two angels are entering to ask the disciples why they are gazing into the sky instead of going on to Galilee, as Jesus told them to do.

Cover the top two-thirds of the bulletin board with blue paper, to represent the sky. Add clouds, too. Cover the bottom third with green and brown paper to represent the hilltop. Add flowers, animals and insects, and you might research the kinds of creatures that make their home on mountains. Cut out two large feet, and staple them at the top of the bulletin board, as if the rest of Jesus' body is out of the picture. Then add the disciples (or just their faces) below.

Tradition gives each disciple a unique expression, as if to say that each person's response to mystery is unique, as if to say that one person, over the course of a lifetime, responds in a different way each time the person encounters the mystery.

You could make eleven apostles, or you could have each student create her or his own face out of paper, crayons, markers and so on, and add them all, grouped together in a crowd. Attach them at angles to face up toward Jesus' feet. Add the angels, not looking up, but straight at the viewer of the bulletin board.

The same faces can be used for Pentecost. Replace Jesus' feet with an image of fire. Perhaps the flames can form the shape of a dove. Add a tongue of fire over each person's head. Red, fuchsia and orange foils are perfect.

At Pentecost, sky images can be removed and walls and windows added, perhaps with a door flinging wide open so that the disciples can spill outside and begin their work as the body of Christ enlivened by the Spirit. The disciples were hiding in fear behind locked doors when the Spirit came down—and then they opened the doors and at the Spirit's bidding ran into the streets to begin telling everyone the good news about Jesus.

Flowers and greenery can stay in place—it's a Jewish and Christian custom to spread fresh cut grasses and flowers through the home at Pentecost, to open windows and doors and to erase the barriers between inside and out. God's Spirit knows no barriers. God's Spirit fills the whole world.

Perhaps the paschal candle could have a "cloud" of crabapple or spirea or black locust blossoms placed nearby. The cafeteria staff or some other school chefs might prepare cloudlike foods for lunch—mashed potatoes, vanilla pudding, meringues, ice cream, whipped cream. (Don't laugh—such "edible prayers" are an old custom for the festival.)

*A*scension is often a day for an all-school liturgy, and in some places students participate in a balloon launch. That's a fun activity that catches the imagination and gets eyes gazing into the skies—but what is the message here? That Jesus is gone? That it's fine to litter the earth with bits of plastic?

By all means, organize outdoor activities for Ascension Day. Ascension and Pentecost are picnic days in many places. Perhaps the day's liturgy can end with everyone tossing a grain or two of incense on a bed of burning charcoal outside. That will turn eyes upward.

*A*n old custom for the day is to march in procession around the parish boundary or just around church property. In England this was called "beating the bounds," since the boundary markers of the property were checked and cleaned of weeds. Ascension Day is a perfect day for a procession, complete with banners on poles, handheld flowers and bells, perhaps even a brass band. The cross and paschal candle can go at the front of the procession. On a rainy day simply walk in a circuit around the classroom or through the halls. Sing you favorite "Alleluia." That's a way of putting into motion those words of Paul that the "fullness of Christ fills all in all."

The Solemnity of Pentecost

On the Jewish calendar, Shavuot, the feast of Weeks, falls 50 days—seven weeks—after Passover. (Another name for Shavuot is Pentecost, from the Greek word for 50.) These seven weeks are the time of the grain harvest in many Mediterranean lands. This most important crop of the year must be abundant and the harvesting successful.

A stand of grain is extremely vulnerable just before it is gathered in. When grain ripens, it grows brittle and is easily broken by wind, easily rotted by rain. The 50 days in Jewish lore are a time of pensiveness, of holding one's breath until the harvest has been safely brought into storage.

Even in more northerly climates we know the anxieties of spring. When will the fields dry out so that we can plant? When will the rains come so that the seed will sprout? A hailstorm can wreck an orchard, a cold snap can kill newly hatched chicks, and a dust storm can asphyxiate a herd. On the old Catholic calendar the "Rogation Days" (from *rogare,* "to ask") were celebrated just before Ascension Day with processions through the fields and a litany of supplication as a prayer for God's providence during the seedtime of the year.

Pentecost became a celebration of the end of anxiety—a feast of fulfillment that the barley harvest had been gathered in safely. Not that many weeks ago the earth seemed lifeless, but in time the ground softened, the buds blossomed, and the Passover arrived. Now that the season is complete, the days have gotten long and warm, trees are green, and the earth has grown fruitful.

For centuries, among Jews and Christians alike Pentecost was a premier day for decorations. Signs of the season were interpreted as reminders of God's covenant with humankind, as emblems of the life-giving Spirit. Customary at

Pentecost were branches of fresh foliage, bundles of green grasses and reeds, and a large number of familiar flowers, especially the fragrant kinds that bloom at this season—roses, poppies, peonies and irises.

The custom still lives on in central and eastern Europe, and the practice of carrying leafy branches on Pentecost makes a wonderful connection between this red-vestment Sunday and the one eight Sundays earlier, Palm Sunday, when budding branches were carried. Branches from trees and bundles of green grasses remind the church of phrases from the Pentecost sequence— *dulce refrigerium* ("sweet refreshment"), and *in aestu temperies* ("mildness in the summer heat"). These are attributes of the Holy Spirit.

Many Byzantine churches use small birches and poplars in their Pentecost decorations, especially by doors. Some Jewish synagogues spread floors with sweet-smelling hay and decorate the ark holding the scriptures with tree branches. We might try something along those lines in the classroom or at least in the prayer corner—the custom has too much history to fall into disuse.

Bundles of grasses will not wilt the way newly green foliage wilts and so are more useful as indoor decorations. Subtropical trees such as eucalyptus are not quick to wilt. In the temperate zone, willow and oak has a bit more staying power than maple. Any cutting of branches is a pruning operation and needs to be done correctly to insure the health of the tree. It's best to cut branches flush, leaving no stub. (The stub prevents the wound from healing properly.) A clean cut requires strong, sharp pruning shears.

Prayer Corner Idea

*C*ity folks substituted paper roses and foliage for the real thing in their Pentecost adornments. The art of cut paper added a lovely dimension to Pentecost, and even when real foliage was available, the paper flowers, birds, fruits and others handmade ornaments would be used to festoon whole small trees cut and brought inside. In past generations, Christmas wasn't the only season for decorated trees. The folk-craft of cut paper is a favorite the world around, and it's fairly easy to find books of patterns and instructions that make use of, for instance, Chinese, Mexican or Polish designs.

*A*t this season people feasted on the first pickings of their gardens— asparagus, peas, lettuces and herbs, rhubarb and strawberries. With herds giving birth on lush pasturage, the abundance of dairy products transformed winter's fast into summer's feast.

A Hebrew title for Pentecost is Yom ha-Bikkurim, "the day of first fruits." A first fruit is an offering to God of the first of each harvest. Following Passover

A Bulletin Board for Pentecost

Climbing Mount Sinai

After the Jewish people escaped slavery in Egypt, they traveled to Mount Sinai where they received God's holy law. In the nineteenth chapter of the book of Exodus we read that, at the bottom of Mount Sinai, after three days of preparation, "Moses brought the people out of the camp to meet God." "To meet God"—imagine that!

At Passover the Jewish people celebrate their freedom from slavery. At Shavuot, 50 days later, they celebrate the great day that they met God on Sinai. For Christians, too, the 50 days following Easter are a journey toward meeting God. A song for these days is "Veni, Sancte Spiritus," "Come, Holy Spirit."

The Lord God descended on Sinai in fire and wind. So, too, at Pentecost the Holy Spirit of God descended on the church in fire and wind. Especially during the final weeks of the Easter season you might want to depict Mount Sinai on a bulletin board, or else have student artists create a model of Sinai from papier-mâché, modeling clay or another substrate. It will look like a volcano if you follow the description in the book of Exodus, which describes the holy mountain "wrapped in smoke . . . like the smoke of a kiln," topped with God's fire, shaking with earthquakes and blasts of thunderous noise.

Each student depicts herself or himself, perhaps simply as a paper figure with a name written on it, perhaps using a photo, gathered in a circle hand-in-hand around the mountain. At Pentecost, tongues of God's holy fire, signs of the Spirit, can be placed over each person's head.

Jewish tradition says that the base of Sinai, where the people waited, was verdant with life. It's customary at Shavuot to decorate homes and synagogues with fresh green grasses, foliage and flowers—and also to eat one of the amazing byproducts of late spring's lush verdure—dairy products (usually in the form of cheese blintzes and cheesecake). God promised to bring the people to "the land flowing with milk and honey," and sweetened dairy dishes are a first taste of that wonderful land.

Christians borrowed this tradition for Pentecost. Be sure to add to the base of your "Sinai" an abundance of greenery and also depictions of cows and their calves as well as beehives. And be sure at Pentecost to share with students some cheesecake or ice cream for your own taste of "the land flowing with milk and honey."

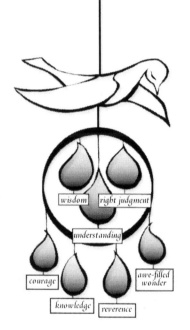

a daily offering of barley was made to God, and at Pentecost the offering changed to the first sheaves of ripe wheat.

In Jewish and Christian folklore, Pentecost is also associated with strawberries, apricots and cherries—the first of the summer fruits. This is just about the time of year these fruits grow ripe in the warmer places of North America, and markets everywhere have them in abundance. Even in the north, June brings serviceberries, which at one time were a principal source of vitamins in the Native American diet.

*D*uring the Pentecost novena, how can the cafeteria staff (or a few cooperative parents) help students "taste" Pentecost? Eggnog, strawberry cheesecake and cheese blintzes were just about invented as Pentecost delicacies. Sweetened dairy foods are the "milk and honey" we share as a sign of our arrival in the "promised land" of the settled days of summer.

Other ways of making ready for the festival throughout the novena are to read and perhaps illustrate or act out the readings proclaimed on Pentecost Eve. These include the story of the Tower of Babel; the people's arrival at Mount Sinai to, in the words of Exodus, "meet God"; and the vision in the book of the prophet Ezekiel of the dry bones that take flesh and come alive.

*A*ny of the signs of the Spirit can be employed to ornament the classroom throughout the Pentecost novena. The word *spiritus* in Latin means "wind," and so windsocks, pennants, kites or any vehicle that is buoyed by the wind is perfect at Pentecost. Some students create in the classroom a mobile featuring the "seven gifts of the Holy Spirit" (derived from Isaiah 11:2–3: wisdom, understanding, right judgment, courage, knowledge, reverence, awe-filled wonder) and/or the "nine fruits" (Galatians 5:22, although sometimes "twelve fruits" are listed and the terms for the gifts vary: love, joy, peace, patience, kindness, generosity, faithfulness, gentleness, self-control). The pieces of the mobile could be shaped like tongues of fire, and then hung from the overhead light fixtures.

Fire and light are also the Spirit's signs, and the festival has been a time in many cultures for bonfires and fireworks, as well as for calmer, safer displays of light, such as the crafting of floating candles to set on a river or pond. A Pentecost barbecue also makes safe use of fire. If the date and time is chosen correctly, this is a wonderful opportunity to bring together the parish school children and the students in the religious education program.

June and July

Entering into the Mystery of Early Summer
In Summer, Go with the Flow
Sun and Seashells: Images of Summer

Entering into the Mystery
of Early Summer

*I*n Christian poetry summer gets favorable attention while winter gets a bum rap. Winter is often regarded as an image of everything lousy about human existence, and the lousiest of all is death.

Think of C. S. Lewis's *The Lion, the Witch and the Wardrobe.* The world under the reign of the White Witch had been unending winter. When the lion Aslan roars to reclaim the kingdom, Christmas arrives, spring's foretaste, and then the spring itself arrives and the stage is set for Aslan's self-sacrifice.

*I*ronically, some of the loveliest and strongest summertime images are used within the liturgy during winter. At the church's winter festivals several customary practices jump the gun on summer. Greenery and flowers and candles and even spiced breads and drinks are used to make it seem as if death has taken a holiday.

In the words of several traditional Christmas carols, nightingales return from their winter roosts and chase the night away with song. Thorny brambles burst into roses. The stable is filled with Maytime perfumes that beguile the senses and invite all creatures to drink deeply of Christ, as a bee is beguiled by a flower's fragrant nectar.

*T*he language of liturgy delights in opposites and in contrasts as images of paradox. Expressions of paradox can make daunting concepts accessible and even charming.

Paradox is a fitting image of the incarnation of God in human flesh and blood, of what a Renaissance lyric described as "summer in winter and day in night," of what the poet G. K. Chesterton called the "things that cannot be, and that are."

So, what do the liturgical poets have to say when summer finally rolls around, when the year has completed the passage from dark December to June's bright verdure? Summer images, for the poets, are signs of the "fullness of life" promised by the Lord, a (literally) *wholesome* life to be lived now and not only in the future. The fullness of life is a birthright bequeathed by baptism.

The season's warmth and bounty and light make the world more hospitable and life-sustaining. In this, summer has become for the church an image (reflecting Revelation 22) of our existence in heaven, within God's holy city, that place of abundance and healing and endless day. Just as the cold months evoke homey images of "cocooning," the warm months are a time for opening windows, opening doors, getting outside, traveling, visiting, family vacations, pilgrimage.

The summer festivals on the liturgical calendar essentially return to the scene almost all the familiar "playthings" that are used at Christmas: greenery, flowers, trees, images of fire and water, and an abundance of circular or spiral things, including breads, wreaths and crowns. At Christmas these are used to delight in opposites. As springtime turns into summer, the images are used to celebrate the fulfillment of the promise.

June

1 Memorial of Justin, martyr

2 Optional memorial of Marcellinus, presbyter, martyr, and Peter, exorcist, martyr

3 Memorial of Charles Lwanga, catechist, martyr, and his companions, martyrs

5 Memorial of Boniface, bishop, religious, missionary, martyr

6 Optional memorial of Norbert, bishop, religious, missionary, martyr

9 Optional memorial of Ephrem of Syria, deacon, doctor of the church

11 Memorial of Barnabas, apostle

13 Memorial of Anthony of Padua, presbyter, religious, doctor of the church

19 Optional memorial of Romuald, abbot, religious founder

21 Memorial of Aloysius Gonzaga, religious

22 Optional memorial of Paulinus of Nola, bishop

Optional memorial of John Fisher, bishop, martyr, and Thomas More, married man, martyr

24 **Solemnity of the Birth of John the Baptist**

27 Optional memorial of Cyril of Alexandria, bishop, doctor of the church

28 Memorial of Irenaeus, bishop, martyr

29 **Solemnity of Peter and Paul, apostles**

30 Optional memorial of the First Martyrs of the Church of Rome

First Sunday after Pentecost: **Solemnity of the Holy Trinity**

Second Sunday after Pentecost: **Solemnity of the Body and Blood of Christ**

Friday following the Second Sunday after Pentecost: **Solemnity of the Sacred Heart of Jesus**

Saturday following the Second Sunday after Pentecost: Memorial of the Immaculate Heart of Mary

In Short, in Early Summer

- Make sure to plan a year-end event—a barbecue, trip to a museum, a boat trip, or a potluck supper—that brings together all parish students and their families. Pick a day already sacred on the church's calendar, and use the occasion as your focus.

- You'll need to spend some time "decommissioning" the classroom before summer vacation and getting materials into storage. Allow students to take part in this process.

- The annual flagging of energy as the weather warms up has claimed many a good intention. Especially at this time of year, don't bite off more than you can chew.

- This time of year is filled with "processional" events that deserve ritual action and ornamentation. (The biggest of these is graduation.) For instance, begin and end a class trip with prayerful song. Safely hang pennants on the bus. "Ornament" participants with buttons or specially designed T-shirts.

- A class yearbook or almanac is a yearlong project, and it doesn't need to be under the control of an outside company. Homemade ones are just as valuable. When yearbooks (or other school memorabilia, such as rings) are distributed, make it a ceremony, with a sung psalm, a rite of blessing, and good order.

- Especially if there are several weeks between Pentecost and the end of the school year, you might "summerify" the room by simplifying, cleaning and putting away much decoration, and then perhaps adding a few signs of summer, such as seashells and clouds, as well as images of the sun and stars.

- If you like to use plenty of the liturgical vestment colors in season, during summer the greens you use might be lighter and livelier than winter greens. Add sunny yellows, a wide range of blues and aquamarine.

- A bulletin board might be dedicated to advertising summer activities in local libraries, museums, civic centers and nearby parishes. Also, a bulletin board might recap highlights of the year. These boards are more than ways to share information—they are focuses of prayer, signs of promise and hope, and could be ornamented with seasonal symbols.

July

1 Optional memorial of Junípero Serra, presbyter, religious, missionary

3 **Feast of Thomas, apostle**

4 Optional memorial of Elizabeth of Portugal, married woman, queen

5 Optional memorial of Anthony Mary Zaccaria, presbyter, religious founder

6 Optional memorial of Maria Goretti, virgin, martyr

11 Memorial of Benedict, abbot, religious founder

13 Optional memorial of Henry, married man, ruler

14 Memorial of Kateri Tekakwitha, virgin

15 Memorial of Bonaventure, bishop, religious, doctor of the church

16 Optional memorial of Our Lady of Mount Carmel

18 Optional memorial of Camillus de Lellis, presbyter, religious founder

21 Optional memorial of Lawrence of Brindisi, presbyter, religious, doctor of the church

22 Memorial of Mary Magdalene, apostle to the apostles, disciple of the Lord

23 Optional memorial of Bridget of Sweden, married woman, religious founder

25 **Feast of James, apostle**

26 Memorial of Anne and Joachim, parents of the Virgin Mary

29 Memorial of Martha, disciple of the Lord

30 Optional memorial of Peter Chrysologus, bishop, doctor of the church

31 Memorial of Ignatius of Loyola, presbyter, religious founder

Early Summer Ordinary Time
- Seasonal vesture color: *green*
- Some complementary colors: *gold, orange, rose, blue, teal*

*I*n Summer, Go with the Flow

Following Pentecost the liturgical calendar names the weeks "Ordinary Time." The number of weeks of Ordinary Time between Pentecost and the end of the school year can vary from year to year from as many as five or six to none at all. Read between the lines in this book to figure out how you will treat these weeks this year.

*I*f Easter Sunday falls on or before April 11, Pentecost comes in May and these Ordinary Time weeks include Memorial Day and the feast of the Visitation of the Blessed Virgin Mary to Elizabeth. In any year, the two Sundays following Pentecost—the solemnities of the Holy Trinity and of the Body and Blood of Christ—are white-vestment Sundays. The Sunday vesture may still be white but the weekday color has shifted to Ordinary Time green. (The 50 days of Easter are plenty. Easter decorations need to be taken down immediately following Pentecost.)

You may choose to spend these Ordinary Time weeks taking down and packing away seasonal materials, instead of putting new ones up. See what's said beginning on page 44 regarding storage.

This may be Ordinary Time but it's far from ordinary. Even if you can't put this chapter to full use because summer vacation begins soon, take a moment to find out what you may be missing in these marvelous weeks of springtime turning into summer. Of course, summer school, vacation Bible school and other parish summer programs will find what's said here and in the August chapter useful in celebration of the liturgical year.

*L*iturgically speaking, summertime kicks off with the marvelous Pentecost story from the Acts of the Apostles. A blast of the Spirit's fire and wind sends the disciples outdoors into the light, freeing them from their fears. The Jewish pilgrims gathered in Jerusalem for the Pentecost festival were astounded by the commotion.

In North America we've largely lost the custom of carrying leafy branches to celebrate Pentecost, but the practice remains strong in many parts of Europe. That practice in Poland and in Lithuania has led to the popular name for Pentecost and the days that follow as "green days." Lush green foliage signifies the completion of the earth's paschal transfiguration begun on Palm Sunday, when, by custom, budding branches were carried.

 **Display Idea**

If you used a bare tree or grape vine or other leafless woody material through the year as a carrier for seasonal ornamentation, it won't look right now. Either take it down or leave it in place and glue paper or cloth leaves to the branches. (You might do this in synch with the blossoming and leafing out of branches in your neighborhood.)

The "green days" following Pentecost and the entire month of June are just about "bustin' out" with festival days, especially immediately following the summer solstice. And why not? These are the lushest, floweriest, most verdant days of the year, when springtime peaks. The new foliage has yet to be disfigured by summer's insects and scorching heat. The world seems ripe but not yet rotting.

At this festive time of year the school calendar—in contrast—is winding down. Everyone in school may be hankering for vacation to begin. Typically in the classroom as the weather warms, energy gets directed away from year-long patterns of prayer and celebration. End-of-the-school-year activities will demand some attention, although it may be difficult to muster enthusiasm. It may just seem that everything's topsy turvy.

The trick here is not to impose additional observances on an overcrowded calendar but to recognize in year-end activities images consonant with the liturgy. If possible, when scheduling for the year, give some priority to the June festivals. As an example, the usual picnic that ends the year and kicks off summer school can be scheduled for June 24, Midsummer Day—the solemnity of the Birth of Saint John the Baptist—complete with the decoration and raising of the midsummer pole as they do this day in Sweden.

The procession traditionally held on the solemnity of the Body and Blood of Christ is another expression of the church's penchant for getting into the great outdoors during summer. The eucharistic Body of Christ, by custom,

A Bulletin Board for Summer
Tobiah's Journey

Find the book of Tobit in the Bible. Some Bibles don't include it, and some locate the book in the apocrypha, the nonbiblical but revered writings.

The story begins at Pentecost and tells of a journey—perfect for summer. Raphael is an angel sent by God to protect Tobiah (Tobit's son) on his travels, and so Raphael has become a patron of travelers. (Tobiah doesn't know that Raphael is an angel until the very end of the story; all along Tobiah thought the angel was a relative—and in a sense, that's what Raphael was.)

The travelers have another companion, Tobiah's dog. We hear about the dog at the beginning of the journey and then at the very end when everyone arrives home safely.

On the journey Tobiah met Sarah, the love of his life. They got married, and so Raphael is also a patron of romance, of newlyweds, of happy families, even of in-laws.

Cover the bulletin board with summer colors. Or leave up the flowery background you had in place during the Easter season. Add a large summer sun. Add the angel Raphael and Tobiah and his dog. Often portrayed is the time that Tobiah caught a large fish. Tobiah was told by Raphael to save a portion of the fish to place on his father's eyes when he returned home. (His father, Tobit, was blind.) Tobiah followed Raphael's advice and Tobit was able to see. And so Raphael also became a patron of anyone who takes care of the sick.

Students can draw depictions of their hopes for the summer— where they think they will travel, who they intend to visit, what they want to learn and accomplish, what activities will keep them busy. Each student then signs her or his name. These depictions are gathered around the central image of Raphael and Tobiah. Then say this prayer:

God of Tobiah and of his
*   faithful dog,*
God of all travelers,
send your holy angel to be our
companion this summer.

In our work, bring fruitfulness.
In our adventures, bring safety.
In our coming home, bring
contentment and peace.

In all that we do,
lead us to the joys of heaven,
where you live and reign
for ever and ever. Amen.

is carried through the streets over a bed of flowers and fragrant herbs. Arbors of foliage and sweet grasses mark stations along the route.

Of course, strewing a processional route with flowers and herbs is not something unique to this day. It's a practice for any procession, such as the procession with a patronal image, beneath bride and groom at their wedding, beneath the body on the way to burial. Only a few generations ago graduates carried flowers, a marvelous tradition worth restoring.

*T*he winding down of the school year brings a number of other "processions": class trips, the drive to and from the prom (and the hairdresser or tuxedo rental store), perhaps to and from a year-end barbecue or picnic, the awards ceremony and commencement exercises.

*A*ctivity Idea

One way to ornament such "processions" is to "decorate" the folks involved in the movement. That's one reason for caps and gowns as part of the visuals of celebration. A button or badge or other wearable sign naming your school, such as a T-shirt, is perfect for class trips and outdoor parties. Blessing this gear is the right thing to do to begin the event. Decorate the cars or buses used to transport students—although safety is the first consideration here.

*J*ust following the summer solstice (which falls on June 20 or 21) come the church's two great solstice festivals, the Birth of John the Baptist (June 24), and the solemnity of Saints Peter and Paul (June 29). This time has the

traditional name of "Midsummer," and these days, among our ancestors, overflowed with special foods, games and other traditions kept with the same exuberance as at the winter festivals.

Even though it's likely that summer vacation has begun by the time Midsummer arrives, the days are too important and too delightful to leave uncelebrated. A year that makes a big fuss over the winter solstice but ignores the summer solstice is unbalanced. Especially households and students deserve a chance to assemble and celebrate these summer days.

Many places have discovered the late June solemnities as the perfect time to bring together all the students in a parish, whether in public, private or parochial schools, for a merry celebration.

*I*nterestingly in the United States and in Canada, the civic calendar has its largest national holiday at this time of year. When the founding fathers of the United States proclaimed festivities for Independence Day, they turned to the traditional Midsummer practices of erecting bonfires, having fireworks displays, ringing bells and otherwise marking the turning of the year with noisemaking and illumination.

The setting up of "liberty trees" (a kind of maypole), a custom that has fallen by the wayside, is a variant of a Nordic Midsummer tradition. Either a rooted tree is decorated and illuminated for the occasion or a tree is cut down, stripped of lower branches (making it pole-like), ornamented with ribbons and flags, and set up in the town commons as the focal point of the celebration.

In our own day there are few stronger moments that capture a sense of the turning of the year than a fireworks display on the Fourth of July, especially when it's over and folks are heading home. At that moment many of us feel just a little bit older. The end of the school year is such a moment, a time for all ages to gather, a time that links everyone in the parish community with the school community, a time that needs ritual expressions, songs and decorations, perhaps even special foods. What's on the menu in your school?

Sun and Seashells: Images of Summer

Summer directs our gaze outdoors. What do you see outside the classroom? Any way to improve the view? Any improvements students can help bring about?

Display Idea

*P*ay attention to your environs. Schools near mountains, within a large city, near a cranberry bog, near soybean fields, near a harbor, near a river—each school has a different heritage to reflect. Still, city schools deserve something of the country and vice versa. City schools are under obligation to acquaint students with agrarian images. Suburban schools cannot remain aloof to the concerns of the city. "Twinning" and "sister school" programs help break down some divisions, and your school's twin or sisters might cooperate in creating and sharing decoration for the classroom and might join in festival activities.

One teacher brings the outdoors inside at this season by hanging African cloth handprinted with designs of birds overhead in great swaths—something that was found for a bargain price at a local fabric store back in February, African American Heritage Month. The same cloth is used again in September, its greens, blues and golds just the right colors for summer. Another teacher hangs a fishing net from the light fixtures—found on a trip to Cape Cod one year—and into this net go fishes and other sea creatures the students designed from origami paper during Lent.

*T*he grain harvest is a prominent early summer image springing from the scriptures. We don't ordinarily think of the harvest as a summertime event, but in fact the wheat harvest in most locations ripens early rather than late in summer.

Christian cultures match the summer grain harvest to a festival that coincides with the harvest in that region. In some places Pentecost becomes the harvest festival, true to its biblical origins. On the former Roman Catholic calendar, Pentecost was followed by the "summer ember days." (Ember days were marked by fasting in thanksgiving for the seasonal harvest.) The many scripture readings for the Ember Saturday following Pentecost revolved around the first fruits of the grain harvest and were also related, rather wonderfully, with the ordination to the orders of ministry in the church.

In many places to this day, June 29, the solemnity of the apostles Peter and Paul, does the honor as the festival of the wheat harvest. Again, the harvest is seen as an image of the many gifts needed to build up the church. Peter and Paul represent all apostles, a word that simply means "those who are sent on a mission." Further north, at the far reaches of locations where wheat can be grown, August 6 or 15 does the honor as a harvest festival. The mystery of those days is explored beginning on page 79.

In school you might take your cue from this practice by connecting the harvest of grain with end-of-the-year awards and honors. Saints Peter and Paul, the "pillars of the church" might be two of your honored guests at the awards ceremony each year, perhaps their presence signified by some fine iconography hung in a place of honor. Especially you will want to include an image of the parish-school patron.

In a Colorado school the local fields are full of ripe, golden wheat each year at graduation time, and every June it seems the right thing to ornament classrooms with some of this wheat. Graduates carry a bundled sheaf of it as they enter for the ceremony and then place the sheaves around an image of the parish-school patron saint.

Do you know the traditions surrounding "corn dollies"? These are ornaments woven from wheat, sometimes in geometrical shapes and sometimes in the shape of crosses, crowns and scepters. Although in America "corn" means the same thing as "maize," in England "corn" is a generic term for any grain. "Dolly" means "effigy." A full-fledged "corn dolly" is wheat and other grains woven into a figure of the Lord of the harvest, complete with regal trappings, who would be set on a "throne" to preside as the personification of the harvest over the harvest-time festivities.

All of this would be far-fetched except the folkcraft of weaving grain has been growing in popularity. It's fairly easy to find books and kits for making corn dollies, although some of this has gotten confused with, thanks to the name, the craft of making dolls out of cornhusks.

 **D**isplay Idea

A crown or wreath fashioned from wheat is a splendid ornament during several seasons. In one school a "robe" is made of wheat and other dried grasses and is placed over the statue of the Blessed Virgin throughout harvest time.

*T*he image of the sun is associated in the gospels with John the Baptist. A pun is at work here, although some background is needed to appreciate the pun: Jewish lore (echoed in the final words of the book of the prophet Malachi) claims that the prophet Elijah will return to prepare the way for the Messiah. The Lord Jesus said that "if you are willing to accept it, John the Baptist is Elijah who is to come" (Matthew 11:14). Now, the name Elijah in Greek is Elias. The word for the sun is *elios.* Elijah, the prophet who ascended into heaven in a fiery chariot, is identified with the sun.

Elijah's feast on the Byzantine calendar and among Carmelite communities is July 20. Carmel is the mountain on which Elijah challenged the prophets of the god Baal to a fiery contest. The mountain is a place of pilgrimage, and Christians built a monastery there. The feast of Our Lady of Mount Carmel (July 16) falls just a few days before Saint Elijah's Day, and there isn't an American city without an Italian or another community that makes of this day a great festival and street fair.

*A*s every Jewish boy, John the Baptist was circumcised eight days after his birth. In joy his father, Zechariah, sang the words that begin "Blessed be the God of Israel" and so are known by the Latin word *benedictus,* "blessed." The church sings this song every morning, and it includes these lines that tell of an astounding sunrise:

> *By the tender mercy of our God,*
> *the dawn from on high will break upon us,*
> *to give light to those who sit in darkness and in the shadow of death,*
> *to guide our feet into the way of peace.*

John's birth is celebrated at the onset of summer, June 24. His terrible death is remembered as summer wanes, August 29. John the Baptist is, in a sense, summer's patron. The images associated with him, such as seashells (often shown in his hand as he baptizes), the desert, the lion (a "voice in the wilderness"), locusts and honey (John's food), the river and the summer sun, as well as images associated with his biblical doppelganger, the prophet Elijah, fit summertime hand-in-glove.

The Blessed Virgin Mary is another of the "patrons of summer," and we give her special attention in the August and September chapters of this book.

*A*nother (although more obscure) patron of the summer is the archangel Uriel, whose name means "God's fire" or perhaps "God's lion." The other seasons have angelic patrons, too, according to tradition. Autumn's patron is Michael, who battles against the forces of darkness and who is to ferry the dead into paradise at the end of time. Raphael, the healer and guide, is a wonderful patron during winter. Gabriel, naturally, is spring's patron. Not only did Gabriel bring the good news to Mary, an event we celebrate as spring begins, but Gabriel is imagined to be the announcer of the resurrection.

Michael, Raphael and Gabriel are mentioned in the Bible, but Uriel is mentioned in the apocryphal second book of Esdras, a strange eschatological book, similar to the book of Revelation, bits of which are used here and there in the liturgy and quoted by Jesus in the gospels. Uriel is pictured as flame or else as a winged lion. A male lion's golden mane is sometimes imagined as flame. In the ancient imagination, when the sun enters the summer sign of Leo the lion, its heat is intensified.

*W*e have here a wealth of scriptural images to employ in celebrating the summer. Other summer signs revolve around the sea and other bodies of water. In a corner of the classroom, especially if students spend time on the water or if the school is located near a body of water, might go an image of Jesus in the boat calming the storm.

*D*isplay Idea

Boats and fishing equipment have become symbols of the fishermen apostles Peter (June 29) and James (July 25). Of course, Paul's journeys (his day is also June 29) gained him the ship and anchor as two prime emblems. The seashell is a sign of John the Baptist, and a scallop shell has become the apostle James' chief symbol.

In medieval times travelers along the great pilgrimage routes in France and Spain would wear a scallop shell as a plea for hospitality in the towns they passed through. The shrine of Saint James in Compostela in northwestern Spain was one of the farthest flung destinations on the pilgrimage route. (The route is still traveled by religious pilgrims and backpackers every summer.) The scallop became so associated with James that the French word for it remains *coquille Saint Jacques.*

*T*he month of July brings other patrons of travel and of summertime hospitality. There's Benedict (July 11), whose holy rule claims that guests are Christ-come-to-visit. Kateri Tekakwitha (July 14) suffered from inhospitality in a kind of limbo, rejected by many of her own people and never accepted by the French missionaries. Martha (July 29), who with her sister Mary and brother Lazarus opened her home to Jesus, is a patron of homemakers and cooks.

Summer school and vacation Bible schools have in July a number of guiding lights in these saints. Images of the saints—as many as you can find, along with their symbols—might be gathered in the prayer corner or even placed throughout the room.

*P*erhaps the most beloved of July's saints is Mary Magdalene. Her feast day is July 22. To the end, Mary was loyal to our Lord when other disciples fled. She was commissioned by the Easter angels to proclaim the good news to the disciples. She makes the perfect patronal figure for summer school.

Mary Magdalene has been called "apostle to the apostles." Artists' renderings usually show her holding a crock of myrrh because she kept watch by the tomb of the Lord and was prepared to anoint his body as a final act of love. She's often also shown holding an egg, sometimes a red-dyed egg—an Easter egg! Like Easter eggs, like all of Jesus' disciples who live true to their baptismal commitment, Mary proclaims the resurrection.

Resources

Available from LTP

Liturgy Training Publications, the publisher of this book, offers a number of splendid resources that go hand-in-hand with *School Year, Church Year.* To order, contact LTP, 3949 South Racine Avenue, Chicago IL 60609; 1-800-933-1800; orders@ltp.org; fax 1-800-933-7094; www.LTP.org.

Every classroom will want to display the *Year of Grace* liturgical calendar poster. A laminated version is available. Notebook-size versions of the poster are available in packs of 25, perfect for distributing to each student. The calendar's art is meant to be a stunning addition to the visuals in the classroom. Some people keep the calendar in a frame and use stickers or foil stars to mark off each day.

Companion to the Calendar is a gem of a book that gives ready access to information about entries on the *Year of Grace* calendar (the seasons, solemnities, feasts, and memorials). The book also includes information about other Catholic days and observances, the civil calendar, and Jewish and Muslim days. This book was written to be accessible to those with about a fifth-grade reading level, although nothing here patronizes children or adults. *Companion to the Calendar* lies flat and can be left open to each day. The book would look great on a bookstand near the poster calendar. Some classes read each day's entries out loud to start the day.

Blessings and Prayers through the Year: a Resource for School and Parish by Elizabeth McMahon Jeep and Mary Beth Kunde-Anderson, music consultant, is a beautiful hardcover book with a full-color illustrated interior and a ribbon to mark your page. This essential classroom resource contains blessings, prayers, and simple rituals for every season, occasion, and need that arises in both school and parish life. The book has a clear, easy-to-follow format and offers helpful background information and ideas for preparing for ritual and prayer. Included are two CDs, one with music and vocals to teach the songs, and the other with musical accompaniment only. There are also music pages for teaching and playing in groups. Classes can begin using this valuable resource at any time during the year.

About Daily Prayer

Children's Daily Prayer. This best-selling annual book provides texts for prayer in the classroom for every day of the school year. The book is designed to be used by students. Also included are monthly meal prayers, end-of-the-day prayers, and prayer services to celebrate the seasons and special days.

Sunday Prayer for Catechists provides weekly Gospel reflections that relate to the experiences of catechists, Catholic school teachers, and even parents. Each page provides the Sunday Gospel reading, as well as a short reflection that is aimed toward those who catechize with young people of all ages. This resource makes an excellent gift for catechists or Catholic school teachers, and may be used as a jumping off point for prayer or discussion among groups of catechists or teachers.

About Masses with Children

Children's Liturgy of the Word. An annual book from LTP, providing materials to use when children are dismissed from the assembly during Sunday Mass to celebrate the Liturgy of the Word. For every Sunday and holy day of the year, you will find scripture background and preparation notes for the adult prayer leader and a detailed order of prayer with full text of a homily/reflection.

Directory for Masses with Children. Everyone who prepares liturgy for children and children for liturgy should possess and understand well this document published in 1973 by the Roman Congregation for Divine Worship. (You'll notice the way the title of this document is worded: "*with* children" and not "*for* children.")

Lectionary for Masses with Children. Volumes for Years A, B and C of the Sunday lectionary, and one for weekdays. Please note: The Church is awaiting a new version of the *Lectionary for Masses with Children,* which will use scripture based on the *New American Bible.* Until this new version is approved and available, the current edition may still be used in the liturgy. However, it may no longer be reprinted by publishers.

My First Holy Communion by Melissa Musick Nussbaum with art by Laura Montenegro. In words and pictures, this book invites children to learn and to love the words that we all say and sing at Mass, and to receive Holy Communion with understanding.

Sunday Morning by Gail Ramshaw introduces little ones to the wonder of our God and to what the Church does on Sunday in a way even the youngest child can appreciate. The words and phrases used in Sunday liturgy are presented in people-centered art swirling with detail. Multicultural illustrations paint stories of God's love for all people, which we hear in the Liturgy of the Word. Use this with preschool or day care classes, first Holy Communion preparation, and children's Bible classes. You'll discover it will open hundreds of ways to talk about and explain Sunday worship.

We Learn About Mass by Gerard Moore is a cost-effective resource to use with second, third, fourth, and fifth graders preparing for their first Holy Communion or Christian initiation. The perfect supplement to any diocesan approved religious education textbook, it is also a helpful resource for parents looking for ways to discuss and guide their child through the liturgy. This book is also available in Spanish.

We Learn About Mass, Teaching Edition, by Gerard Moore with additional material by Jean Marie Hiesberger. This teaching edition of the child's little workbook, *We Learn About Mass,* instructs teachers, catechists, and parents with notes and ideas on how to teach the meaning of the Mass to children. For easy reference, this book has reprinted each page of the children's version and placed the teacher's notes in the margins. Special notes and activities for each age level (second through fifth grade) have also been included. This book is also available in Spanish.

About Sundays, Feasts, and Seasons

In addition to the *Year of Grace* calendar, *Companion to the Calendar,* and *Blessings and Prayers through the Year,* here are other wonderful resources for celebrating the Church's year.

Advent Calendar Activity Sheet. Color activity sheets that help children and families to celebrate Advent, using a unique Advent wreath design. Available in packs of 16 from LTP.

At Home with the Word. An annual book with the Sunday scriptures, including discussion and ideas for living the Christian life.

Bible Stories for the Forty Days by Melissa Musick Nussbaum. Stories bring to life the "paschal" Bible characters.

Build Your Own Bethlehem: A Nativity Scene and Activity Book for Christmastime by Gertrud Mueller Nelson with Peter Mazar provides the beautifully illustrated cut-out characters children will need to build their own Bethlehem.

Child of God by Gertrud Mueller Nelson. A book for birthdays!

Create Your Own Christmas Season Booklet Activity Sheet. Color activity sheets that help children and families to learn about the Sundays, solemnities, and feasts of the Christmas season. Available in packs of 16 from LTP.

Fling Wide the Doors! An "Advent" calendar that runs till Epiphany! In large and small versions.

Forty Days and Forty Nights. A lenten calendar with doors to open from Ash Wednesday until Easter. Inside the doors you'll find all the animals of the Bible.

The Garden of the Good Shepherd: A Sticker Calendar to Count the Fifty Days of Easter by Peter Mazar, illustrated by Tomie de Paola, provides the ideal way to teach young people, from preschoolers on up, about the entire season of Easter.

Keeping the Seasons, Reproducibles for Advent-Christmas / Celebremos los tiempos litúrgicos, Recursos reproducibles para Adviento-Navidad CD-ROM with bilingual reproducible catechesis and art for the seasons of Advent and Christmas.

Keeping the Seasons, Reproducibles for Lent-Triduum-Easter / Celebremos los tiempos litúrgicos, Recursos reproducibles para Cuaresma-Triduo Pascual-Pascua CD-ROM with bilingual reproducible catechesis and art for the seasons of Lent, Triduum, and Easter.

Winter Saints by Melissa Musick Nussbaum. Stories of people who inhabit our winter calendar.

Winter: Celebrating the Season in a Christian Home by Peter Mazar. Traditions of the time from Advent to Carnival.

Catechetical Resources

A Is for Altar, B is for Bible by Judith Lang Main.

The Catechesis of the Good Shepherd in a Parish Setting by Tina Lillig. A practical introduction to this method of catechesis.

The Catechetical Documents: A Parish Resource. A collection of the church's documentation on catechesis and religious development.

Celebrating the Lectionary. A series of five age-graded books from LTP that provide 15 to 20 minutes of catechesis on the Lectionary and liturgical year for each Sunday and holy day.

The Good Shepherd and the Child: A Joyful Journey by Sophia Cavalletti, et al. A method for fostering a young child's religious development through the child's innate wonder and awe.

History's Golden Thread: The History of Salvation by Sophia Cavalletti. Helps the catechist experience and relay the scriptures as an unfolding story.

Illustrated Psalms and Prayers / Salmos de Alabanzo Ilustrados. Three psalms presented bilingually with beautiful, vivid illustrations.

Journals of the Catechesis of the Good Shepherd 1984–97. Reprints of the newsletter of the Catechesis of the Good Shepherd.

Living Liturgy: Elementary Reflections by Sofia Cavalletti. In this book, the founder of the Catechesis of the Good Shepherd, Sofia Cavalletti, provides background for catechists who work with children, focusing on the liturgy's history, symbols, meaning, and centeredness in Christ.

Mustard Seed Preaching by Ann Garrido offers the essential themes of the Catechesis of the Good Shepherd as a guide to preaching to children and to the heart of the child in each of us.

The Religious Potential of the Child: Experiencing Scripture and Liturgy with Young Children by Sofia Cavalletti. This classic book describes the profoundly biblical and sacramental way of religious formation for children ages 3 to 6, known as the Catechesis of the Good Shepherd. This experience of adults and children dwelling together in the mystery of God is Montessori-based and is deeply respectful of the nature and spirituality of young children who make their way to God in freedom and joy.

The Religious Potential of the Child, 6 to 12 Years Old by Sofia Cavalletti. For educators and catechists of the older child, particularly illuminating the child's relationship with the mystery of God. Even those not familiar with the Catechesis of the Good Shepherd will find in these pages wisdom and insight into the religious life and needs of older children.

Saving Signs, Wondrous Words by David Philippart. A pleasure to read! Introduces the signs and gestures of the liturgy.

We Learn About Our Parish Church by Teresa Marshall. For children 7 to 12 years old, this little booklet introduces them to the church building and its furnishings and to the mysteries they express.

We Learn About Our Parish Church Teaching Edition by Teresa Marshall. Ideas and background for teachers, catechists, and parents to help children get the most out of their little book with the same title.

Other Art Sources

Bee Still Studios
www.beestill.org

The art of Brother Michael O'Neill McGrath—on postcards, greeting cards and posters—is available from his studios. Modern-day and ancient saints receive a fresh treatment.

Bridge Building Icons
PO Box 1048
Burlington VT 05402-1048
1-800-325-6263
www.bridgebuilding.com

This is an excellent source for posters and icon reproductions of various sizes, of both traditional and contemporary icons and sacred images, especially sacred images portraying Christ and Mary as Native American. Good holy cards are available here, too, and most of the images can be purchased as refrigerator or filing cabinet magnets.

Josephite Pastoral Center
1200 Varnum Street, NE
Washington, DC 20017
202-526-9270
http://www.josephite.com/pastoralcenter.html

This organization publishes an annual calendar with images and information for each month taken from African American history and heritage.

yzantine Icons
of Syria Skete
ms Way
53805
1-800-814-2667
http://www.skete.com

Over 700 mounted icons are available, including reproductions of classic images from Greece, Turkey and else-
where in Europe.

The Printery House
Conception Abbey
37112 State Highway VV
PO Box 12
Conception MO 64433
1-800-322-2737
www.printeryhouse.org

This is a good source for icon reproductions (in various
sizes, including large sizes for the classroom), holy cards
(to distribute to students) and greeting cards.

Tree of Life Imports
6941 Calumet Avenue
Hammond IN 46324
1-800-300-3335
http://thetreeoflifeimports.com

Here you will find sacred images imported from El
Salvador and Guatemala, especially a good selection of
crosses. The images are brightly colored and in a style sure
to appeal to children. (Most of them tend to be small, so
be careful about scale in your classroom.) Tree of Life
Imports works hard to employ native artisans and to pay
them just wages.

St. Andrew's Abbey Ceramics
PO Box 40
Valyermo CA 93563
1-888-454-5411
customerservice@abbeybooksandgifts.com
http://www.abbeybooksandgifts.com/

This is a source for ceramic plaques of angels and a wide
variety of saints, done in a colorful and whimsical style
that will appeal to younger children. Some of the newer
saints—whose images are difficult to find—are here:
Saint Elizabeth Ann Seton (United States), Saint Andrew
Kim (Korea) and Saint Lorenzo Ruiz of Manila (Philippines), for example. Images of biblical events are also available: for example, Pentecost, the baptism of Jesus, the
wedding at Cana. A good selection of Old Testament figures is available, too.